BIBLICAL ETHICS AND SOCIAL CHANGE

BIBLICAL ETHICS
AND
SOCIAL CHANGE

Stephen Charles Mott

New York / Oxford
OXFORD UNIVERSITY PRESS
1982

Copyright © 1982 by Oxford University Press, Inc.

Library of Congress Cataloging in Publication Data

Mott, Stephen Charles.
  Biblical ethics and social change.

  Bibliography: p.
  Includes index.
  1. Christian ethics.   2. Social ethics.
3. Ethics in the Bible.   I. Title.
BJ1251.M66   241   81-11026
ISBN 0-19-502947-X   AACR2
ISBN 0-19-502948-8 (pbk.)

Printing (last digit): 9 8 7 6 5 4 3 2 1

Printed in the United States of America

In memory of
Royden Cross Mott
1908–1979

PREFACE

When one is asked to recommend a thorough treatment of the biblical basis for implementing social change, few books come to mind. The writings of Walter Rauschenbusch (and his social gospel contemporaries) as well as the promising Third World treatments are addressed to a situation different from that facing most contemporary American readers. The most pertinent of Rauschenbusch's writings, moreover, are out of print. Further, readers often perceive in such writings particular theological or political stances—social gospel, immanent theology, Marxism—which stand in the way of an open reading for many who seek biblical support. And the recent resurgence of evangelical interest in applying Scripture to the problems of society has mainly produced writings aimed at a popular audience.

The divergence between the academic disciplines of Christian social ethics and biblical studies has been noted by several authors recently.[1] James Gustafson describes biblical ethics as "a complex task for which few are well prepared; those who are specialists in ethics generally lack the intensive and proper training in biblical studies, and those who are specialists in biblical studies often lack sophistication in ethical thought."[2] For an introduction to the principles of the use of the Bible for ethics, I recommend *Bible and Ethics* by Bruce Birch and Larry Rasmussen as particularly helpful in showing the varied ways in which the Scripture provides authority for ethical discourse and the use of the total canon in arriving at valid conclusions about the ethical teachings of the Scriptures.

I would also like to identify an approach to the social application of the Bible which has been particularly fruitful for my own ethical understanding. The interpretation of Scripture begins in the life experience of listening in faith as the Word of God is read and taught and of obedient conduct guided by this Word. Among the truths experienced in this way, the biblical message of justice creates a basic loyalty to the poor and weak and a commitment to their defense. Scripture is then interpreted in the light of this biblically formed understanding.

The Bible is read with the expectation of answers to questions of social justice and human oppression. Accordingly, J. Andrew Kirk writes that the starting point of any theological interpretation must coincide

> with the bias of the Christian gospel itself ("good news to the poor . . . release to the captives . . . liberty to those who are oppressed," Luke 4.18). . . . There is no option; theology must be done from out of a commitment to a living God who defends the cause of "the hungry" and who sends "the rich empty away" (Luke 1.53).[3]

But the interpreter of the social ethics of Scripture brings to the text not only a disposition shaped by his or her own experience and background. The interpreter's own focus on social need has led to an increased interest in all that can be known about social and economic structures and ways of expressing and evaluating social norms. In aid of greater methodological self-consciousness in interpretation, modern sociological and ethical categories are applied to the materials of the Bible to suggest new possibilities of meaning and to provide a means of assessing the applicability of the results of exegesis to contemporary discussion. When such terminology does clarify the meaning of Scripture, biblical interpretation finds a new vocabulary with which to address current problems. Sometimes, however, the categories are dissonant with the

text, and analysis makes it apparent that the passages have little
immediate relevance to modern questions. Then for Scriptural guidance we must depend upon the more general framework of values
and attitudes in the biblical witness, and can arrive at a clear-cut
Christian position only after extended study of these general claims
in the light of historical and current empirical information.

As an example of this approach, comparative economics provides the category of property arrangements in the traditional co-
operative village.[4] This property system supplies an understanding of Hebrew land tenure which will be missed by exegetes who,
although possessing considerable linguistic and textual skill, approach Scripture with assumptions based on either the economics of
western private property or of socialism or who ignore economic
considerations altogether.

Thus one interprets Scripture with knowledge of sociological,
economic, and ethical categories employed elsewhere to understand
socio-economic structures and conflicts. Careful exegesis and reflection reveal which principles are helpful in understanding the social
phenomena and norms of biblical thought. These non-biblical con-
structs aid the understanding of Scripture and are tested and
refined where the biblical Word relates to them; where it does not
relate, they are set aside.

In the following pages we shall see that the heart of biblical
thought mandates efforts to correct economic and social injustices
in our communities. The emphasis in this book on the use of
political authority to achieve justice should complement the stress
upon the witness of the church as counter-community which is
found in many recent writings.

The first part of the book builds a biblical theology of social
involvement. Chapter 1 shows the recognition in Scripture of the
social reality of evil, as reflected both in its concepts of "the world"
and in its acknowledgment of the existence of evil supernatural
powers. Chapter 2 finds social responsibility at the core of biblical
faith in the grace of God present through the death of Christ and
argues that in the early church responsibility for the neighbor extended beyond the Christian community. Chapter 3 shows that

love, the expression of grace and the basis of Christian ethics, consistently points to the existence of human rights based on the divine bestowal of dignity upon every person. In Chapter 4 biblical justice is seen to be in continuity with love, rather than constituting a separate ethical pole, which explains its egalitarian disposition toward oppressed groups. The fifth chapter brings biblical theology into the perspective of history with the idea of the Reign of God, conceived as only partially present yet at work in all spheres of life; particular attention is given to the effect of Jesus' earthly ministry upon social reality.

The second part of the book treats the variety of ways in which Christians bring about social change. The dangers of relying on any single approach are pointed out, and the contribution of each such approach is demonstrated. This part of the book deals with crucial questions faced by the church today, including "the primacy of evangelism, the relationship between reconciliation of man to man and reconciliation of man to God, and the precise nature of evangelical socio-political involvement."[5] Chapter 6 highlights the importance of evangelism for moral character and as the motivation for justice, while pointing out the unbiblical thinking of those who would rely upon evangelism alone for social change or subordinate other missional activities to it. Christian community (Chapter 7) provides necessary support for the individual in mission and also serves as a visible sign of the new community God is creating. Chapter 8 uses the concept of "strategic noncooperation" in discussing nonviolent forms of action for situations in which normal modes of public change are blocked. On the other hand, the argument from the New Testament for a posture of absolute nonviolence is questioned (Chapter 9), and the theoretical context for political revolution is described. The final chapter of the book argues that, despite the ease with which it can be coopted or distorted, political reform can be defended as a necessary instrument of biblical justice.

The readers for whom this book is intended will have had some theological training and may be working in (or preparing for) pastorates and other posts of Christian leadership, service, and learning. It is hoped that scholars will be interested in the book both as

a synthesis of biblical studies and ethics and as a developed presentation of social ethics from an evangelical perspective. The topical
arrangement facilitates use as a textbook, although the intended
horizon of the book extends beyond such use.

This book has received substance and spirit from my wife,
Sandra R. Mott. She has made the book possible not only through
her love and support but also in her competence as wife, mother,
and professional nurse and teacher. She is a dear companion and
also a trusted consultant for many aspects of my work.

I must thank my daughter Sarah, for much clarification of argument and wording was done in those times when she was a baby
and I had nothing else to do but hold her and think. And one of
the added comforts of working on the book at home was being able
to gather around me my older children, Adam and Rachel.

I want to express my gratitude to Gordon-Conwell Theological
Seminary for granting me a sabbatical leave during 1977 when I
researched and wrote the final stages of the book, and I am ap-
preciative of the support over many years of my colleagues on the
faculty. I want to thank Corinne Languedoc, faculty secretary, for
her skill in making order out of my drafts in all their stages and for
her personal support as a leader of Christian social action. I am
grateful to Jan Neumeister and Kathleen Horak for their outstanding work in typing the final copy. I must acknowledge my
great debt to the students of Gordon-Conwell Theological Seminary, with whom I have worked on the ideas of the book for over a
decade. Only a few times have I been able to document their contributions, and not only by raising questions but also in offering
their own knowledge, they have contributed as much to me as I to
them. I appreciate particularly the careful work on the indices by
Robert L. Renfroe, my student assistant in 1981–82.

Both the reader and I are indebted to Charles W. Scott, Religious Books Editor of Oxford University Press. Out of his understanding of the intent of the book and of the English language, he
has lent greater clarity to the argument through his suggestions.
Cynthia A. Read and Curtis Church also provided valuable edito-
rial assistance on the style.

It is in memory of my father, Royden Cross Mott, that I dedicate this book. From him, and from my mother, Katherine Hyde Mott, I learned the natural association of faith and social compassion. Much of my father's pastoral ministry was spent with those whose lives were lived on the edge of the community: across the river, on the other side of the tracks, on the back country roads. Among his flock were the lonely old man in his shack, the obese single parent and her children living on macaroni and gravy, the large black family with their illnesses and their burly, brave, illiterate father without a job and without a winter coat. My father battled the liquor industry which took his people's money and fueled their weaknesses, and he challenged the YMCA and the hospitals which would not let them in. The Psalmist, the prophets, Jesus, John Wesley, Charles Dickens, Mom, and Daddy are blurred together in these memories; some taught the others so that they all taught me. My father combined active social love with a ministry of revival. Why? Because he lived his sermons, and his sermons received their life from the wrinkled pages of the Word of his God—and mine.

Beverly, Massachusetts   S.C.M.
December 1981

Notes to Preface

1. Cf. Bruce C. Birch and Larry L. Rasmussen, *Bible and Ethics in the Christian Life* (Minneapolis, Augsburg, 1976), 11–44.
2. James M. Gustafson, "The Place of Scripture in Christian Ethics: A Methodological Study," *Interpretation* 24 (1970), 430.
3. J. Andrew Kirk, *Liberation Theology. An Evangelical View from the Third World* (Atlanta, John Knox, New Foundations Theological Library, 1979), 205.
4. Cf. P. J. D. Wiles, *Economic Institutions Compared* (New York, Wiley, 1977), 41.
5. Athol Gill, "Christian Social Responsibility," in *The New Face of Evangelicalism. An International Symposium on the Lausanne Covenant,* C. R. Padilla, ed. (Downers Grove, InterVarsity, 1976), 89, 99.

ACKNOWLEDGMENTS

The author and publisher are grateful to the following for permission to reprint (with revisions):

The Society of Christian Ethics for portions of "God's Justice and Ours," which appeared originally as "Egalitarian Aspects of the Biblical Theory of Justice," in *The American Society of Christian Ethics Selected Papers 1978,* edited by Max L. Stackhouse;

Christian Scholar's Review for "Biblical Faith and the Reality of Social Evil," which appeared in the volume 9, number 3 (1980) issue.

Biblical quotations from the Revised Standard Version of the Bible are used with the permission of the Division of Christian Education of the National Council of the Churches of Christ in the U.S.A.

CONTENTS

ABBREVIATIONS

Bauer, *Lexicon* [5] Walter Bauer, *A Greek-English Lexicon of the New Testament,* 5th ed., trans. and ed. by W. Arndt, F. W. Gingrich, and F. Danker

Brown, Driver, Briggs, *Lexicon* Francis Brown, S. R. Driver, and Charles A. Briggs, eds., *A Hebrew and English Lexicon of the Old Testament*

KJV King James Version

NEB New English Bible

RSV Revised Standard Version

TDNT *Theological Dictionary of the New Testament,* G. Kittel and G. Friedrich, eds.

I

A Biblical Theology of Social Involvement

Chapter 1

BIBLICAL FAITH AND
THE REALITY OF SOCIAL EVIL

In the time of Jesus, violence and oppression led people to see underlying the lawless deeds of humanity a structure of evil, personified by fallen angels. Some Israelite visionaries believed that events of the days of Noah explained their own. The bloody warriors then raging over their Mediterranean world were like the giants in Noah's day, the offspring of the rebellious chief angel, Shemihaza, and other "sons of God" who followed him. The treacherous technology of the making and using of metal and weapons had been taught to humankind by Azazel, another chief of angels. In response to the pleas of humanity, God had provided (and would again provide) deliverance. God sent the mighty angels Michael and Gabriel to "bind Azazel" and "to bind Shemihazah and his companions," so that the evil on the face of the earth might be destroyed and a new age of justice and truth brought in (*1 Enoch* 6–11).[1]

The explanation of the injustices of history through reference to angels may seem unrelated to the economic and political problems of our communities. But, as we shall see, this overshadowing community of evil, described by New Testament writers as "the powers," is cited frequently in recent efforts to provide a biblical account of the contemporary social situation.[2] Such personages as Shemihaza and Azazel, along with the New Testament concept of *the world* (*cosmos*), may help us to see that injustice and other evils not only depend upon the decisions of individuals but also are rooted in manifestations of culture and social order. This recognition affects our understanding of the spiritual struggle and victory in which we participate, for God has "disarmed the powers and the authorities and made a public mockery of them, leading them captives in Christ" (Col. 2.15). These biblical concepts relate to phenomena which can be sociologically described and they extend rather than nullify personal responsibility in society.

THE WORLD AS THE EVIL SOCIAL ORDER

A basic way of describing evil in the New Testament uses the term *cosmos,* "the world." This word refers to the order of society and indicates that evil has a social and political character beyond the isolated actions of individuals.

It is unfortunate that *cosmos* has been translated in English Bibles as *world,* which primarily refers to a physical place. The Greek term, *cosmos,* however, essentially means *order, that which is assembled together well.* In this sense it is used in a variety of ways. Adornments which make a woman beautiful are thought to "make her orderly." So 1 Peter 3.3 admonishes wives not to let their "external adornment [or *order (cosmos)*] be with braided hair, gold ornaments, or dressing in robes." From such usage comes our term *cosmetics.*

The term naturally came to be attached to the most important ordering of earthly life, the social order. It referred to the structures of civilized life and specifically the civic order represented by the city-state, which among other things secured the bonds of friendship in the face of the threat of social chaos (Plato, *Prot.* 322c).[3] As *cosmos,* the universe itself is a city-state. Plato wrote, "Heaven and earth and gods and people are held together by sharing and friendship and self-control and justice; therefore the universe (*to holon*) is called cosmos, not disorder (*acosmia*) or licentiousness" (*Gorg.* 508a).

The New Testament uses *cosmos* in a variety of ways. Among these, it can mean all people (John 3.16), the inhabitants of the universal social order. But most striking and most important theologically is a usage which picks up the meaning of social order which we have discussed, but with a difference. For classical Greece *cosmos* protected values and life, but in the apocalyptic thought patterns of first-century Judaism, and particularly of the New Testament,[4] *cosmos* represents the twisted values which threatened genuine human life. For Plato the order stood guard against licentiousness; now the order is the intruder bearing immorality. Paul writes that to avoid the immoral persons of the social order (*cosmos*) one would have to leave human society (*cosmos*) altogether (1 Cor. 5.10). Ephesians 2.1–2 provides another example. The author refers to the individual "trespasses and sins" of the Gentile readers of the letter and then describes the greater order of evil after which their individual acts were patterned:

> And you he made alive, when you were dead through the trespasses and sins in which you once walked, following the course of this world [*cosmos*], following the prince of the power of the air, the spirit that is now at work in the sons of disobedience. (*RSV*)

There is no radical distinction between the actions of the person as an individual and as a social being. Evil exists in the society outside the individual and exerts an influence upon him or her (cf. Rom. 12.2 with *aiōn*).

The basic fiber of society is comprehended in the New Testament use of *cosmos*. It includes the system of property and wealth: 1 John 3.17 speaks of "whoever has the world's means of livelihood[5] (*bios tou cosmou*). . . ." It thus includes necessary economic relationships; Paul admonishes his readers to "make use of the world" (meaning the essential functions from which one cannot get away) but not to "overuse" it (1 Cor. 7.31). The world also has a stratification of class and status. Reference is made to the poor, foolish, weak, and lowly of the world (Jas. 2.5; 1 Cor. 1.27–28). Paul associates the world with status distinctions based on religion (Gal. 6.14–15 [circumcision]; cf. Gal. 3.28 [slavery and sexual status]).[6] The world has its "wisdom" (1 Cor. 1.20), its system of learning. The political rule of societies also belongs to this order (Matt. 4.8). In Revelation 11.15 heavenly voices shout, "The kingdom of the world has become the kingdom of our Lord." *Cosmos* here is grammatically parallel to "our Lord." Both terms indicate the sovereign force (subjective genitives): "the kingdom ruled by the world has become the kingdom ruled by our Lord." The government had been controlled by the evil social order but was now to be subject to Christ. Finally, the most characteristic social aspect of *cosmos* in the New Testament is a system of values which are in opposition to God.

> Love neither the world nor the things of the world. If one loves the world, the love of the Father is not in that person. Because everything that is in the world—the desire of the flesh and the desire of the eyes and the boasting of wealth—is not of the Father but is of the world. (1 John 2.15–16)

C. H. Dodd writes that the *cosmos* is "human society in so far as it is organized on wrong principles." It is characterized by the sensuality, superficiality, pretentiousness, materialism, and egoism which are the marks of the old order.[7]

In this usage, *cosmos* is not a place. It is a collectivity which in many Johannine references is personified: it loves, hates, listens, knows, and gives.[8] This does not mean that *cosmos* is simply the sum total of human beings. We are told to hate it and to hate all people would contradict God's example of loving the world in the sense of *humanity* (John 3.16). The *cosmos* we are to hate is human values and conduct insofar as they are organized in opposition to God. Evil is in the very fabric of our social existence.

THE EVIL SUPERNATURAL POWERS

In Ephesians 2.2 it is stated that our individual sins were patterned not only after the evil social order, but also "according to the ruler (*archōn*) of the domain of the air." Evil exists external to the individual not only in the order of society but also in the social and political roles of powerful supernatural beings. We are to put on the armor provided by God because "our battle is not with flesh and blood, but with the rulers [*archai*], the authorities [*exousiai*], the rulers of the order [*kosmokratores*] of darkness" (Eph. 6.11–12). These opponents are not human; they are not "flesh and blood." They are "the powers." Their titles denote that they wield great power.

Who or what are these powers? To understand the powers which come between human beings and God, two things should be kept in mind. The first is the pervasive awareness of power in Hellenistic thought. The second is the angelology of the Jewish tradition. The Hellenistic world understood life as an expression of forces. To be able to do anything, one needed to participate in some force. Abstract power without a concrete attachment was inconceivable. The power must come out of something. It was primarily understood as belonging to the gods and the demons (or angels) who upheld the social order.[9] Plato stated that the deity maintains the virtue of the universe through the justice and self-control of *rulers* (*archontes*) appointed by the deity. Plato identifies these rulers as gods and demons (*daimones;* not evil) (*Leg.* 10.903b, 906).

The belief in angels was a part of this Hellenistic outlook. God's care and control of everything in creation from the stars to the elements, from individuals to nations, was directed through angelic agents. The universal care of the angels was presented with the most detail in the Jewish apocalyptic literature. *2 Enoch* 19.4–5 (first century A.D.) speaks of

> angels who are appointed over seasons and years, the angels who are over rivers and sea, and who are over the fruits of the earth, and the angels who are over every grass, giving food to all, to every living thing, and the angels who write all the souls of men, and all their deeds and all their lives before the Lord's face.

Like Plato's *archontes* the angels are responsible for morality. In the *Book of Jubilees* (*ca.* 120 B.C.) the watchers, who are linked with angels, instruct humankind in justice and righteousness (4.15). The powers and principalities in the New Testament are angelic beings; they are not yet depersonalized into social forces or principles.[10] I stress this background, not to bring the occult into the understanding of institutional evil, but because it shows the political and social significance of the powers. 1 Peter 3.22 makes this connection, speaking of the subjection to Christ of "angels and authorities and powers" (cf. Rom. 8.38). Greek translations of the Old Testament helped pave the way for the association of angels with the Hellenistic terminology of power by translating Hebrew references to angels as *power* (*dynamis*) and *rule* (*archē*). "The Lord of Hosts" becomes "the Lord of Powers (*dynameis*)."[11] Two listings of the classes of angels in apocalyptic literature include all the different powers mentioned in Colossians 1.16 and Ephesians 1.21: rulers, authorities, powers, dominions, and thrones (*1 Enoch* 61.10—first century A.D. but possibly later—and *2 Enoch* 20.1).[12]

The terminology for describing these angelic guardians is also used for human rulers, and we should note that these terms do not always refer to supernatural powers. There is no indication, for example, that such powers are involved in the authorities discussed in Romans 13. The familiar statement that the powers crucified Jesus is based on 1 Corinthians 2.8; but whether the "rulers" in this verse are cosmic or human is extremely difficult to determine, as the context provides little indication.

But since the government is a major factor in the control of human life, it is not surprising that those celestial beings charged with "the good government of the world" (*2 Enoch* 19.2) play significant roles in political life, which in these societies incorporated to some degree most of the activities of the community. Each of the nations has its own angelic ruler and guardian.[13] In Daniel, Michael is a celestial prince "who has charge" over Israel. He contends with the corresponding custodians of Persia and Greece. These angels (*archōn*, LXX) guard and represent the earthly states (10.13, 20–21; 12.1).[14]

In the New Testament the powers are fallen. They are linked with Satan (Eph. 2.2; 6.11–12), and Christ triumphs over them (Col. 2.15). They use their authority over the governments to attack the Christians. Paul's discussion of the persecutions and tribulations of the believers (Rom. 8.35) is the context for his assurance that the angels and rulers (*archai*) cannot separate us from the love of God in Christ Jesus (vv. 38–39).[15] The powers can afflict Christians by working through political and social bodies. The Book of Revelation depicts in bizarre imagery the complete control of the political apparatus of society by the Satanic power structure.[16]

A category of "the powers" called *stoicheia* (Gal. 4.3, 10; Col. 2.8, 10) merits our attention at this point: their relationship to the Law, understood here as the pattern of the created world, further shows the influence of the powers throughout the social fabric of the universe. *Stoicheia,* meaning *the elements,* basically referred to the physical elements—earth, air, fire, and water.[17] But since all forces tended to be viewed as animate, the elements came to be regarded as personal beings or as controlled by personal beings.[18] In apocalyptic writings angels are associated with the forces of nature.[19] In *2 Enoch* 16.7 (cf. 15.1) angelic beings are called "elements." There is evidence that *stoicheia* were venerated as gods or angels, and the New Testament letters to Galatia and Colossae support this conclusion.

In Galatians and Colossians the *stoicheia* are personal supernatural beings associated with the Law. In the former letter the *stoicheia* are likened to guardians and house managers who had kept the people in slavery (4.2). Subjection to the *stoicheia* was at the same time subjection to the Law: "When we were minors, we were *enslaved by the* stoicheia *of the world"* (4.3); but God sent the Son "that he might redeem those who were *under the Law"* (4.5). Paul has said that angels were mediators of the law (3.19); the references to *stoicheia* make sense if interpreted as angelic custodians of the Law.[20] In Colossians, the *stoicheia* appear to be identified with "the powers." After warning his readers against a philosophy which is according to the *stoicheia* (2.8), Paul goes on to give his reasons: the readers have been brought to fullness in Christ, "who is the head of every *power* (*archē*) *and authority* (*exousia*)" (v. 10). God has nullified the legal charge against them and its demands, "by nailing it to the cross. God disarmed the *powers and the authorities* and made a public mockery of them, leading them as captives in Christ" (vv. 14–15). Paul describes this false philosophy; it includes matters of food purity, holy days, self-abasement, and, significantly, the worship of angels (vv. 16–18). Paul then asks why, if they have died to the *stoicheia,* they are again submitting themselves to these regulations.

The situation addressed in both Galatians and Colossians is comprehensible if we see, as has been suggested, that the churches are confronted with a syncretistic form of Jewish Christianity. The angels who brought the Law and administered it also control the seasons and the harvests. The principles of the Mosaic Law, including its separatist injunctions, were incorporated into the forces of the universe at its creation; following the law requires worship which is in harmony with the seasons and scrupulosity in the choice of foods. Angelic beings who administer both nature and the Law are venerated out of fear and the desire to be in accord with the universal Law.[21] As the Law permeates the structure of the customs and institutions of society, so do the powers; and with them, so does evil.

SOCIAL REALITY

The biblical concepts of *cosmos* and the supernatural powers comprise an objective social reality which can function for good or for evil. Careful observation of institutional life suggests ways in which the powers and the *cosmos* protect or threaten human life in the spheres attributed to them in the biblical world. A mystery of evil appears in our social life. The existence of an evil order ruled by supernatural beings must either be accepted or rejected on faith, but such reality would not be dissonant with our social experience. Our concern here is not to settle the cosmological question of whether angels and demons should be demythologized but rather to come to terms with the social material to which their biblical existence points. The *cosmos,* a more pervasive theme in the New Testament than the powers, represents the social structuring of evil without necessitating recourse to the symbolism of supernatural personages.

An examination of the objective characteristics of social reality can help us understand how there can be an intermediary locus of evil. One obvious characteristic of social life is that *its formal elements are much older than the individuals who constitute it.* Even in our very mobile society the continuity outweighs the changes by far. The symbol system, the customs, the traditions, the basic laws, the technology, the techniques for getting things done and distributing power were here long before we came and will be here long after we are gone. A law is passed in 1830. Certainly, a great deal of individual reflection and responsibility went into it. But once it is on the books, much less thought is necessary to keep it in force. Yet it can be a powerful factor in human life, affecting the fortunes of individuals for generations. Its good or evil qualities continue despite the lack of attention to it during succeeding years. People go into business and enter a kind of enterprise which existed long before they started and may continue long after they retire. It will go on with little regard to their personal morality, for "business is business." We die, but society goes on.

This social longevity is beneficial. We could not invent the wheel or discover metallurgy anew in each generation. The stability of society requires that we build on the solutions of previous generations.[22] As a consequence, however, the evils of those earlier generations continue as well. Another characteristic of social life, therefore, is that it not only goes on, but does so with relatively *little dependence on conscious individual decision making or responsibility.* Ellul tends to overstate the case, but his description of the French bureaucracy illustrates our point very well.

> From the very moment that a general policy decision has been made by the minister, it escapes his control; the matter takes on independent life and circulates in the various services, and all depends eventually on what the bureaus decide to do with it. Possibly, orders will eventually emerge corresponding to the original decision. More frequently, nothing will emerge. The decision will evaporate in the numerous administrative channels and never really see the light of day. Everyone knows of ministerial orders getting nowhere simply because they were blocked—purposely or not—somewhere along the line.

Everybody is merely concerned that his political-economic-social sector should function well, without crisis or stoppage; everyone has his sector and fails to know the whole.

All a chief [of a modern state] can do is to give a general directive, ordinarily not incorporating concrete decisions, and therefore not entailing true responsibility for the concrete acts emerging at the other end. New decisions taken at every level are necessarily the anonymous fruits of several bureaus, technicians, and circumstances. Ultimately, every decision becomes independent of all individuals.[23]

Similar observations can be made of bureaucracy in the private sector. A former president of the Midas Muffler Corporation spoke of the executives that he had known in the corporate world:

They are strapped, rigidly and cruelly constrained to their functions as heads of corporations, and secretly they are barely hanging onto a position in which they alone hope that no one will discover that no one pays very much attention to them after all. Do you know the word "fungible"? It merely means that one part can be replaced with another, a replacement part; a muffler, for example, is a fungible item. So indeed are corporate chairmen and presidents—and they know it. . . . They are anonymous because they perform no particular function of individual merit.

Corporations, he went on, are "a circumstance of large, impersonal forces over which no one seems to have much control."[24]

Who is responsible for the evil in such a bureaucracy? We become more conscious of evil as what people suffer than evil as what people do.[25] Social life includes objective realities which evolve according to their own laws.[26] A man works for the gas company. The nature of the job and of his skills forces him to travel in the field away from his family. His absence becomes a pivotal factor in the break-up of the family. The job requires his absence, and no one can point to a certain person who made the job be that way.

Some of our greatest evils are characterized by this absence of conscious individual decisions on the critical issues. One thinks of the horrible evil of American slavery. Even those who appeared to be the better and more considerate people of the society not only acquiesced in it but supported it. The moral choices took place on minor issues—whether to take 150 slaves rather than 200 on a particular ship. The major issue of the evil of the institution of slavery itself was seldom faced or considered.

Our churches are not exempt from this moral myopia. The members of an all white church in a racially mixed neighborhood may assert that they are aware of no thoughts or acts of discrimination on their part. They may need to see not merely that their outreach really extends only to whites but also that, in a society which tells blacks in countless ways that they are not accepted in equality or association with whites, they must take the initiative if they are to be any different from other white institutions in this respect.

We are socialized into the acceptance or the avoidance of major ethical issues. Our socialization reflects the moral conscience of others who share our position in society, and our ethical reasoning is shaped before we actually come to reflect upon life or make conscious moral decisions. In Reinhold Niebuhr's terms, virtue is being defeated at a lower level.[27] In short, social life consists of group ways of thinking and acting in which every individual participant's decisions are but a small portion of the development of the whole.

Finally, social life often consists of *complex problems for which there seem to be no solutions.* Every attempt at solution only creates serious problems at another point. Jürgen Moltmann calls these patterns "vicious circles" and speaks of the "hopeless economic, social and political pattern formations which drive life toward death." He appropriately suggests that in them we sense the presence of the demonic in our lives.[28]

Examples of these vicious circles abound. There is the cycle of deprived children who become depriving parents, of welfare payments which are necessary to sustain life but which do not produce a free life, of arms races begun to preserve peace but which lead to avoidable and meaningless wars, of the stand-off in world trade between workers in industrial countries and workers in others hurt by trade policies designed to protect the former. We can also think of our drive to solve our material problems through technology and growth while in the process depleting our resources and threatening the ecological balance. Certainly, rational analyses of the problems are needed and can help, but beyond what we can analyze there is the mystery of evil, which defies our understanding and thwarts our efforts to improve people's lives.

In describing social reality and social evil our intention is by no means to argue against individual responsibility for our social life. The powers are able to rule because individuals follow their influence and conform themselves to the world-order in actions which are system serving rather than system critical. The objective social situation and individual choice exert influence on each other. Social entities came into being through individual decisions; they result from the conscious decisions of individuals over the years. But they also are powerful influences upon our choices. Jesus recognized the interrelatedness of the social source of evil and individual responsibility. "Woe to the world because of temptations to sin! For the coming of temptations is necessary; nevertheless woe to the person through whom the temptation comes" (Matt. 18.7). We must admit to unknowables in this matter of responsibility. One of the most challenging problems in ethics is to assign responsibility for the exploitation which goes on around us, which we participate in or fail to correct, yet fail to acknowledge. "How many times can a man turn his head, pretending he just doesn't see?" One way to increase individual responsibility is to increase awareness of social evil: this is our concern.

Our social systems are not eternal or absolute but reflect the ambiguous nature of humankind and the angelic guardians of culture. Our institutions are not just a constraint on sin (a conservative attitude toward institutions); they themselves are full of sin. The structures of social life contain both good and bad. Because of the hold of self-interest we will tend to see only the good in those social forms which favor our interests unless we have a strong theology of sin. Our social life is fallen with us, and no social system is beyond the need of reform or perhaps even of reconstitution.

A qualification must be made at this point. One cannot evolve a total theology of culture from the concept of the fallen order of society and of the fallen powers of the world. These concepts must not be understood to mean that society, government, or other institutions are evil or demonic in themselves. We cannot do without institutions. They are integral to human life. This point is not always made clear in discussions of the powers. The New Testament passages that we have examined deal with a battle for the *control* of creation, of which the social life of humanity is a part. In this battle God has the advantage—the opponents are God's own creatures and appointees. They cannot create; they can only thwart. They must start with the materials, powers, and designs made by God. As indicated in the Prologue to John, even in the darkness exists the divine creation.[29] "The light shines in the darkness, and yet the darkness did not overcome it" (John 1.5).

Earthly authorities are appointed by God and serve God (Rom. 13.1, 4), but government is marred by the disobedience and opposition of the angelic lieutenants, a disobedience which is more in evidence at some times than others and which will culminate in the demonic capture of the state at the end time (Rev. 13). But even then that rule is under God's permission (Rev. 13.5). The claim of the Devil in the wilderness that the authority and glory of the kingdoms have been entrusted to him (Luke 4.6) should be treated for what it is, a claim of the Devil. The fallen angels have authority only to the degree that they are serving God. It is a characteristic of the demonic powers to deny their divine source and claim to be on their own.[30] The world-order and the evil presence of the powers are never *synonymous* with the concrete forms of social and institutional life. Institutions function both to enslave and to liberate human existence. The powers are always present along with enslavement and death in small or large degree; but their real existence is behind the scenes in a system of hostile values vying for control of the life of the world.

IMPLICATIONS OF EVIL RESIDING IN SOCIETY

In its teaching about the world the New Testament provides direct witness for a conclusion that should be inferred from our theology of sin. If sin is as pervasive as we say that it is, if it violates a divine intent which is not removed from history, if it is not tolerable in life but a force which is viciously destructive of person and society, if it is not only against the will of God but against nature,[31] then it will affect not only our personal motivations, decisions, and acts, but also our social life. It will powerfully influence our customs, traditions, thinking, and institutions. It will pervert our *cosmos.*

The consequences of acknowledging the presence of evil in institutions are considerable. Our attitude to society will be changed. Our struggle with evil must correspond to the geography of evil. In combatting evil in the heart through evangelism and Christian nurture we deal with a crucial aspect of evil, but only one aspect. Dealing with the evil of the social order and the worldly powers involves social action, action in the world. Christian social reform has been effective when there has been a sense of a stronghold of evil in society which must be resisted. Evangelical reform in the past century was characterized by this perspective, particularly in the struggle against slavery. William Knibb, a British missionary who was a hero in the struggle for abolition in Jamaica, wrote upon his arrival on that island, "I have now reached the land of sin, disease, and death, where Satan reigns with awful power, and carries multitudes captive at his will."[32] His mission board, like many Christian bodies before and since, failed to discern the intrusion of evil into the prevailing practices of social life. Aware of the anger of the powerful planters at amelioration proposals, they wrote to Knibb: "You must ever bear in mind that, as a resident of Jamaica, you have nothing to do with its civil or political affairs; with these you must never interfere." "The Gospel of Christ, as you well know, so far from producing or countenancing a spirit of rebellion or insubordination, has a directly opposite tendency."[33]

The discovery that evil resides in the social order as well as in our personal life confounds the common inventory of besetting sins. "Stealing, gambling, profanity, desecrating of Sunday, murder, lasciviousness, or whatever is eternally wrong"[34] is a typical list of what is often considered public unrighteousness. The biblical sins of economic exploitation or oppression or hoarding of wealth from the poor have vanished. But the prophets spoke out not only against sinful personal relationships but also against breakdowns of complex social relationships between groups with unequal shares of power. Thus they attacked broad economic patterns, such as the consolidation of the holdings of peasants into vast estates of the rich (Isa. 5.7–8). In Scripture, sin includes participation in social injustices or failure to correct them. Yet insensitivity to social evil often dulls comprehension when this dimension is encountered in the reading of Scripture. Isaiah 1.18 (*KJV*) is familiar:

> Come now, and let us reason together, saith the Lord: though your sins be as scarlet, they shall be as white as snow; though they be red like crimson, they shall be as wool.

Some familiar hymns use the striking wording of this verse: "Whiter than snow, whiter than snow, wash me and I shall be whiter than snow." But do we recognize that the sins spoken of are specific social evils? The preceding two verses state:

> Wash yourselves; make yourselves clean; remove the evil of your doings from before my eyes; cease to do evil, learn to do good; seek justice, correct oppression; defend the fatherless, plead for the widow. (*RSV*, cf. v. 23 also)

"The heart is deceitful above all things, and desperately corrupt" (Jer. 17.9, *RSV*) is a familiar verse. Less well known is the fact that the first example of this condition Jeremiah gives is "he who gets riches but not by justice" (v. 11). The biblical witness provides the key to the identification of the characteristics of the fallen social order and the marks of the social holdings of the powers.

The Christian should become sensitive to sin arising from social conditioning. Social evil lies close to home. The powers which rule through the *cosmos* speak with a familiar voice. As mentioned above, the sociology of knowledge has shown us the degree to which, through socialization, our class position affects the way we think. According to John Bennett, the interests of class distort the day to day decisions of the ordinary citizen more than do his or her individual interests.[35] But we are also conditioned in our outlook by considerations of race, sex, and national loyalty. We should examine our inner selves to discover these biases.

The recognition of the habitation of evil in social life will affect our activity in the world. It will change the mode of Christian citizenship from passive obedience to active responsibility. We can no longer discharge our responsibility by passively accepting the status quo (the order which is) as the will of God. John Calvin spoke of "public evil," in which vice was protected by custom and laws; "either the affairs of men must be altogether despaired of, or we must not only resist, but boldly attack prevailing evils. The cure is prevented by no other cause than the length of time during which we have been accustomed to the disease" (*Institutes,* Prefatory Address, 5). It is in this context of the corruption of the system that the Christian is enjoined to be the salt of the earth (Matt. 5.13), resisting corruption just as light resists and combats darkness: "You are the light of the world" (v. 14).

We serve a different order, the Reign of Christ, which he sets up in contrast to the prevailing way of life in the social order as supported by the fallen powers. To the old order there must be enmity; according to James 4.4, to be a friend of the fallen order is to be an enemy of God.[36] We are to follow the Lordship of Christ who judges the world and conquers it. Christ's victory over the powers is sure; he has disarmed them (Col. 2.15). The hostilities still continue, however, for it is only at his return that "every power and every authority and power" will be brought to an end (1 Cor. 15.24).[37] By faith we live in Christ's victory, yet we must continue to struggle.

This struggle against the hold of the forces of evil is expounded in the Letter to the Ephesians. We are to fight the demonic powers which rule the world by arming ourselves with truth, justice, peace, and the Word of God (6.10–18). We are to expose the unfruitful works of darkness, taking the offensive against sin (5.11). The many-sided wisdom of God will be made known to the "rulers and authorities in heavenly places" through the church (3.10). In his interpretation of these passages, Heinrich Schlier sees the church opposed to the principalities, as a haven of justice and truth. Human history is seen as a great struggle between the principalities and the church, ending in the downfall of the demonic spirits.[38] The church is to be engaged in a battle against evils within the social structure, because they mark the points of these powers' penetration into our history.

Mobilization for social change follows more clearly, however, from the mandates and models associated with God's activity in the world than from the theology of the cosmos. The direction of our efforts is suggested by such themes as the scope of Christian love, the implications of divine grace, the mandate to justice, and the dimensions of the Reign of God.

THE ACTIVIST WHO TAKES SIN SERIOUSLY

A conviction of the existence of evil in the social system can lead to one of two responses according to a typology worked out by Max Weber.[39] Weber called both patterns "asceticism." Asceticism is a mode of religious response in the face of a larger society given over with little restraint to self-seeking. The goal of ascetics is to achieve mastery over fallen nature. To achieve this control, they structure the whole of life in an effort to be conformed to the will of God. Asceticism produces a systematic, methodical character and an avoidance of what is purposeless and ostentatious.

Weber identified two very different forms of asceticism. One he called "other-worldly asceticism," the other "inner-worldly asceticism." Of the two, inner-worldly asceticism was the most likely to provide leverage for evolutionary social change. Inner-worldly ascetics, best represented in certain types of Puritanism, apply their concern about sin and spiritual discipline to a mastery of life around themselves, rather than to defeating sin within. Other-worldly ascetics flee the world. Inner-worldly ascetics face the world, extending the quest for the mastery of evil to all aspects of the human condition.

Because inner-worldly ascetics reject the existing world-order, the world is their place of mission. The theocentric viewpoint on which their criticism of the world is based is also the source of a calling to glorify God in the world. The energies committed to the struggle with evil within are channeled into vigorous support of this outward mission. For the Calvinists, for example, in addition to a specific calling in daily work, there was also a general vocation in the world to work for the establishment of a society of justice and mercy.[40] Calvinism everywhere formed voluntary associations for deeds of neighborly love and was engaged in a systematic endeavor to mold society as a whole.[41]

Evangelical Christianity has borne several marks of the inner-worldly ascetic pattern. Although in the twentieth century the drive for social righteousness has frequently been lacking, the unmatched commitment to worldwide missions is a form of activism expressing that religious energy and discipline in financial sacrifice, physical suffering, vocational choice, and prayer. The plethora of supportive organizations is also characteristic. Even separatist patterns in church polity and personal ethics can be seen in part as a methodical discipline to support the mission. Accordingly, zealous activity has been directed not to saving one's own soul but to setting one's redeemed soul to save the world. In ancient Israel one also sees a separated people with a mission to the nations. In the Bible, the notion of the separation of a people from the world is but the corollary of the revelation of the Lord to a people who will become the bearer of the living truth and a missionary to all humanity.[42]

Biblically informed concern about sin thus provides a piety capable of energizing effective social action. Vigorous and systematic social involvement requires not that Christians weaken the structure of their piety but rather that they carry it through to its natural social consequences.

Finally, there is a danger that an awareness of evil may lead to nothing more than dogmatic condemnation of the surrounding society. But social evil also means the fear, the humiliation, the suffering, and the loss when people hurt people. God knows that hurt and cries out against it. We do not know what sin is until we weep with the weeping of the earth. We are in touch with the substance of justice when the hunger for righteousness within us is one with our anguish at human suffering. Then we know more fully what it means that Christ was "made sin" for us.

Chapter 2

GOD'S GRACE AND OUR ACTION

"A piety of works" is an idea about social action which discourages many Christians from becoming involved. To work actively to make changes in society seems to them to reflect a lack of trust in God's providential care. Instead of relying on the power of Christ's work to change lives and to change history, social activists are accused of first depending upon their own works to initiate change and then trusting in the programs of social change thus produced. Christian social action is suspected of being a religion of works separate from, and not growing out of, God's saving work in Christ.

From a different perspective, the radical demands of Jesus (or of his contemporary interpreters) are not effectively acted upon by many Christians because fulfilment seems beyond their personal resources.

But despite suspicion on the one hand and fear on the other, Christian social action, indeed all Christian conduct, properly understood, is grounded in the grace of Jesus Christ. Because of sin, we are dependent upon God's power through Christ working for us, in us, and through us. Christian social action builds on everything that the Scriptures say about the grace of God in salvation. As a form of Christian ethics, it starts with the cross, with appropriation of atonement.

CHRISTIAN ETHICS GROUNDED IN GOD'S ACTS OF GRACE

> By sending the Son in the likeness of sinful flesh and to take away sin, God condemned sin in the flesh in order that the just requirement of the Law might be fulfilled in us who walk not in conformity with the flesh but in conformity with the Spirit. (Rom. 8.3–4)

Grace preceding Christian ethics. Every system of ethics must have some ultimate basis of goodness and obligation; God is the basis of Christian ethics.

But why does God have that authority over us? Why do we keep God's commandments? If we wish to respond by means of a coherent presentation of theology, there is more than one approach. One could start with human need. One could start by considering God's character, God's sovereignty, and God's intentions in creation and history and in the Law. But the question can be answered in terms of spiritual autobiography. The "why" now does not call for purely rational explanations, rather it asks why in fact you as a person seek to obey this God. It was with this question in mind that Karl Barth stated that God does not have authority over us because of a particular definition of God. We recognize this claim because God is "the God who is gracious to us in Jesus Christ."[1] Barth here has encapsulated a central truth of New Testament theology and ethics. Our obedience to God is inextricably bound up with our reception of divine grace in and following conversion.

"Clean out the old yeast," writes Paul, "in order that you may be a fresh batch just as you are, without fermentation. Because Christ our Paschal lamb was sacrified" (1 Cor. 5.7). Paul demands that the behavior of the believer conform to his or her identity as a Christian. "Without fermentation" is the character of the Christian through conversion and baptism, based on Christ's sacrificial act for us. "Clean out the old yeast" describes the ethical duty of the Christian to conform to this reality. The "old yeast," as the context shows, is vice, particularly sexual immorality, but also such things as rapine and greed. In this exhortation the Christian is told to "become what you are."[2] Our ethical behavior is to correspond to what God has enabled us to be by adoption and grace based on God's historical, once-for-all act in Christ's death and resurrection. Be (imperative) what you are (indicative) in Christ; thus we are given an "indicative and imperative" ethical appeal. We could call it "grace and ethics."

Romans 6 is a classic passage illustrating this relationship of grace and ethics. A section on grace, demonstrating our union in baptism with Christ's death and resurrection (vv. 2–10), is followed by a section of instructions on the obedient behavior that this union impels (vv. 12–23). Verse 12 is the link between the two sections: "Therefore let not sin reign in the death of your bodies so as to obey its desires." Yet even within the ethical section statements of grace and ethical imperatives interpenetrate.[3] "Do not put the parts of your body at the disposal of sin as tools of wickedness but put yourselves at the disposal of God" states the imperative (v. 13a). In the phrase that follows, Paul presents the state of reality, the situation of grace, on which the injunction is based, echoing the thought of the first part of the chapter: "as those who have risen from death to life" (v. 13b).

We find an outstanding example of this biblical perspective in the second chapter of Philippians. Confronting rancor and self-centeredness in this church, Paul argues that this conduct denies the grounding of their new life. A spirit of love and putting others before oneself (vv. 2–4) is what corresponds to the "incentive of love" (v. 1)[4] at the heart of their faith. Their mind-set should express the core events of love which have made possible their relationship with Christ,

> who, although he was in the form of God, did not consider being equal with God something to take advantage of, but he humbled himself by taking the form of a slave, being like us. And when he appeared in human form, he humbled himself and became obedient unto death, indeed, death on a cross. Therefore God has raised him to the loftiest heights and granted him the name which is above every name in order that at the name of Jesus every knee should bow. . . . (vv. 6–10)

Ernst Käsemann, in an important article on this passage, argued that Paul is not urging a self-conscious imitation of Christ, but participation in the ethos of this drama of salvation—the source of their being as Christians.[5]

John 3.21, for a final New Testament example, states that "those who do what is true come to the light that their deeds may be clearly seen as being done in God." What are "deeds done in God"? They are deeds rising out of and in harmony with a relationship with God.

Grace appears as the foundation of ethics in the Old Testament also. "For ancient Israel, the basic motive for ethical action of a particular kind is the obligation to respond to the activity of God on her behalf."[6] The covenantal structure provides the form. The earlier Hittite covenants already had a historical prologue which told of the benefits which the lord had in the past bestowed upon vassal people who had no claim to them; having received these benefits, the vassal is bound to obedience.[7] Thus the Decalogue begins, "I am the Lord your God, who brought you out of the land of Egypt, out of the house of bondage" (Exod. 20.2, RSV). The conduct mandated in the laws which follow is required in response to what God has done. The Decalogue begins by recalling the deliverance as the focal point of the whole history of Israel, and the Law is the charter of that which has resulted from this deliverance. Even the persistent formula "I am Yahweh" serves to recall the great events of history in which this name was revealed, continually underlining the motivation to respond to God's acts of grace.[8]

The priority of God's grace to ethics, in the sense that the root is prior to the stem reflects the sovereignty of God. As Victor Furnish points out, righteousness is not something under our control; rather we are controlled by it. Righteousness does not involve what we do on our own; rather it is the power of God in whose services we stand. Righteousness as created and shared by God is the presupposition, not the goal, of obedience. Paul's ethic is thus radically theological; it "presupposes that man's whole life and being is dependent upon the sovereign, creative, and redemptive power of God."[9]

The first question regarding the motivation and obligation of the believer is not "What ought I to do?" but "What has God done for me?" "What am I, as a believer in Jesus Christ, as a member of his church to do? The answer is, 'I am to do what I am.' "[10] The authority which God's commands have over us, our understanding of their meaning, and even the ability to carry them out, all stem from the reality that it is our salvation in Christ which now defines our basic identity. These dimensions of God's demand are actualized as, in faith, gratitude, loyalty, and love, we "are ourselves"—our newly created selves.

To base Christian ethics on God's activity for us is not to imply that God no longer addresses our conduct with words of injunction. The Word which reveals to us the deeds of God also declares their meaning,[11] and with that declaration of meaning come the commandments of God for our conduct.

But the grace of God expressed in the Law (and in creation) did not produce the corresponding conduct in humanity. Christ's restoring work points to the words of Scripture and makes them live. God's demand is heard no longer as charging us with our inability to fulfil it, condemning us to death. Hearing what God has done for us, we now can understand and carry out what God would have us do. We are set free by the act of Christ so that, in the words with which we opened this section, "the just requirement of the Law might be fulfilled in us" (Rom. 8.4). The plenary authority of Scripture remains the norm for all aspects of life, addressing us with specific demands of God.

The indicative and imperative formulation emphasizes the indispensability of grace for ethics, but it also indicates that ethics is crucial to grace. Ethics is not an appendage to grace, and ethical admonitions are not one of several ways in which theology can be applied. The ethical as much as the dogmatic is the substance of the revelation and work of God.[12] "God's claim is regarded by the apostle as a constitutive part of God's gift."[13] What God is creating is a new realm of social existence, a believing and obedient human community. In Christ the new Israel is found. Creating and urging new ways for human beings to relate is not an implementation of God's plan; it belongs to the essence of God's work in Christ.[14] The indicative only exists in conjunction with the imperative.

Grace empowering and invoking Christian action. God's redeeming grace has two aspects. 1. Grace is God's power *for us,* the work of pardon and justification through atonement by the Son. 2. Grace is also God's power *in us,* the work of sanctification by the Spirit of God, as well as the Spirit's work in drawing us to repentance and transforming us.[15]

As God's power in us, grace gives us strength to be what we cannot be in ourselves. The Spirit empowers us to act ethically, including social action, as grace "reigns through righteousness for eternal life" (Rom. 5.21). The obedience invoked by what God is and does is not dependent upon our wills alone, for God works in us through both our will and our actions for God's own purpose (Phil. 2.11–12). Karl Holl, in an essay on the distinctive elements of Christianity, notes that grace "creates an inner affection, a feeling of gratitude which must find expression and for which the highest is not too much to do."[16] This affection is the source of the naturalness, the spontaneity of action rising out of a relationship with God.

When a prostitute embraced Jesus at supper, her affection aroused suspicion (Luke 7.36–50). Having come to anoint Jesus, she stood behind him crying. Apparently overcome by her feelings and without premeditation, she washed his feet with her tears. She wiped them with her hair, inviting shame by letting down her hair in public. She "continually kissed" (imperfect tense, v. 38) his feet—a sign of complete submission, further humiliating herself for Jesus.[17] Jesus' acceptance of these actions at a meal was itself an indication of forgiveness for her sin. To explain the situation and to teach a beautiful and enduring lesson, Jesus told a parable about a creditor who forgave the debts of two debtors, one who owed him the equivalent of nine dollars, the other ninety dollars. The point of the story is that those who are forgiven more will love their benefactors more (vv. 42–43).

For purposes of our present discussion of grace, it should be noted that the term for forgiveness (*charizesthai*) used in these two verses is the verbal form of the noun for grace (*charis*); basically it means *to be gracious to*. Grace is the power which frees one for love and action. From where does the force of the prostitute's love come? It comes from the grace which she has received.

CHRISTIAN ETHICS CORRESPONDS TO GOD'S GRACIOUS ACTION

Christian ethics is a response to the grace of God that we have received in Jesus Christ. What is the nature and content of our ethical response? "We love, because God first loved us," states 1 John 4.19.[18] Once more we see the pattern of grace preceding our ethical action. Our action is grounded in God's action: our ability to love is preceded by our reception of God's love. "We love *because* God loved us." Verse 10 clarifies the form of God's love: God loved us and sent the Son as the expiation for our sins." But we have more than the basis of ethics here. Our action corresponds in kind to God's action. We *love* because God *loved* us. The content, the nature of God's grace determines the content and nature of our acts. Our response is love because God's grace is manifest as love. Karl Barth writes that we are to do what responds to God's grace. With our actions we are to render account to it.[19]

Ephesians provides a similar teaching: "Become imitators of God as much loved children and conduct yourselves in love, just as Christ loved you and give himself on behalf of us" (5.1–2). We are loving in our conduct because its foundation is the love expressed in Christ's sacrifice for us. The command in this passage to imitate God as children reiterates the lesson. As children copy their parents in appearance and conduct, we are to be like God in love. The preceding two verses have the same thought.

> Let all bitterness and anger and wrath and clamor and slander be put away from you along with every vice. But become kind to each other and compassionate, being gracious [or forgiving, *charizesthai*] to each other just as God in Christ was gracious [*charizesthai*] to you. (4.31–32)

Because God has been gracious to us, graciousness is to characterize our relationships with others. We are to carry out to others the pattern of God's actions for us.

The presence of God's grace in us as a power reproducing itself is a key to understanding a paradox: a faith which opens itself to the worst of sinners yet confronts them with the highest of moral standards. The ancient foe of the church, Celsus, sneered at the Christian God, who seemed to him to be like a robber baron who gathered only criminals around him. Yet in the relationship between the indicative of grace and the ethical imperative we are bidden to live the life of Christ himself (Rom. 6.5–12); we are to share the life of the new Adam, the focus of the new creation, the embodiment of the human ideal.[20] Holl marvels at this faith, which holds that God extends a total self-offering to the sinner; yet on this relationship of grace the most exacting ethic conceivable is built. This forgiveness brings the sinner into a close and warm relationship with God and at the same time establishes a morality in which God's own perfection provides the model (Eph. 5.1).[21]

SOCIAL ACTIONS OF GRACE

Karl Barth states that grace demands that we do in our own circle that which God does by Christ. We should attest to God's creating, reconciling, and redeeming acts by deeds and attitudes which correspond to them.[22] What is "our circle"? It is as broad as the sphere of human relationships in which we participate, which today is not less than global. Our circle includes, certainly, intimate relationships and persons needing to hear of Christ's redeeming love. Yet we cannot exclude our extended social and political relationships and responsibilities, including those social forces which so frequently oppress. As we saw in Philippians 2, in which Paul applied the lesson of the great drama of salvation to the strife in the church, we are to act out what God has done, in the context of our own lives.

The parable of the hardhearted servant is a warning to us. Jesus tells the parable of a minister (*doulos*) of a king who had been forgiven by his lord a debt of ten million dollars (Matt. 18.23–35); yet this official then imprisoned a fellow minister who owed him a debt of twenty dollars. When the king heard of this act, he put the minister in prison. The story comes to a climax with this statement by the king: "Should you not have had mercy on your fellow minister as I had mercy on you?" (v. 33). Jesus drives the point home with a severe warning: "Thus my heavenly Father will do to you if you do not each forgive your brother or sister from your heart" (v. 35). The minister did not enact what the king had done to him, and so the king did to him as he had done to his fellow minister.[23]

Because we have received grace at an enormous cost through Christ's death, grace must characterize all our human relationships. The reception of grace puts one under a heavy responsibility: "You only have I known of all the families of the earth; therefore I will punish you for all your iniquities" (Amos 3.2, *RSV*).[24]

In the Law of Moses, God's act of grace in the deliverance from Egypt is frequently invoked as the basis for commands to do justice to the socially and economically weak:

> You shall not pervert the justice due to the sojourner or to the fatherless, or take a widow's garment in pledge; but you shall remember that you were a slave in Egypt and the Lord your God redeemed you from there; therefore I command you to do this. (Deut. 24.17–18, *RSV*)

Because they had received justice from the Lord, they were to extend justice to others.[25]

The special grace of God in Christ's death and resurrection quickens our impatience with oppression and affliction. Because Christ was subjected to the depth of suffering and oppression in his death yet was raised victoriously, we can hope that the vicious circle of human suffering may be broken through by the sovereignty of God.[26] Because in God's grace we "have experienced healing in our life together, we cannot be content in the knowledge that there is brokenness and suffering in the world."[27]

The objection may be raised that since God's grace in Christ brought us salvation, the activity which would most appropriately result from it would be testimony through evangelism, so that others may share our blessing. Certainly, evangelism is in this sense a basic response to grace; it would seem impossible to be grounded in the grace which brought us to life and not want to share it with others. But to limit our obligation to evangelism is not only to underestimate the scope of God's work of reconciliation (to which we will return in later chapters), but also to miss the fact that Scripture calls for a broader response to grace. 2 Corinthians 8 and 9 delineate the social implications of grace and illustrate the characteristics described throughout this chapter.

> You know the grace of our Lord Jesus Christ who although he was rich became poor in order that by his poverty you might become rich. (2 Cor. 8.9)

In this powerful summary of the drama of salvation, which is reminiscent of Philippians 2.6–10, Paul supplies the highest motivation for our action, connecting it here more closely than in any other passage with the redemptive gift of Christ,[28] yet the action it calls for is a collection for the poor in the Jerusalem church. Paul wrote these two chapters to prepare the church of Corinth for the collection upon his arrival.

The point is that God's grace towards us is to find expression in our grace to the poor. As the following chart indicates, grace (*charis*) moves back and forth between God's grace imparted to Christians and Christians' grace in their contribution to the poor.

God's charis	Christians' charis
8.1	8.4
8.9	8.6
9.8	8.7
9.14	8.19

The correspondence of the human grace to the divine is noted at the beginning of chapter 8. Paul speaks of the grace of God (v. 1) which has been given to the churches of Macedonia (where Paul is as he writes these chapters). That grace enabled the Macedonian

Christians to give despite their own affliction and poverty (v. 2). They even surpassed the example set forth in the book of Acts of giving according to one's ability; they gave beyond their ability. They begged Paul that they might have a part in his collection (v. 4). They "asked for the act of grace and the sharing which is the contribution for the saints." God gave *charis,* and they responded with *charis* in giving to meet the material needs of the poor.

This application of *charis* to both the giver and the receiver, to the benefactor (here God) and the beneficiary (the Christians) is common in Greek writings, in which *charis* has a reciprocal meaning.[29] The benefactor's *charis* is a gift; the recipient's *charis* is gratitude. But we have more than reciprocity. Grace in these chapters remains God's power. God's grace flows into them and emerges as their grace toward the poor. God's benevolent act does not merely "inspire" the response, it actually creates the ability to respond— it is both the reason and the power for the response.

Thus in chapter 9.8 and 14 it is difficult to distinguish between God's grace and that of the believers. "God is able to cause you to have every grace in abundance in order that in every respect at all times by having full sufficiency you may have ample means for every good deed" (9.8). Grace abounds for them; every good work comes from it; yet it is grace imparted by God. Further, because of the liberality of their sharing (9.13), the poor recipients will long for them "because of the surpassing grace of God" in them (9.14). The grace is God's but the poor have seen it in the Corinthians' contribution of money. God supplies the resources which they distribute (9.10–11). The true actor in the collection is God.[30]

Giving to the poor is one of the gifts of the Spirit. In chapter 8 Paul states that he is sending Timothy to the Corinthians in order to complete "the same act of grace" in them that the Macedonians had performed (v. 6). Paul makes this request: "Just as you have all things in abundance—faith and speech and knowledge and full zeal and the love from us in you—so I exhort you to have *this* grace in abundance" (8.7). Moffatt describes this statement as a call to exercise grace in all areas of the Christian life. Paul is saying that the Corinthians have an opportunity to distinguish themselves in liberality as in the other gifts of the Spirit.[31] They already have power to speak about their faith and insight into its meaning; but grace must also affect the relationship of the rich to the poor.

Paul's language is difficult in this verse (8.7). He starts with a comparison ("*as* you have all things in abundance—faith and speech . . . and the love from us in you"); but instead of completing the comparison ("so . . ."), he ends the sentence with these words: "*that* (*hina*) you have this grace in abundance." Most interpreters supply a verb of exhortation, as we did above, "*I exhort you that you have*. . . ." But Georgi reads the verse just as it stands, seeing it as a noteworthy case of a comparative clause amalgamated with a purpose clause (which still has its imperative function). "As you have all things in abundance . . . *in order that* you may have this grace also." One purpose for their possession of the charismatic gifts of faith, speech, knowledge, and zeal is that they may also have the gift of giving to the poor.[32]

As indicated in the verse with which we began this section, Paul uses the contrast between poor and rich to illustrate Christ's great acts of grace and to give weight to this exhortation (8.9). As in Philippians 2, this verse shows the character of the power which vitalizes them as Christians. Care for the poor will demonstrate their love if it is genuine (v. 8).[33] They only have to be reminded of Christ's love. If truly grounded in the event of Christ's total self-giving on behalf of the helpless, our response to those who are weaker than we are can hardly be begrudging or niggardly. Jonathan Edwards made this comment on the verse:

> Considering all these things, what a poor business will it be, that those who hope to share those benefits, yet cannot give something for the relief of a poor neighbor without grudging! that it should grieve them to part with a small matter, to help a fellow-servant in calamity, when Christ did not grudge to shed his own blood for them![34]

The goal that Paul sets for them is a basic principle of social ethics which we too readily ignore.

> I am not asking that there be release for others and distress for you, but out of equality in the present time your abundance should go for their lack that [at another time] their abundance may go for your lack, the purpose being, that there *may be equality.* (vv. 13–14)

The goal is equality (*isotēs*) among the churches.

Paul ends this passage by returning thanks (*charis*) for God's ineffable gift, the whole spectrum of grace (9.15). This is the nature of Christian social action: God's grace in us expressed in human relationships.

SOCIAL ETHIC OR COMMUNITY ETHIC?

1 John describes the illegitimate response to God's grace, the one which denies the source. "If anyone says that one loves God and hates one's brother or sister, this person is a liar" (4.20). Even more specifically: "Anyone who possesses property in the world-system and sees one's brother or sister having needs and closes away from them one's heart, how can the love of God dwell in this person?" (3.17). Christianity demands a compassionate response to the poor. Without this response one cannot have assurance of salvation. The meaning of the epistle seems unmistakable. It makes unconditional for the Christian the code of maintenance of the poor already found in Deuteronomy and Leviticus.

But does 1 John imply a social ethic? Are the recipients of this love all the poor or only the Christian poor? The passage at first reading would seem to indicate the latter. *Brethren,* as used in these verses, is the common designation used by Christians for one another in the early church, a term familiar in the circle of Johannine Christians (cf. John 21.23). They are brothers and sisters because they have gained the same heavenly parent by being born again through faith (1 John 5.1–2).[35] *Brother* means fellow Christian just as *brother* or *neighbor* meant fellow Israelite. Thus 1 John would appear to present not a social ethic but a community ethic, advocating responsibility to the Christian community rather than to society in general. The same objection can be raised regarding Paul's collection for Jerusalem; it was for the poor of the *saints* (2 Cor. 8.4). According to a recent interpretation, even in the beautiful and powerful passage in Matthew 25 ("inasmuch as ye have done it unto one of the least of these my brethren"; v. 40, *KJV*), *brethren* may have the restricted meaning of Christian missionary. Elsewhere, also in a missionary context, Matthew uses "these little ones" in reference to needy Christians to be helped, who are identified with Christ (10.40–42).[36]

This restriction of reference in these New Testament passages has been noted by many who interpret the obligation for sharing in material goods as directed primarily to the fellowship of those in Christ. Some of these interpreters see little in the New Testament that points to a Christian responsibility to the larger society.

But we cannot rest with these qualifications. 1. We are not at present even carrying out our responsibility to the Christian community. How many in the ghetto are our Christian brothers and sisters, not to mention poor Christians overseas? In addition, we cannot get at the social and economic roots of their problems without community-wide efforts which would affect all in the community, whether Christian or not.

2. We must put the limited social perspective which we have noted in the above passages together with the principle of love for the enemy. Jesus broke away from the traditional restrictions on love for one's neighbor. In Matthew 5.43–48 and in the parable of the Good Samaritan, he specifically and directly rejected the concept of a qualitatively different responsibility for those in one's own group as opposed to those outside the group; one's neighbor (or brother or sister) is anyone in need—not only the fellow member of one's community (cf. Rom. 12.20). Therefore to be consistent and faithful to the whole of Scripture and particularly to be true to these teachings of Jesus, we would have to generalize and universalize the teachings of 1 John, 2 Corinthians 8 and 9, and Matthew 25 and see them as material for a social ethic. They be-

come a standard and example of the love which we must apply to all people.

3. A denial of love to non-Christians was not intended in 1 John and the other passages. John's intention is to supply principles for the Christians in their relationship to those around them, and thus the focus is upon the Christian community. The early Christians had no one upon whom they could depend but each other. Not many of them were socially advantaged (1 Cor. 1.26). They were hated (1 John 3.13) and could expect no love from the world.[37] But if the question of the larger sphere of responsibility were raised, *brother* or *sister* could be replaced by *fellow man* or *fellow woman*.

4. Paul also gives evidence of this universal application. In 2 Corinthians 9.13, he says that their contribution will cause the saints to praise God for the Corinthians' "obedience to the gospel of Christ and their liberality of sharing to them *and to all*." That *all* here means all people and not just all Christians is supported by the similar Pauline statements mentioned below. The principles of 2 Corinthians 8 and 9 have application beyond the Christian community.

Galatians 6 also deals with giving, in this case giving to the teachers of the Word (v. 6). (The "teachers of the Word" may be the Christians in Jerusalem [cf. Rom. 15.27].) Paul ends his exhortation with the words, "Let us do what is good to all people, but especially to the household of faith" (v. 10). The terminology *doing good* (*ergazesthai to agathon*) in Greek means kind concrete acts of helping others, not merely having right relations, or not being bad. This care is commended especially to the Christian community, and specifically to Christian teachers, but "defines only the minimum of love's responsibility, not its farthest extent." The first part of the verse states the presupposition that love is "for all."[38] Specific attention is given to the needs of the church with the assumption that the general social responsibility is already understood and accepted.

This obligation to both local and universal loving care is mentioned twice in 1 Thessalonians. "May the Lord cause you to increase and abound in love to each other and to all" (3.12). "Strive always for what is good for each other and for all" (5.15). Our attention is called to those who are close to us and who depend upon us, but this responsibility is not qualitatively different from our responsibility to all people. The community ethic both draws upon and implies a social ethic.

CONCLUSION

The reception of God's grace will affect our attitudes toward the weak and oppressed and needy—those for whom we have the power to do good as God did for us. We should be mindful of our own situation: "When we were still weak, Christ died for the ungodly" (Rom. 5.6). This grace in our lives will cut down the pretension and resentment which keep us from caring for those in need. The Apostolic Father Ignatius warned, "Let us not be lacking in feeling for his kindness, for if he were to imitate our way of action, then we would exist no more" (*Magnesians* 10.1). If we look upon those who are on welfare the way God looked upon us, we can no longer subscribe to the bigoted notion that the needy are deserving of their lot. If our own worth depends, as it must, "on what God has done in Jesus Christ, then all our claims to superiority crumble into dust. According to Paul, we are all saved by welfare." [39] An attitude of grace toward society will cut through the rationalizations and stereotypes used to defend the advantaged positions of our class, race, or sex. The spirit of suspicion and resentment will be replaced by one of generosity and readiness to help. The attitude of grace will lead to a new political consciousness and a political orientation which does not merely reflect the interests of our own social class.

To expect a group of people to have a social attitude which cuts across its self-interest is utopian from the standpoint of political sociology or Marxist critique or even Christian realism regarding the natural state of humanity. But we are speaking of what is possible for God as people yield themselves to God's grace. And God's grace is sufficient; the dowry which, like a bridegroom, God bestows on those married to him supplies the needed social virtue: "I will betroth you to me with justice, with right, with steadfast love, with mercy" (Hos. 2.19). [40]

Chapter 3

LOVE AND SOCIETY

LOVE AS GRACE

Love is the preeminent New Testament virture. Significantly, it is also the fullest expression of God's grace. Both grace and love are expressed in actions which go far beyond the call of duty, but love ties the lover to the beloved with a greater bond of affection.

Love's connection with grace is important for an understanding of its biblical meaning. The deepest significance of the love upon which our Christian faith is based is not its ethical quality, but the fact that the lover was God, the sovereign lord of life. As Stanley Hauerwas has said. "God does not exist to make love real, but love is real because God exists. God can come to us in love only because he comes to us as God, the creator, sustainer, and redeemer of our existence." Thus our ethic is not an "ethic of love" but an ethic of adherence to Jesus Christ.[1]

In the previous chapter we noted that the response and correspondence of our conduct to grace are basic to biblical ethics. Love describes both God's action and our response: "We love because God loved us" (1 John 4. 19). "Walk in love as Christ loved us" (Eph. 5. 1). "Who loved him more?"—"The one to whom more was forgiven" (Luke 7.42–43). Love begins in God's act of grace.

> In this is love: not that we loved God, but that God loved us and sent the Son as expiation for our sins. (1 John 4. 10)

"The liberating and transforming grace of God is active as love, and Christ's death ('for us,' 'for our sins') is the decisive actualization of that love in history."[2] In 1 John this love is extended and completed in the believer's love for other people.[3] John Wesley wrote:

> There is no motive which so powerfully inclines us to love God as the sense of the love of God in Christ. Nothing enables us like a piercing conviction of this to give our hearts to Him who was given for us. And from this principle of grateful love to God arises love to our brother also.[4]

Human love cannot be compelled by the will of another nor created by self-discipline; love is a simple response that goes out to the other person. Love is a creation of grace. The capacity to love is a gift of God, but more than that, it is activated by the action of love upon us. We receive love from beyond ourselves or we do not have it at all.[5] If a child is not loved, he or she is deprived of the capacity to love—thus the tragic spiral of parents, deprived as children, recreating their own misery in their children. The recipients of deep and genuine love gain personal security and insight into personhood which enable them to love better. Correspondingly, the love in our lives reflects our openness to the love of Christ.

How than can love be commanded, as it frequently is in Scripture? Our responsibility for loving is not negated by love's origins in grace. The ability to respond in love is a reflection of our basic character.[6] We can repress our deepest feelings or we can allow them to be expressed. Thus the will is important in encouraging conditions favorable for love, as is repentance.

CHRISTIAN ETHICS GROUNDED IN LOVE

That love is the pattern of life into which we are reborn in Christ is a dominant theme in the New Testament.

> Affliction produces endurance; and endurance produces character, and character produces hope. Now hope does not disappoint us

because the love of God has been poured into our hearts through
the Holy Spirit, whom God has given to us. (Rom. 5.3–5)

The first fruit of the Holy Spirit is love (Gal. 5.22). The Spirit is
not an aid to doing good; it is the power of new life which creates
love if one gives it room.[7] This supernatural infusion of love into
our lives produces the character upon which eschatological hope is
based. The relationship of grace to works according to Paul is seen
here: we are not saved by works; we are saved by God's grace-
which-produces-works, which is God's love.

Love is the "new commandment" of Jesus. "A new commandment I give to you that you love one another; even as I loved you,
that you also love one another" (John 13.34, *RSV*). This passage,
set at the time of Jesus' Last Supper with his disciples, provides a
bridge between love as grace and the central place of love in Christian ethics. The love command is not unique in the history of
ideas; what is new is its relationship to the redeemer who calls
forth a new world which makes love possible. In this verse (as
elsewhere in John) *as* (*kathōs*) includes both comparison and cause:
"That you should love each other *as and because* I loved you." Jesus'
love is both the source and the measure of their love. The model
(*hypodeigma*, v. 15) for love is given in his act of washing the disciples' feet. To follow his example does not mean literally to imitate this act. Instead, his service penetrates our lives and liberates
us to serve others as we become aware of their needs. The second
that (*hina*) in v. 34, unlike the first, indicates purpose. "I loved
you *in order that* you should love each other." Jesus' great acts of
love for us are done so that we will love actively.[8]

When this love is actualized, the other demands of God upon
us are being fulfilled. Paul writes, "Love does no harm to the
neighbor; therefore love is the fulfilment of the law" (Rom.
13.10). Paul's statement echoes Jesus' great summary of our moral
duty. "Which is the greatest commandment?" " 'You shall love
the Lord your God with your whole heart and your whole soul and
your whole mind.' . . . The second is similar: 'You shall love
your neighbor as yourself.' Upon these two commandments hang

the whole Law and Prophets" (Matt. 22.38–40). These two commandments taken together provide the grounds for the demand of God upon us. We can compare 1 John 4.20: "If someone should say, 'I love God,' and hate his or her brother or sister, this person is a liar." "If one loves God one is not free to decide whether to love the neighbor or not."[9]

The second command, to love your neighbor, is a quotation from Leviticus 19.18. Its crucial importance for the early church can be seen in the fact that it is quoted four other times in the New Testament (not counting the Synoptic parallels to this passage): Matt. 19.19 (where it is added to the second half of the Decalogue); Rom. 13.8–10 (where it fulfills the law and sums up the second half of the Decalogue and "any other commandment"); James 2.8 (where it represents the "royal law"); and finally, Gal. 5.14 (where it again is said to be the fulfilment of the law, following Paul's statement in verse 13 that our freedom in Christ is not an opportunity for selfishness, but that we are rather to be slaves to each other in love).

In the light of such instructions, a Christian ethic, and with it a Christian basis for social action, obviously must be established in love. The following representative phrases are crucial to an understanding of the meaning of New Testament love: "as Christ loved us" (Eph. 5.1); "as yourself" (Matt. 22.39); "whatever you want people to do to you" (Matt. 7.12); "aims not at its own advantage" (1 Cor. 13.5). Love is measured against the two strongest forces that we know: God's love for us in Christ and our own love for ourselves.[10] Love seeks the good of the other person, of every person, looking to his or her well-being and not to our own self-benefit; this is the minimal statement of Christian love. But as grounded in God's sacrificial love and measured against the depth of our own self-seeking, love achieves its highest expression in self-sacrifice for the good of other persons.[11]

THE SOCIAL IMPORTANCE OF LOVE

The worth of human life. The most important implication of love for social action is that it provides the evidence for the worth of human life.

> When we were still weak, at the right time Christ died for the ungodly. But one will hardly die for a just person though perhaps one will dare to die for a good person. But God demonstrates love for us in that when we were still sinners Christ died for us. Therefore, now that we are justified, how much more will we be saved by God from the wrath! Because if when we were enemies we were reconciled to God through the death of the Son, how much more, now that we are reconciled, will we be saved by his life! (Rom. 5.6–10)

Paul Ramsey states that the lesson of God's love is "Call no man vile for whom Christ died."[12] In this passage the Apostle Paul notes that to give one's life for the good and righteous is an extraordinary heroism. God's love is seen in the fact that when we were weak (sickly), when we were sinners, when we were enemies, Christ died for us. This shows us how much we are valued in God's love; we therefore have confidence in the face of the future judgment. The basis of the argument is that, by ordinary human standards, it is astonishing that anyone would die for the vile and unworthy. The dignity of all persons is fixed firmly in God's love for them. The highest basis of human worth is God's love. Abel's value was established when God asked Cain, "Where is your brother?" (Gen. 4.9).

The far-reaching character of the ethics that Jesus taught corresponds to the nature of these actions of God's for our atonement. Christ goes beyond the neighbor ethic to a universal ethic. (By *neighbor ethic* is meant an in-group ethic which teaches a higher ethical responsibility toward those belonging to one's own group.) His command, "Love your enemies" (Matt. 5.43–44), continued but sharpened a principle already present in the Law, in the form of the responsibility to the resident alien (cf. Lev. 19.18; Deut. 10.18–19). The only reason he offers for this command is that our love is to be grounded in God's providential love for all. "Become sons of your Father in heaven," who sends rain and sunshine on both the bad and the good (v. 45). "Be perfect as your heavenly Father is perfect" (v. 48). Perfection is here a perfection in love, a love which can be extended impartially to all.

Our attitudes toward all people are important in this passage. Furnish notes the parallel between loving only those who love us and greeting only our brothers and sisters (Matt. 5.45–47). In the ancient world to greet someone meant to affirm his or her existence as a person and in relation to oneself. To love the enemy, to greet the enemy, suggests "acknowledging their presence and the bond that exists between oneself and them." [13] Love thus means recognition of the common humanity of all persons.

Two attributes define us in our relation to one we love. The first, which we have been describing, is our *attitude* revealed in the dignity and status that we assign to the loved one. The second is *intention,* the behavior that we intend toward the loved one in contributing to what is good for him or her. [14]

This second characteristic is emphasized in Luke's account of the command to love our enemies. Luke places the command to "do good to those who hate you" in a position parallel to "love your enemies" (6.27), and there is a similar parallelism in verses 32 and 33. The terms used for *doing good* in these verses (*kalōs poiein* and *agathopoiein*) in Greek ethics have specific reference to concrete acts of helpfulness in social relationships. [15] We are directed to love in the mode of deeds of mercy and kindness. "For Jesus love is not just an attitude, but a way of life. Love requires the real expenditures of one's time, effort, and resources." [16]

Both these characteristics must be present in genuine love. Paul warns of the shallowness of deeds performed without a loving attitude (1 Cor. 13.3). Conversely, we can mask our lack of performance by self-satisfaction with our loving attitude. I may think that I love the neighbors on my block, people in need, or all people, because of the presupposition that Christians are loving. I always speak kindly, and I would be available if called upon for my help. In the meantime I am too busy with the more important affairs of my "calling" in life. But the call for help of course does not come because the extent of my love is not seen; it remains within me, unexpressed. The following illustration wryly expresses the point.

> A cartoon once showed a picture of a woman lying in her sick bed, obviously in misery. In the sink were stacked piles of dirty dishes. A huge basket of clothes to be ironed sat nearby. Two dirty children were fighting in one corner, and in the other sat a cat which was licking milk from a bottle that had been broken. A smiling woman stood in the doorway, and the caption under the cartoon pictured her as saying, "Well, Florence, if there is anything I can do to help, don't hesitate to let me know."[17]

Jesus' great account of the active love which breaks out of in-group limits is the story of the Good Samaritan (Luke 10.29–37). The parable is told in response to the question "Who is my neighbor?" (v. 29). The astonishing answer is that the neighbor is the one least likely to be so considered: a Samaritan; or if you are a Samaritan, a Jew. Your neighbors include the "neighbor" who would seem to be excluded by definition: the enemy, the opposing ethnic, religious, or economic group. It is any person in need whom one encounters.

The parable also stresses the concrete expression of neighborly love; it is introduced with Luke's version of the double commandment of love (vv. 25–28). But in Luke it is not Jesus who states the commandment of love but the questioning lawyer. Jesus affirms that the lawyer has correctly identified the basis for obtaining eternal life according to the Law (vv. 25–26, 28); "*Do* this and you will live," continues Jesus (v. 28). The emphasis in the Lukan account is not on knowing what love is but on love's activity; the parable of the Good Samaritan confirms Jesus' point.[18] The parable does not deal with optional behavior, Christian electives, but with what people who expect eternal life will be found doing as a matter of course. The lawyer correctly perceives that the one who recognized the neighborly relationship was "the one who showed mercy to him." Jesus' response ends the narrative: "Go and *do* likewise" (v. 37).

People are candidates for our love because they are our fellow *human beings,* not because they are members of the same community or have some other special characteristic beyond being human. Love's evaluation of the other person "as of irreducible worth and dignity extends to everyone alike." There is something in every person which *claims* our acknowledgment of value, our love.[19]

God's love for all people is not the only source of universal human value. Dignity was bestowed upon humanity in the fact of the Incarnation. As a human being Christ shared our lot, and in him the potential glory of humanity is seen (Heb. 2.5–18). Basic to the idea of human dignity is the biblical assertion that human beings are created in the image of God. Scripture draws out the ethical implications of this divine image, for example in reference to murder (Gen. 9.6). And in the wisdom literature of the Old Testament, the fact of a common creator, if not the image, is the basis for equality between classes and for kind and just treatment of the poor and slaves.

> If I have rejected the cause of my manservant or my maidservant, when they brought a complaint against me; what then shall I do when God rises up? When he makes inquiry, what shall I answer him? Did not he who made me in the womb make him? And did not one fashion us in the womb? (Job 31.13–15, *RSV*)[20]

Several authors have distinguished dignity which is *appraised* from dignity which is *bestowed.* An appraised dignity is based on the recognition of notable characteristics in a person. Bestowed dignity is imparted to a person, but not necessarily recognizable.[21] Human value based on the love of God for all people is bestowed dignity. Human worth may seem to be appraised dignity, since the human race, created in God's image, must possess certain qualities which enable it to carry out its mandate to "have dominion" over the rest of creation (Gen. 1.28). But as the concept functions in the ethical texts to which we have referred, the value accruing

to humanity through its creation in God's image is in fact bestowed by God. All people are honored because their common creator and loving protector is God.

The idea that human dignity is based on appraisal is opposed
by those who feel that to grant any inherent human nobility would
take away from the glory of God. Differing opinions as to the
extent to which this divine image has been effaced by the Fall
present further problems. Also, self-interest and greed can block
the perception of dignity in others. Oppressors use the perceived
worthlessness of their victims to rationalize their own subhuman
treatment of them. Finally, appraised dignity can be attributed on
the basis of a romantic idea of humanity in general or of certain
groups in particular. When sentimentality is replaced by a more
realistic viewpoint, the basis on which honor was granted may be
undercut. If a minority group subject to mistreatment is judged
on the basis of its value in the sight of God, however, this deeper
foundation will stand firm against any stereotype or misconception.

When the dignity of all people is established in the love of
God, and especially in the offering of Christ, this not only connects human value to the source of all grace, it also posits worth
in what, in terms of appraised dignity, might be seen as the most
worthless of all human conditions. No one is so sinful or so de-
praved as to be beyond the love of God.

Dignity bestowed through the cross upholds rather than negates whatever nobility people have by creation. When we think
of others in the light of the love God has for them, we see qualities
we might otherwise miss.

The assertion that dignity is bestowed on all people by virtue
of the atonement does not necessarily entail acceptance of the doctrine of the universal availability of grace (that Christ died for all).
In fact, even those who hold the doctrine of limited atonement
(that Christ died only for the elect) believe that behind this offering lay God's love for *all* people. As an illustration of this belief:
A French philanthropist, out of his great love for Americans, establishes a scholarship program to enable Americans to study in
Paris. His motivation is love for all Americans, but the places can

only be filled by some, who are chosen at random without reference to qualifications or abilities.[22] A stipulation of the gift is that the program is open to participants from all groups in society.

This story illustrates the Calvinist doctrine of predestination and limited atonement. The doctrine has an equalizing aspect, in that the elect are chosen without regard either to virtue in themselves or to their place in society. Moreover, according to this doctrine no one but God knows who are his elect. Thus one cannot assume that any particular person is or is not among the elect. And therefore, just as in evangelizing one must witness to every person as possibly elect, so one must accord to each person the dignity of one for whom Christ died.

In summary, one of love's greatest contributions to social responsibility is the establishment of the value of every person. John Wesley used the following illustration to demonstrate the implications of the scriptural injunctions to honor all people and to love all people:

> A poor wretch cries to me for an alms: I look and see him covered with dirt and rags. But through these I see one that has an immortal spirit, made to know, and love, and dwell with God to eternity. I honour him for his Creator's sake. I see, through these rags, that he is purpled over with the blood of Christ. I love him for the sake of his Redeemer. The courtesy, therefore, which I feel and show toward him is a mixture of the honour and love which I bear to the offspring of God; the purchase of his Son's blood, and the candidate for immortality.[23]

Love the basis of justice. There are two important aspects of the New Testament statement that love is the fulfillment of the Law. 1. Love is the meaning of the Law. 2. The Law provides content for love.

That love states the meaning of the Law is the emphasis in Matthew's version of the Great Commandment. Only in Matthew does Jesus state that upon those two commands of love "hang the whole Law and Prophets" (Matt. 22.40). And Matthew ends the story with these words, giving them an emphasis which recalls the comment on the Golden Rule in Matthew 7.12: "this is the Law and the Prophets." For Matthew the Great Commandment of love is the key to the right interpretation of the whole Law.[24] Commitment to God and the good of the neighbor is what every part of the Law is about. The other commands of Scripture have their moral meaning as they are integral to a total attitude of preparation to love God in everything and of genuine respect for one's fellow humanity.[25] Love thus serves as the measure of every requirement of the Law.

But it is also significant that love fulfils the Law, and not something else. It is the Law of God that love brings to completeness. Love is a commitment to the good of the other, but it does not in itself specify what that good is. The implementation of love must depend upon a theory of human needs and of values and of how they are interrelated.[26] In appealing to love one also must specify with what understanding of morality one loves.[27] The morality that directs the way in which one loves in the Bible is the Law of God, articulated in the Old Testament and clarified in the New.

An essential part of the Law, the meaning of which love discloses and the content of which is made complete in love, is justice. Jesus regarded it as one of the more important parts of the Law (Matt. 23.23). Justice is a virtue, as it is present in love; and it also articulates love's completion.

Love creates images of itself potent for discerning social responsibility. Three elements in Christian love contained seeds of the recognition of human rights: equality, respect, and perception of common needs.

Since Christian love for all people is based on characteristics which are shared by all—God's love in Christ, God's providence, the image of God, a common creator—this love does not take into consideration those particulars which make one individual seem greater or lesser than another. The result is a basic equality in which the well-being of one neighbor is as valuable as that of any other.[28] In terms of inherent worth or dignity before God all persons are equal. Kierkegaard saw this clearly:

> Your neighbor is every man, for on the basis of distinctions he
> is not your neighbor, nor on the basis of likeness to you as being
> different from other men. He is your neighbor on the basis of
> equality with you before God: but this equality absolutely every
> man has, and he has it absolutely.[29]

Love is particularly unconcerned with worldly factors such as
social status. The letter of James makes this point. Over against
such considerations as status and class James cites the love command. Concerning discrimination against the poor in the church
and the economic exploitation and political and religious harass-
ment of the Christian poor by the wealthy (James 2.1, 5–7),[30]
James writes: "If, however, you carry out the Royal Law according
to the Scripture, 'You shall love your neighbor as yourself,' you do
well. But if you show partiality, you commit sin and are condemned by the law as transgressors" (vv. 8–9). Black Christians,
in the face of its denial by an oppressive white society, found
their essential human equality and dignity upheld in the love of
Christ. In one of the most moving passages in recent theological
and ethical literature James Cone describes this experience.

> Through Jesus Christ they could know that they were *people,* even
> though they were bought and sold like cattle. Jesus Christ was
> that reality who invaded their history from beyond and bestowed
> upon them a definition of humanity that could not be destroyed
> by the whip and the pistol.[31]

Love not only deals with each person on an equal basis, it
respects the human dignity ascribed to and shared by everyone.
This involves both a perception of what humanity was meant to be
and respect for this potential in every person.

A prerequisite for such caring for the humanity of each person
is the acknowledgment that everyone else is similar to me both in
needs and in capacity for enjoyment. "The first step to regard our
neighbor as ourself is to see that he is as real as oneself, and that
his reality has the same sort of actual structure and quality as our
own."[32] Norman Porteous translates Exodus 23.9, ". . . because
you know what it feels like to be an alien."[33] The chosen people

are reminded that all persons are alike in ways that are likely to be forgotten, such as the capacity to feel pain and affection, and to desire self-respect.[34] Love is denied when we rationalize someone else's suffering as less important than ours. We may see poor people living in circumstances which we would never choose yet convince ourselves that they are content and can be left alone. ("I was in Alabama in the Army. I spent a lot of time around the Negro sharecroppers. They're happy.") A sharecropper or a Latin American peasant feels just as deep a void at the death of a child as do we. The suffering people of the world do not have less refined sensitivity to hunger, or cold, or the pain of sickness. Che Guevara's last letter to his children addressed this implication of love: "Above all, always be capable of feeling deeply any injustice committed against anyone anywhere in the world."[35]

A desire for the well-being of each person leads to the idea of basic rights for each person. The concept of human rights reflects the three aspects of love that we have just described: love as equality, in that rights are possessed by all; love as respect, in that rights help preserve human dignity; love as perception of common needs, in that rights work to protect the minimal conditions for life together.

William Ernest Hocking says that the historical process of making life more humane requires the search for principles which people can know as they are confronted by the complex moral demands of their mutual relations.[36] The implications of love have to be spelled out so that they will be permanent and normative rather than changing with situations, subject to rationalization, distortion, or ignorance. In social relations rights define a basic minimum of human values from which to start.[37] These implications of love are stated as fixed duties which must be insisted upon even for those who do not wish to be loving or to recognize the authority of God or to recognize the authority of God on this point.

Some Christians have difficulties with the concept of rights. Rights are viewed as secular in origin, with an emphasis on humanity over God and on freedom over responsibility.

While more than an extrapolation of Christian love, the development of the concept of rights was influenced by the Christian perception of the value of the person. Although the terminology of natural rights was Stoic in origin, the motivation for its development was Christian. Human rights are a crystallization of the claims that a person has when valued as an end. Paul Ramsey states, "These so-called natural rights are measured out historically to men in the West by the supernatural measure which gave the meaning of obligation in Christian ethics. By its very nature Christian love counts men to be things of value, ends to be served in spite of everything."[38] Early Protestantism, and especially Puritanism, played an important role in the development of the modern concept of rights. Rights of individuals which protect them from oppression by the larger community developed from the medieval concern for the needs of the human community.

Although the Bible does not have a catalogue of duties called "human rights," it does reveal claims of justice which function as rights for each member of the community; some translations perceptively translate the justice terminology at times as *rights* (e.g., Jer. 5.28: "They do not defend the *rights* [*mišpāṭ*] of the needy," *RSV*). The later practice of specifying rights in a catalogue or bill is an important development, for it more clearly identifies the agreed-upon minimum in social relations. If there had been a biblical list of human rights, it might have begun with such items as these: the sanctity of life; the right not to be permanently deprived of land; equality in the means of livelihood and where this is not possible, equality of opportunity; the right to rest from work one day in seven; the right of a servant of God not to be the servant of anyone else; the right to be protected from the arbitrary exercise of power; equality before the law or equal subjection to the law of all classes.[39] The implications of some of these tenets go beyond even the rights provided in modern liberal states.

According to the theology of love and human dignity that we have developed, human rights are not claims against the sovereignty of God; rather, respect for human rights is an implication of recognizing God's supremacy. For since human dignity is bestowed, based in God's love, the rights necessary concretely to protect and express that dignity are also bestowed. God is the provider and protector of human rights; we accept them as duties as we perceive God's love and acknowledge God's authority over us.

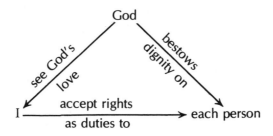

Rights are not a claim of a person against God; they are God's claim on us.

Rights, properly defined, are as much a matter of responsibility as they are of freedom. Every right implies a duty. Rights free us from indignity and oppression and at the same time mandate respect for others. Their limitation is in their concentration on the individual versus the common good of the community; herein lies the risk of freedom and the weakness as well as the strength of the early Protestant contribution.

Defined and acknowledged rights are an essential element of justice. The language of rights is the language of political criticism. The American Revolution drew its ideology and stated its cause to the world in terms of human rights. A social program can be built upon rights but not on a vague conception of the worth of the individual alone. One must draw out the broader implications of this worth in order to have a social ethic.

One needs justice in addition to love to carry on what love starts but cannot finish alone. Love is the greater factor, but justice is a necessary instrument of love. Ramsey defines love as "regarding the good of any other individual as more than your own when he and you alone are involved" and justice as "what Christian love does when it is confronted by two or more neighbors." [40] Since love affirms that the well-being of each person is as valuable as that of each other person, love itself cannot present a reason for preferring the cause of one neighbor over another. It responds equally to both. We assume that we have particular moral obligations to certain individuals: spouses, children, parents, members of the church. How can these relationships be affirmed in terms of love? How can love take into account the special needs of particular people? It is justice which aids love in these considerations because it deals with the individual needs of my neighbor as a member of the community, in the context of his or her special claims, for example as a child or a parent, as impoverished or a victim of discrimination.[41]

Justice carries out what love motivates. It is "the *order* which love requires."[42] As order, it shapes the kind of society to which love points. Because of the reality of sin, we cannot simply leave it to each individual in each situation to act on the impulses of love. Justice is not a different principle, in contradistinction to love; rather it expresses in terms of fixed duty and obligation the appropriate response to love in certain social situations. Loving actions may take place in an evil society, for example in a slave society. But if the order of society is not changed—if "the rich remain rich and the poor poor, and nothing in the fundamental relationship is changed"[43]—then love itself is thwarted. Love cannot rest until it "will breathe a peculiar spirit into the existing world-order."[44] The institution perverts the love within it; therefore structural changes are needed to "make love more possible."[45] Love provides the impulse to change through justice.

Love transcending justice. Love must persist even after it has propelled us into the realm of justice. "Love can only do more, it can never do less, than justice requires."[46] It transcends justice because it is that which gives justice its moral meaning. Paul wrote, "If I divide up and distribute my possessions . . . and do not have love, it is of no benefit" (1 Cor. 13.3). Such a disposal of one's property could be an appropriate response to the claims of justice. In the Septuagint version of the Psalms such an act of distribution to the poor, using the same verb (*psōmizein*), is called *justice* (*dikaiosynē* [Heb.: ṣ^edāqāh]) and is highly praised (Ps.

112.9, LXX). Yet unless a loving attitude of respect for the neighbor motivates justice, the act is empty.

Love also transcends justice because love's work is never done. Love produces moral actions which cannot be ordered by justice. A familiar example is that of the soldier who throws his body on a grenade to save his companions. One can never say that one has fulfilled the love command. How could one say that one has so loved God with one's whole heart, soul, and mind that one will not attempt to love God even more?[47] The precepts of Jesus have the disturbing characteristic of rendering it impossible ever to say categorically that you have kept them.[48]

Love is needed in any movement for justice. When justice is seen as the instrument of love, love may undercut the self-interested disposition that hinders a perception of true justice. Further, love is needed to protect the individuals who might otherwise be sacrificed to a cause, even a just cause. A Christian involved in bitter social conflict, whether violent or not, must retain his or her concern for the individual person. The Christian is distinguished, not only by commitment to justice, but also by commitment to love over and above justice. Exploitative slumlords are still persons, although they are persons under great temptation, and economic power is a corrupting force. Rauschenbusch made this distinction and attacked capitalism, not the capitalist. Our sensitivity to social evil helps us view the opponents as persons like us with human frailties.

The demands of personal ethics still apply in the midst of the imperatives of social ethics. Social ethics may demand activities which will hurt the personal interests of the individual involved (the economic interests of the slumlord may suffer), but love can soften the blow and prevent the transference of hate from the structure to the individuals caught in it. Saul Alinsky said that he had learned not to confuse power patterns with the personalitites involved—in other words, to hate conditions, not individuals.[49] Reinhold Niebuhr put it well:

> One of the most important results of a spiritual discipline against resentment in a social dispute is that it leads to an effort to

discriminate between the evils of a social system and situation and the individuals who are involved in it. Individuals are never as immoral as the social situations in which they are involved and which they symbolize.[50]

The creative power of love. Paul Ramsey notes that love has the capacity to create community, whereas the ethics of enlightened self-interest or mutual interest—the utilitarian ethic—can only preserve it. Since this ethic is based on common interest, it can get no further than common interest. A person or cause which contributes to the community or to me is protected by my obligation to the community. But what of areas that lie outside what is perceived as common interest: where there is no community, where there are no visible ties to what is good for the whole or for me personally? It is the work of Christian love to respond in these areas, the work of reconciliation. "Only Christian love enters into 'no man's land' where dwell the desperate and the despised outcasts from every human community and brings community with them into existence."[51] General Booth wrote, "No one will ever make even a visible dint on the Morass of Squalor who does not deal with the improvident, the lazy, the vicious, and the criminal. The Scheme of Social Salvation is not worth discussion which is not as wide as the Scheme of Eternal Salvation set forth in the Gospel."[52]

Christian love cuts through many secular concepts of right in a way which is consistent with its character as the ethical content of grace. Robert Funk has noted that in one type of parable told by Jesus there are two respondents in the story. The first represents the normal standards and expectations of justice. This person is on the right side of the fence religiously and socially. An example is the elder brother in the parable of the Prodigal Son in his reaction to the effusive reception of the younger brother. The other respondent is one who does not expect anything and has no right to expect anything according to everyday logic: those who were hired at the eleventh hour, the uninvited street people at the banquet, the younger son, the victim on the road to Jericho. Jesus always sides with the latter. The fortunes of the respondents are always transposed in relation to their expectations. "Jesus announces a fundamental reversal of the destinies of men."[53]

This reversal, which finds expression in biblical justice, reflects again the influence of grace upon Christian love. For the justification of the ungodly offends the sensibility of everyday moral perception. To those who assume because of their relation to the Law or ethics that they are in a right relationship with God, Paul announces that the righteousness of God is separate from the Law and that this is demonstrated by the resurrection of Jesus, which vindicated him who was cursed according to the Law (Gal. 3.13). The expectations of everyday moral sentiment are thrown into disarray.[54]

This moral shift brings with it a demand for action. As we have already seen, the point of the parable of the Good Samaritan is the obligation to *do* mercy. Furnish concludes his discussion of the parable with these words: "Obedience in love establishes relationships where none were conceivable or possible before."[55]

Christian love is different from Hellenistic benevolence, which was based on the institution of reciprocity.[56] A worthy recipient was considered to be one capable of making a concrete return of gratitude. But Jesus renounces gifts which anticipate a return (Matt. 5.42, 46). Instead of equity and reciprocity, he challenges us to a unilateral and self-sacrificing acceptance of the burden.[57] Love compels us to go beyond institutional security in search of those strayed from the fold, but those little ones are brought to institutions created by love which take them in and keep them safe. The ancient church gave shape to its love in a social organization in which every person had dignity.

Extrapolation of love for an individual. In practice love brings Christians into social involvement through the carrying out of the full implications of love for an individual. The first contact of Christian love with social action is what John Stott calls a "simple uncomplicated compassion" which spontaneously serves wherever it sees need.[58] But if we see a person in dire poverty or one who has been hurt by prejudice, and we love that person, there comes a time when that love must consider the causes of the misery of the loved one—a time when love not only binds the wounds but turns to stop the attack. If every time the Good Samaritan went down that road from Jerusalem to Jericho, he found people wounded and did nothing about the bandits, would his love be perfect? Spontaneous, simple love, following the dictates of its own concern for persons in need, grows into a concern for the formal structure of the society. It expands from attention to single individuals to the interaction of groups with which the individuals are caught up.

There are no limits to the extent of social action which can be extrapolated from genuine love. Troeltsch argues that this explains what happened in the ancient church. It was primarily concerned with social problems affecting its own life; but the problems all had to do with institutions which were part of the state: its legal system, its ordering of property, its social structure. The church was thus forced to confront the state.[59]

> To love one's neighbor means to concern oneself with his need for bread, clothing, shelter, economic security, peace, education, and freedom, as well as his fundamental need for Jesus Christ.[60]

Chapter 4

GOD'S JUSTICE AND OURS

JUSTICE AND GRACE

Together, love and justice make up the most important and most characteristic component of biblical ethics. The Bible is full of the language of justice. Its presence is often veiled from the English reader by the ambiguity of the terms *righteousness* and *judgment*. The following chart shows the chief Hebrew and Greek words which approximate our term *justice*.

	Original term	Translation in English Bibles
Hebrew	ṣ^edāqāh mišpāṭ	righteousness, justice justice, judgment
Greek	dikaiosynē krima krisis	righteousness, justice judgment, justice judgment, decision, justice

A rule of thumb is that when one sees *righteousness* or *judgment* in the context of social responsibility or oppression, one can assume that *justice* would be a better translation.

Our justice corresponds to God's justice just as our grace corresponds to God's grace (Chapter 2) and our love to God's love (Chapter 3). In 2 Corinthians 8 and 9, after encouraging them in their collection for the poor with the promise of the sufficiency of God's grace, Paul reminds them of God's justice for the poor.

"God distributes, God gives to the poor. *God's justice* lasts for ever."
Now God who supplies seed to the sower and bread for food will
also supply and multiply your seed and cause the harvest of *your
justice* to increase. (2 Cor. 9.9–10)

Our justice corresponds to God's. We are able to give because God
gives to the poor through us, equipping us for this purpose. God's
grace flowing through us is manifested in the form of justice.

In Scripture, the people of God are commanded to execute
justice because God, after whom they in grace and love pattern
their lives, executes justice. Since God has a special regard for the
weak and helpless, a corresponding quality is to be found in the
lives of God's people (Deut. 10.18–19). The justice which they
are to manifest is not theirs but God's, the "lover of justice"
(Ps. 99.4). In deciding a legal case between neighbors, judges are
told not to show partiality, "for the decision of justice belongs to
God" (Deut. 1.17). When justice is properly executed, people are
the agents of the divine will (cf. Isa. 59.15–16).

Justice is a chief attribute of God. God is the one who vindi-
cates the oppressed and defends the weak. "The Lord works vin-
dication ($s^e d\bar{a} q\bar{a} h$) and justice for all who are oppressed" (Ps. 103.6,
RSV). This general statement about God has a particular applica-
tion in the next verse: "He made known his ways to Moses, his
acts to the people of Israel." This refers to the Exodus, in which
slaves were freed and forged into a nation. Psalm 146 repeats this
statement. The Lord "executes justice for the oppressed" (v. 7).
Several images reflect the nature of this justice:

. . . who gives food to the hungry. The Lord sets the prisoners
free; the Lord opens the eyes of the blind. The Lord lifts up
those who are bowed down; the Lord loves the righteous. The
Lord watches over the sojourners, he upholds the widow and the
fatherless; but the way of the wicked he brings to ruin. (vv. 7–
9, *RSV*)

For the poor and the powerless—those for whom, unless God
did something, nothing would be done[1]—God remained the sure
defender. To God they could appeal "to do justice to the fatherless

and the oppressed" (Ps. 10.18; cf. 35.10). "In you the orphan finds mercy" (Hos. 14.3). The truly wise person is one of whom it can be said, "he understands and knows me that I am the Lord who practices steadfast love, justice, and vindication in the earth; for in these I delight" (Jer. 9.24). Those who understand God know that God is on the side of the poor, and this knowledge determines their own position in the social struggles of their day. And if they fail to see the implications of God's character, God makes their responsibility clear through the commands of Scripture.

To those who wonder about the Christian use of such Old Testament passages, it must be pointed out that this justice cannot be restricted to the Old Testament or to any one period, covenant, or dispensation. It precedes, succeeds, and transcends the Israelite theocracy and is the basis of the contemporary Christian social ethic. For it is based on the character of God as king of the universe (Ps. 99.1–4). God "works justice for *all* who are oppressed" (Ps. 103.6). God establishes "justice for *all* the oppressed *of the earth*" (Ps. 76.9; cf. Jer. 9.24). The beneficiaries are not only oppressed Israelites (or Christians). There is one God and therefore one justice for all people and for all time.

Human justice is a manifestation of grace not only in the sense that it is provided by a gracious God, but also because it is similar in nature to grace and to grace's expression in love. In Scripture love and justice do not appear as distinct and contrasting principles. Rather there is an overlapping and a continuity. The importance of interpreting justice as an expression of grace lies not only in the fact that it ties this primary social obligation to the motivation and capacities received in the saving work of Christ; it also has important consequences for understanding the content of justice.

Some theologians have argued that justice and love are two distinct theological principles, some even contending that they reflect a distinction within God's nature. Justice, not love, it is said, is the concern of the state. It is related to God's wrath toward evil and preserves society through the enforcement of morality. According to this understanding, justice is impartial; it renders without favor what is due to each person and is therefore appropriately expressed in political or civil rights, which can be extended equally to all. Basic economic needs are not given the status of rights because a justice which met such needs would have to be partial, taking from some to give to others. In this view, therefore, those who appeal to love in seeking the expansion of the role of government to include concerns of social and economic welfare are said to exhibit a confusion of love and justice.[2] The issue is important. As Reinhold Niebuhr said, "The effort to confine *agape* to the love of personal relations and to place all structures and artifices of justice outside that realm makes Christian love irrelevant to the problem of man's common life."[3] The direction of one's political philosophy will be determined by the outcome.

The idea that love and justice are distinct in principle can be traced both to a confusion of terms which is prevalent in systematic theology and to a failure to analyze the biblical material regarding justice. At some point it became customary to speak of God's judgment on sin as God's justice, in contrast to God's redeeming love. This distinction makes *justice* a static (and conservative) term, while *love* conveys the dynamic action of God. Our point will be made clearer if we use the example of two prominent modes of justice within a social system: distributive justice and retributive (or criminal) justice. The first provides the standard for the distribution of the benefits of the society, the second for the distribution of the penalties (punishment according to one's deserts). In classical soteriology, when God's justice, which demands death for sin, is satisfied by God's love through Christ's vicarious death, this is retributive justice, which is what justice has meant in systematic theology. But the Bible applies the terminology of justice extensively to distributive functions, which in the Bible are continuous with the concept of love. So in atonement, God's righteousness (*dikaiosynē*) (distributive justice) overcomes God's wrath (retributive justice).

Of the Hebrew words for justice, *s^edāqāh* has the sense of a gift, of abundance and generosity,[4] and *mišpāṭ* also often commu-

nicates relief, release, and deliverance.[5] It is highly significant that
ṣᵉdāqāh is never used in Scripture to speak of God's punishment
for sin.[6] It deals with God's *positive actions in creating and preserving
community,* particularly on behalf of marginal members thereof. So
positive (versus punitive) is the terminology used for justice that
according to Exodus 23.7 God says, "I will *not* do justice [Hiphil,
causative, conjugation of *ṣādaq*] to the wicked." *Justice* applies to
the innocent.[7] The justice of God can appear in the context of
judgment, as it does in the prophets. Justice may then represent
God's victory for the innocent or the oppressed, the negative side
of which is the defeat of the wicked or the oppressors, often described with terms other than those of justice. But our point is not
that biblical justice is never punitive but rather that it is not restricted to that function. Justice is also vindication, deliverance,
and creation of community.

A similar observation must be made about *dikaiosynē,* the New
Testament counterpart to *ṣᵉdāqāh.* In Paul the righteousness of
God is the creative power that brings God's gift of salvation and
opens the way into the redeemed community which God is form-
ing.[8] Paul follows the Old Testament pattern in that the power of
judgment is never the righteousness of God but is rather the wrath
(*orgē*) of God.[9]

Accordingly, grace is closely related to God's distributive justice. As people who are weak and oppressed seek the justice of God
to establish their rights, so they seek God's *favor* (*ḥēn*) on the basis
of their weakness and distress.[10] The other term most associated
with *charis, grace,* by the translators of the Septuagint is *ḥesed,*
often rendered in English as *steadfast love* or *covenant loyalty.* While
justice describes the content of covenant and defines the order of
the relationships within the community, *steadfast love* expresses loving faithfulness to a covenant or a gracious kindness within a given
relationship or role.[11] *Steadfast love* is closely associated with justice, and is not a contrasting principle: "Sow for yourselves justice,
reap the fruit of steadfast love" (Hos. 10.12; cf. 2.19; 10.12;
12.7; Jer. 9.24; Mic. 6.8 *et al.*).[12] A justice which includes partiality to those who are afflicted in their social relations extends

the meaning of the creative power of grace and love; received by the weak and alienated, these virtues create community where there is no apparent basis for it, reversing the normal expectations of the world. God's elective love can be described as justice, in the context of the redemption of Israel from Egypt (Mic. 6.5 [ṣidqôt]; cf. Hos. 11.4), for example, or of the deliverance of the lost human race from sin (Rom. 3.23–26 [dikaiosynē]; cf. Rom. 5.8).

When justice is an instrument of love, how does love affect the nature of justice? Because it applies equally to all, demands respect for each, and appreciates the needs and capacity for enjoyment of every person, love gives birth to human rights—the fabric of justice. Justice functions to ensure that in our common life we are *for* our fellow human beings, which is, indeed, the meaning of love.[13]

Love raises justice above the mere equal treatment of equals; biblical justice is the equal treatment of all human beings solely for the reason that as human they possess bestowed worth from God. God's people are commanded to do justice on the basis of what they themselves have received in the gracious acts of God. In a passage in which justice and love are parallel, it is stated:

> He executes justice for the fatherless and the widow, and loves the sojourner, giving him food and clothing. Love the sojourner therefore; for you were sojourners in the land of Egypt. (Deut. 10.18–19, *RSV*)

Since their good lot is attributed to God's grace rather than to their superior claims, in discharging their responsibility to those others who are now the ones in need it is need which determines the distribution of justice, rather than worth, birth, merit, or ability. It is this assumption that all have equal merit which allows justice to be expressed by the principle of equality. Otherwise, egalitarian treatment would be an expression of benevolence above and beyond what people are owed in justice.[14] The presence of grace and love in justice universalizes the formal principle of equal treatment of equals, shows a regard for the needs of each person, and creates the obligation to seek the good of each. The well-being and freedom of each other person becomes as valuable to me as my own.

COMMITMENT TO THE OPPRESSED

Creative justice. In biblical justice, the openness of Christian love to the unlovely is a principle of behavior cutting across the distinctions of society. In its combination of the affirmation of the equal worth of each person in the community with sensitivity to the needs of each person or group, biblical justice is most concerned with those who are on the fringes of the community. It is dynamic justice which can create a free nation out of slaves.

Biblical justice is *creative* justice, in contrast to the *preserving* justice of the Aristotelian type, which is oriented to sustaining people in their place in the community.[15] According to preserving justice, if there is a disruption of the social order, justice is defined in terms of the state which previously existed. The people involved are judged according to their former positions in the community, as determined by considerations of personal ability, merit, rank, or wealth. As they were not equal before, they will not receive equal shares in the benefits awarded in the redress. Marginal people remain marginal *after* justice is finished.

Through the creative power of biblical justice, however, the individual's ability to contribute to the community is not merely preserved but actually created by justice. The point at which Aristotelian justice stops is the place where biblical justice can begin. The difference between scriptural and classical justice lies in the understanding of what is to be the normal situation of society. The Scriptures do not allow the presupposition of a condition in which groups or individuals are denied the ability to participate fully and equally in the life of the society. For this reason, justice is primarily spoken of by the biblical writers as activity on behalf of the disadvantaged.

The principle of redress. To understand justice in the Bible, one must be conscious of the relatively egalitarian nature of the ideal Hebrew community.[16] It was a society of vinedressers and herders—freeholding peasants who had similar resources in orchards, pastures, and habitations. Most significant was the possession by each family in Israel of its own patrimony in the land, the precious means of production. This patrimony (inherited property [naḥ^{a}lâ]) is real property, meant to be held in perpetuity and unsalable. The result is an egalitarian society of independent peasants.[17] In Numbers 26 God dictates the original distribution of the land, to be divided into relatively equal portions, and the prophets also understand the patrimony as a sacred right from Yahweh. Micah condemns those who "oppress a man and his house, a man and his landed inheritance [naḥ^{a}lâ]" (Mic. 2.2). Applying the terminology of political equality to property, Albrecht Alt states that the prophet's view was that "according to the ancient and holy regulation of Yahweh," the property system "was to be and to remain in unconditional recognition of one man—one house—one allotment of land."[18]

By the eighth century B.C., the time of Amos, Micah, and Isaiah, many of the small holdings of the peasants had been absorbed into latifundia (large landed estates) of a new aristocracy (Isa. 5.7–8). Through mortgage foreclosings and oppressive sharecropping arrangements, the peasants lost their heritage from the Lord and their economic and social position. They were disappearing as an independent class, many even passing into slavery (Isa. 3.14–15; Amos 8.4–6). It is in this context that the prophetic call for social justice is to be heard. The task of creative justice was to restore the poor to their position of independent economic and political power in the community.

If such justice is to treat similar cases similarly, it must take a "context-dependent" form in which "identical treatment" is defined with reference to individual needs and capacities.[19] If we are to fulfil the obligation to seek for all persons security of life and well-being, some individuals will need more care than others. If a threat of violence is made on any citizen's life, that person is entitled to special police protection to bring his or her security level nearer to the norm. This "unequal" treatment ensures equal distribution of the right to security.[20] The equal provision of basic rights requires unequal response to unequal needs. Justice must be partial in order to be impartial. Only by giving special attention to the poor and downtrodden can one be said to be following "the principle of equal consideration of human interest."[21]

This close association between special needs and basic rights is supported by the covenantal context of justice. Needs become rights under the provisions of the covenant because the basic needs of all are to be met by the whole community: "If your brother becomes poor and his power slips, you shall make him strong [ḥāzaq in the Hiphil, causative, conjugation]" (Lev. 25.35). The unequal distribution of basic needs violates the normative order which the covenant is to maintain. It is only in this sense that biblical justice can be described, as it frequently is,[22] as rectifying broken covenantal relationships. Justice is not reduced to a formal principle of reconciliation or faithfulness to unspecified types of community relationships. It is restoration of that community as originally established by the justice of God; it is a community of equality and freedom from oppression.

Accordingly, biblical justice is more than an attitude favoring the weak; it implies that each member of the community will in fact be strong enough to maintain his or her position in relation to the other members (Lev. 25.35–36). The special needs to be equalized are thus not only those things necessary for subsistence (food, clothing, shelter, e.g., Deut. 10.18; Isa. 58.7) but also the resources which are preconditions for meeting those needs: land (e.g., 1 Kgs. 21; Isa. 65.21–22), due process of law (Exod. 23.1–3, 6–8), independence from subjugation either as a nation or as individuals (Lev. 25.39, 42; Deut. 23.15–16; 1 Sam. 8.11–17),[23] and participation in legal decisions.[24]

Biblical justice is dominated by the *principle of redress*, which postulates that inequalities in the conditions necessary to achieve the standard of well-being be corrected to approximate equality.[25]

The Lord is the source and standard of such justice: "When they are diminished and brought low through oppression, trouble, and sorrow, he pours contempt upon the princes . . . but he raises up the needy out of affliction" (Ps. 107.39–41, *RSV*). "He raises up the poor from the dust; he lifts the needy from the ash heap" (1 Sam. 2.8, *RSV*). Justice means "vindication by God of those who cannot themselves secure their own rights."[26]

As Psalm 107 indicates, the redress often will not be to the advantage of everyone in the community. The interests of the wealthy who have profited from the distress of the needy, who have indeed created the structures which have produced it, will have to suffer (also 1 Sam. 2.4–10). Their luxury is as much out of line as is the affliction of the poor (Isa. 3.14–26). The new elite have no need or right to continue as a class. "He has filled the hungry with good things and sent the rich away empty" (Luke 1.53).

The goal of redress is to return people to a normal level of advantage and satisfaction in the community, particularly with respect to the capacity to earn a living and to have a reasonably happy life.[27] The restoration of equality in the land was an important element of redress in Scripture. The Year of Jubilees, recorded in Leviticus 25, is the best known of these provisions but its concerns are also reflected elsewhere in the Law and in the wisdom literature,[28] as well as in the prophets. The provisions of the Year of Jubilees exemplify biblical justice. Among its stipulations is the provision that after every fifty years all land, whether sold or foreclosed, is to be returned to the family whose heritage it is (Lev. 25.25–28). The effect of this arrangement was to institutionalize the relative equality of all persons in the landed means of production. It was a strong egalitarian measure and a far-reaching means of redress. When the number of sufferers becomes too large, private charity cannot cope with the ills of society; love then requires structural measures to achieve social justice.[29]

In the prophetic literature the concern for the hereditary egalitarian land system appears in the concept of redistribution. The Book of Ezekiel, written in the context of the exile and the destruction of the old society,[30] spells out what should be done if the people were given the opportunity to begin again. The prophet sets forth a new distribution of the land which would correspond to the first:

> And you shall divide it equally; I swore to give it to your fathers,
> and this land shall fall to you as your inheritance {*naḥᵃlâ*}.
> (Ezek. 47.14, *RSV*)

In this distribution, as with the Year of Jubilees, the property law is based on the concept of landed patrimony. The provision of land for free and independent peasants is understood as normative and is contrasted to previous injustice:[31] "And my princes shall no more oppress my people. . . . Put away violence and oppression, and execute justice and righteousness; cease your evictions of my people. . . . The prince shall not take any of the inheritance of the people, thrusting them out of their property . . . so that none of my people shall be dispossessed of his property" (Ezek. 45.8–9; 46.18, *RSV*). Thus the coming redistribution of the land is presented as a work of justice.

Finally, in Micah 2.1–5 there is a prophecy of social reversal— those who had taken the land would lose it; and if Alt is correct in his interpretation of a difficult text, there is also a prediction of redistribution of land. Alt interprets the references to measuring and dividing the allotment of the land and casting the lot in the assembly of Yahweh (vv. 4–5) as indicating the end of the latifundia of the aristocracy based in Jerusalem. Yahweh will intervene to nullify the unauthorized claims of this controlling group and administer a new distribution of the land. The families who went into slavery will regain property, the division of which will be as equitable as possible.[32] Micah looks forward to a time when, with equal and secure access to the means of production, each person will again sit "under his own vine and under his own fig tree" (Mic. 4.4; cf. Zech. 3.10).

For the advantaged, justice is a duty (and, conversely, a right that marginal groups can claim under God's provision) to bring all who are economically disadvantaged to the point where they have the capacity to participate in the full life of the community: "For there shall be no poor among you" (Deut. 15.4). It is only after the basic conditions for well-being have been met for all that there is room for liberty to use "the rewards of enterprise";[33] the distribution of luxuries according to ability comes only afterward.[34] But the extent of this liberty was limited in Israel by the fact that it was a society of scarcity and because the norm for material possession was sufficiency: neither poverty nor wealth (Prov. 30.8–9; 1 Tim. 6.6–8).

We may summarize this discussion of the principle of redress in biblical justice with the aid of the listing by Vlastos of "well-known maxims of distributive justice":[35]

1. To each according to each one's need;
2. To each according to each one's worth;
3. To each according to each one's merit;
4. To each according to each one's work;
5. To each according to the agreements each one has made.

For biblical justice the first maxim has priority. "According to each one's need" was the basis of redress,[36] and the principle was put into practice in the early church as fulfillment of the Old Testament expectation (Acts 4.35). "According to each one's worth" was not a basis of differentiation since each person has equal worth. "According to each one's merit" pertained primarily to corrective justice, which we shall discuss below; merit of birth or status was not recognized. "According to each one's work" came into play only *after* the basic needs of all in the society were met. "According to the agreements each one has made" had secondary importance in promise-keeping but functioned primarily in the context of the basic covenant with God, which originated and enforced the other valid maxims. To these Scripture adds a further maxim, which, like the first, is a departure from formal equality: "from each according to each one's ability"; it also was expressed in the early church (Acts 11.29). The ability to meet the needs of the poor is provided in God's material blessings.

> Give freely to [your poor brother or sister] and do not begrudge
> him your bounty, because it is for this very bounty that the Lord
> your God will bless you in everything that you do or undertake.
> (Deut. 15.10, *NEB*)

This principle returns us to justice as grace. "God is able to cause you to have a surplus of every grace that . . . you may have ample means for every helpful deed. . . . God will cause the harvest of your justice to increase" (2 Cor. 9.8, 10).

Bias in favor of the oppressed. The priority given to redress on behalf of those who have fallen below the minimum necessary for

participation in social life means that, in the words of Norman
Snaith, there is a "deep-seated and fundamental bias at the root of
[this] ethical teaching."[37] Biblical justice is biased in favor of the
poor and the weak of the earth. This partiality was nowhere more
clearly and succinctly stated than in the prophetic Beatitudes of
Jesus: "Blessed are the poor . . . Woe to the rich . . ." (Luke
6.20, 24). The first principle of justice in distribution is the cor-
rection of oppression. This is the first concern; others follow. In
assessing the level of justice in the society, the needs of the least
advantaged member must first be identified; it is from that person's position that the social system is then evaluated.[38]

Distribution according to needs differs from distribution according to deserts in that deserts are a corollary of some favorable
attribute while need connotes a lack or a deficiency.[39] In Israel
poverty was viewed as an evil and feared. Only later was poverty
voluntarily sought as a desirable spiritual state by ascetics. As
Proverbs puts it, "The poverty of the poor is their ruin" (Prov.
10.15, *RSV*). The poor are given priority only because their
wretchedness requires greater attention if the equality called forth
by the equal merit of all persons is to be achieved. Some arrangements entailing a kind of inequality were permitted, the rationale
being that they were to the benefit of everyone, and particularly to
the least advantaged.[40] One such inequality was in political power—
the need for authority, whether elder, judge, or king. Inherent in
their station was their role in delivering the oppressed (e.g., Ps.
72.1–4). This inequality is tied to the office, rather than the person.

Accordingly, in criminal justice (retributive or corrective) the
norm is the formal equality of all before the law. The bias in favor
of the poor is qualified in this sphere. Before the court the poor
could expect no special recognition above and beyond that of their
rights (Deut. 16.20). In this sense there is to be no partiality to
the rich or to the poor (Lev. 19.15). If a poor person has violated
the covenant, he or she is to bear the prescribed penalty. But the
dominant concern seems to be the power of substantive inequality
(wealth) to corrupt the formal equality of the courts: in the instruc-

tions regarding partiality the focus is frequently on bribes (Exod. 18.21; 23.8; Deut. 16.18–19; 2 Chron. 19.7).

The judges were not to be impartial in the sense of being neutral. They were not to be detached from the issue at hand, but active to see that the law was used for good and not for oppression.[41] A narrow interpretation of the law was not to be used to deny the poor their rights in the land. Job states that it would have been iniquitous for him to have raised his hand against the orphan, "knowing that men would side with me in court" (Job 31.21, NEB). Even if he could have ensured for himself the blessing of the law, it would still have been wrong to afflict the weak.[42]

Because biblical justice shows a bias towards the poor and because it is a socially active principle demanding responsibility on the part of the people of God, we can describe it as the taking upon oneself of the cause of those who are weak in their own defense.

> I put on justice. . . . I was a father to the poor, and I searched out the cause of him whom I did not know. (Job 29.14, 16, RSV)

THE COMMAND TO JUSTICE

God executes justice through the obedience of his people. Apart from descriptions of the justice of God or that of the king who represents God, biblical justice is seen primarily in the commands of God. Justice is not so much what we know, as what we are to do. It goes beyond simply being just in one's personal relationships; it implies an active responsibility to see that justice is done in the community. God sought someone among the people of the land who would, by alleviating the oppression of the poor, the needy, and the alien, "build up the wall and stand in the breach before [God] for the land" (Ezek. 22.29–30). No one was found, and God's wrath was poured out upon them (vv. 10–11).

> Is not this the fast that I choose; to loose the bonds of wickedness, to undo the thongs of the yoke, to let the oppressed

go free, and to break every yoke? Is it not to share your bread
with the hungry, and bring the homeless poor into your house;
when you see the naked, to cover him and not to hide yourself
from your own flesh? . . . If you take away from the midst of
you the yoke, the pointing of the finger, and speaking wickedness, if you pour yourself out for the hungry and satisfy the
desire of the afflicted, then shall your light rise in the darkness
and your gloom be as the noonday. (Isa. 58.6–8, 9–10, *RSV*)

The activism of the language here is striking: "loose the bonds
. . . undo the thongs . . . let the oppressed go free . . . break
every yoke" (cf. Job 29.14, 17). The action goes beyond simple
charity to attack the causes of suffering, and every form of oppression is touched upon. The will of God is that the people of God
be engaged in those actions which will bring to an end human
misery in all its manifestations. The imagery implies the use of
power to effect justice.

The first sphere in which one would expect such power for
justice to be applied is that of government and law. It is to rulers
(v. 10) that Isaiah directs his appeal to "learn to do good, seek
justice, correct oppression; defend the fatherless, plead for the
widow" (Is. 1.17, *RSV*). Justice here means the lifting of oppression. The orphan and the widow are examples of oppression's victims. It is with the king more than any other personage that justice is associated. The chief function of the king was "the
adminstration of justice and especially the assistance given to the
weak against their oppressors."[43]

Because government is the instrument of justice, it may also
become the instrument of injustice. The biblical authors deal with
both possibilities. Jeremiah addresses "the house of the king of
Judah" (Jer. 21.11):

O house of David! Thus says the Lord: Execute justice in the
morning, and deliver from the hand of the oppressor him who
has been robbed, lest my wrath go forth like fire, and burn with
none to quench it, because of your evil doings. (Jer. 21.12,
RSV)

The people of God as a whole share responsibility for justice in society, including the political sphere.

> Hate evil, and love good, and establish justice in the gate; it may be that the Lord, the God of hosts, will be gracious to the remnant of Joseph. (Amos 5.15, *RSV*)

These oracles are addressed to the populace, "the house of Israel" (vv. 1, 4, 25). The gate is the political focus of the Hebrew village. The peasants would gather for legal matters early in the morning at the gate, the only exit from the protected area, as they passed from their homes to their fields. "Whoever desires judgment calls for it, and all willingly respond to the call, for the administration of justice is the affair of everyone."[44] The Lord made the peasants responsible for maintaining justice in the legal processes, even when this was increasingly difficult to achieve. The deliberations in the gates fulfilled judicial, legislative, and executive functions; thus Zechariah enjoins justice in the political system: "Speak the truth to one another, render in your gates judgments that are true and make for peace" (Zech. 8.16, *RSV*). Jeremiah addresses both the civil establishment and the people as well with this mandate:

> Hear the word of the Lord, O King of Judah, who sit on the throne of David, you, and your servants, and your people who enter these gates. Thus says the Lord: Do justice and righteousness, and deliver from the hand of the oppressor him who has been robbed. And do no wrong or violence to the alien, the fatherless, and the widow, nor shed innocent blood in this place. (Jer. 22.2–3, *RSV*)

The prophets, through the inspiration of the Holy Spirit, used every means available to get across to the people the seriousness and the centrality of the command to do justice. All who by grace seek to be God's people will pay heed. The prophets warned that national calamity was the consequence of disobedience to this command, and they promised life as ensuing from obedience (Ezek. 18.5–9). Social justice is a theme that runs through the prophetic literature and into the New Testament, and it is regarded as so crucial to faith that without it other forms of piety are worthless. The imagery is powerful.

> I hate, I despise your feasts, and I take no delight in your solemn assemblies. Even though you offer me your burnt offerings and cereal offerings, I will not accept them, and the peace offering of your fatted beast I will not look upon. Take away from me the noise of your songs; to the melody of your harp I will not listen. But let justice roll down like waters, and righteousness like an everflowing stream. (Amos 5.21–24, *RSV*)

> "With what shall I come before the Lord, and bow myself before God on high? Shall I come before him with burnt offerings, with calves a year old? Will the Lord be pleased with thousands of rams, with ten thousands of rivers of oil? Shall I give my first-born for my transgression, the fruit of my body for the sin of my soul?" He has showed you, O man, what is good; and what does the Lord require of you but to do justice, and to love kindness, and to walk humbly with your God? (Mic. 6.6–8, *RSV*)

Isaiah 1.11–20 similarly contrasts sacrifice and justice. Students of the history of the religion of Israel differ as to whether or not these passages constitute a total rejection by the eighth-century prophets of the sacrificial system. The irony is more biting if the sacrifices were regarded as a good thing perverted. At any rate, the point in these passages is not so much to condemn the sacrifices as to protest the lack of social justice. This injunction took a comparable form in the wisdom literature: "To do righteousness and justice is more acceptable to the Lord than sacrifice" (Prov. 21.3, *RSV*). Likewise, Jesus taught that reconciliation between neighbors must precede the presentation of gifts on the altar of sacrifice (Matt. 5.23–24). The principle behind this teaching calls into question the validity of any type of piety that shuns responsibility for social justice.

Trust in the temple cult was attacked by Jeremiah. The people were deluded in thinking that their failure to do justice would escape punishment because the presence of God's temple would protect them.

> Do not trust in these deceptive words: "This is the temple of the
> Lord, the temple of the Lord, the temple of the Lord." For if
> you truly amend your ways and your doings, if you truly execute
> justice one with another, if you do not oppress the alien, the
> fatherless or the widow, or shed innocent blood in this place,
> and if you do not go after other gods to your own hurt, then I
> will let you dwell in this place, in the land that I gave of old to
> your fathers for ever. (Jer. 7.4–7, *RSV*)

Obedience in carrying out social justice is integral to what it
means to know the Lord.

> Do you think you are a king because you compete in cedar? Did
> not your father eat and drink and do justice and righteousness?
> Then it was well with him. He judged the cause of the poor and
> needy; then it was well. *Is not this to know me?* says the Lord.
> (Jer. 22.15–16, *RSV*)

"Judge" (*dān*) does not really communicate the thought well. This
does not refer to impartial judgment, but to pursuing the cause of
the poor until justice is secured. How can doing justice be said to
be knowledge of God? Because God's concern for the oppressed is
essential to who God is and to what God does in history. Those
who have truly encountered this God in faith will manifest the
same quality.

The challenge of these commands to our own lives cannot be
dismissed on the grounds that they are in the Old Testament.
They are so central to the ethics of the Old Testament that such
dismissal would imply the rejection of *any* ethical demands of the
Old Testament upon the Christian. The Old Testament was "the
Scriptures" of the early church. Far from repudiating the Old Testament, the New Testament taught that every passage in it was
"inspired by God" and, among other things, "useful for . . . education in justice [*dikaiosynē*]" (2 Tim. 3.16). As we have noted,
the teaching of justice in the Old Testament is not bound to a
particular dispensation but is based in the very nature of God,
anteceding, ceding, and succeeding each covenant.

In the Old Testament God reveals God's attitude toward the

weak and what God correspondingly expected of the strong. The New Testament presupposes this revelation and reinforces it. Paul associates the Old Testament obligation of justice with Christian responsibility for the poor (2 Cor. 9.9–10). Jesus in his ethical teaching and practice stands in the tradition of the prophets; one will not understand Jesus or New Testament ethics except in the light of that continuity.

> Woe to you, scribes and Pharisees, hypocrites, because you tithe the mint and the dill and the cummin and neglect the more important parts of the Law: justice and mercy and loyalty. (Matt. 23.23).

Two aspects of this passage are noteworthy: 1. Jesus carries on the prophetic attack on that piety which leaves out social justice.[45] 2. He clearly indicates the place of the Old Testament teachings about justice: they reflect the highest level of Old Testament ethics and are essential to his new order.

The Epistle of James is also pertinent here. It enjoins that which the prophets found to be lacking. "Worship which is pure and undefiled before God is . . . to care for the orphans and widows in their oppressive circumstances" (Jas. 1.27).

JUSTICE AND SOCIETY

The obligation to do justice makes us responsible for the conduct of society in the most comprehensive sense. Wherever there is basic human need, we are obliged to help to the extent of our ability and opportunity. "Do not hold back good from those who are entitled to it, when you possess the power to do it" (Prov. 3.27) sums up the whole teaching and how we are to relate it to our varying circumstances. Our power includes not only our personal resources but also class position and political opportunities. The theme of justice provides the most direct and far-reaching biblical authorization for social action.

Justice is first of all the basic norm for social behavior. All theories of justice—whether based on natural rights or social utility—are in agreement on at least this point: justice is a term regulating our associations with many people; the individual affected by justice exists in society.[46] So the biblical term, $ṣ^edāqāh$, "stands for the norm in the affairs of the world to which men and things should conform, and by which they can be measured."[47]

Justice provides the standard by which the benefits and burdens of living together in society are distributed. It regulates from an ethical as well as a legal and customary standpoint the apportioning of wealth, income, punishments, rewards, authority, liberties, rights, duties, advantages, and opportunities. Behind the structuring of these values of society is a view of human good; it is justice which expresses this view.[48]

Any genuine justice, and any commitment to carrying out justice, must apply to the spectrum of institutional life. For it is the institutions of society which regulate the assignment of the benefits and disadvantages. John Rawls says:

> Justice is the first virtue of social institutions, as truth is of systems of thought. A theory however elegant and economical must be rejected or revised if it is untrue; likewise laws and institutions no matter how efficient and well-arranged must be reformed or abolished if they are unjust.[49]

There are radically different conceptions of justice, as we saw at the beginning of this chapter. Because justice is related to the distribution of the necessities of life, great differences in the human condition will be determined by the view of justice applied. The inequalities in institutions contribute to the different expectations of various groups in the society. Consider the institutions involved in education as an example. Who is to be educated? The sons of the rich and noble families? Some societies take that course, reflecting a view of justice which assigns what is due on the basis of status, financial power, and masculinity. Are blacks to receive as good an education as whites, the poor as the rich? The practice and even the theory of justice in our society has often said no. Should all be educated equally? Or should there be a priority given

to the disadvantaged—the poor, the retarded, and the handicapped—so that a larger proportion of funds is spent on them? Our
concept of justice will determine our answers to these questions.

One cannot deal with the full responsibilities of justice without
dealing with law and public authority. There are areas of justice in
which a community feels there to be a need for special attention:
justice is then expressed in laws backed by the authority of government. The basic structure of the society is shaped by the cumulative effect of social and economic legislation.[50] A society can
hardly be evaluated without attention to its laws; thus justice cannot be separated from coercion, law, and government.

A separation of justice and government would certainly be foreign to the thought of one living in Hebrew society (cf. pp. 73–
74). "The law is slacked and justice never goes forth" (Hab. 1.4,
RSV). The relationship could not be made clearer than the use of
mišpaṭ as a chief term for justice. For mišpaṭ most commonly means
either a legal decision or the legal claim of an individual.[51] In the
plural it signifies *laws* and *ordinances*. Since the biblical command
is to *do* justice, a critical evaluation of our laws will lead to actions
that support, reform, or overturn the existing legal system.

When God's justice motivates us, our basic loyalties and sym-
pathies will be profoundly affected. We can then identify with the
welfare mother whose real income decreases because the legislature
avoids raising taxes by eliminating cost of living increases for welfare recipients. We shall appreciate the viewpoint of the black
worker who fights prejudice to get a job only to lose it because the
economics of treating inflation through increased unemployment
often result in the last hired being the first fired. We shall feel the
discouragement of the laborer who works full time yet remains in
poverty. We shall share the frustration of the Third World laborer
who has seen the government that he worked to elect overturned
in a coup by elitest forces who receive support from a foreign government. We can feel the despair of a father in another land who
sees the marks of torture on the body of his son who died in prison
and wonders why money from a foreign country goes to finance a

dictatorship infamous for its violation of human rights. Our perspective will include the woman whose husband is dying of liver cancer as a result of working with vinyl chloride, which is produced in his country because its production is too strictly regulated in the manufacturer's own country.

A heightened sense of creative justice will cause the Christian to become more sensitive to the needs of the weak; such compassion is certainly a gift of the Spirit. This will cause us, individually and in our institutional involvement, to give priority in our actions and thought to all who stand in a position of weakness with respect to the rest of society.

Since justice is based on the equal worth of each person and one's right to inclusion in the life of the society, every act which favors the oppressed is not therefore automatically just. Justice must work with the whole range of basic rights and duties. We will be returning in later chapters to the question of clashes between basic human rights. But for now we can state that the closer claims are to what is basic to life, dignity, and other aspects of minimal inclusion in community the higher is their degree of inviolability—and the higher is the burden upon us who are called to do justice.

Justice in the life of the Christian is a sign of the work of the Holy Spirit, for Christian justice is distinctive. It demands a willingness to put the interests of others before the interests of one's self and one's class—an impossibility from many points of view. But God is the protector of the poor and God provides such protection through the servants of God. When our deeds are "wrought in God" (John 3.21, *KJV*), God's concerns for the weak in human communities are manifest in us. Thus it is legitimate to ask how we have thwarted the grace of God, if our political choices invariably coincide with those of the rich in our society and not those of the poor and of racial minorities; let us not delude ourselves into thinking that neither the rich nor the poor know where their self-interest lies.

Such justice is not too much to expect from us, whose salvation took place when God looked upon us, who had no rights in the commonwealth of Israel (Eph. 2.12) and, in Christ, took our cause upon God's own self. It is not by chance, but rather it is consistent with the whole pattern of biblical justice, that Paul describes God's great act for us as *justice: dikaiosynē.*

Chapter 5

THE LONG MARCH OF GOD

THE REIGN OF GOD

The Reign of God is a central biblical concept which incorporates the imperative for social responsibility into God's goals in history. Rather than merely an ethical principle, justice is made part of the story of God's provision—the fall of humanity, the coming of Christ, and the final reconciliation of all things under the sovereign rule of God. We can then understand social righteousness in the context of God's patient toil to win back God's lost creation.

The Reign of God is central in Jesus' teaching. That Jesus actually spoke of the Reign in his Beatitudes and parables is largely agreed upon by contemporary scholarship. The Gospels summarize Jesus' proclamation with this phrase: "Repent because the Reign of Heaven has come near" (Matt. 4.17). Matthew uses the same words to show the content of John the Baptist's message (Matt. 3.2). And the concept encapsulates the message of the early church. The Acts of the Apostles ends with Paul under house arrest in Rome proclaiming to those who visited him "the Reign of God and teaching the things pertaining to Jesus Christ" (Acts 28.31; cf. 19.8 and 28.23). The Letter to the Hebrews speaks of the "city" of God (11.10), giving the church a term from Hellenistic Judaism which it would use for centuries to describe the same idea.

The Greek word *basileia,* which is used for *reign* or *kingdom,* means primarily the *act* of reigning rather than the *place* of reigning; thus in most cases it should be translated as *reign, rule, king-ship,* or *sovereignty,* rather than its usual English rendering, *king-dom.* The parallels in the Synoptic Gospels show that the phrase the *Reign of Heaven* is a variant of the Reign of God; compare, for example, Matthew 3.11, Mark 4.11, and Luke 8.10. *Heaven* is a Jewish circumlocution to avoid mentioning the sacred name of God;[1] and the phrase *Reign of Heaven* was probably customary in Matthew's church, which had close contacts with the Jewish syn-agogue. *The Reign of God* is a technical phrase for the idea of the rule of God over history.

OLD TESTAMENT BACKGROUND

Herman Ridderbos states that the New Testament proclamation of the Reign cannot be understood without a knowledge of the Old Testament background. Jesus and John assumed in their preaching that their hearers already understood what was meant by the Reign of God. They stressed its imminence, the fact that it has "come near," and not its nature.[2] In Mark's account, Jesus began his ministry by announcing, "The time has reached its end and the Reign of God has come near. Repent and believe the good news" (Mark 1.15). In this phrase he summarized all of Israel's expecta-tion for the future.[3]

Yahweh's royal power had been described in two ways in the Old Testament. First, God was the guardian and leader of Israel. Moses' Song of the Sea, after proclaiming the Lord's "glorious deeds" (v. 11) in winning deliverance from the Egyptians, ends with the words, "The Lord will reign forever and forever" (Exod. 15.18, *RSV*). Awestruck, Balaam says of this people, "The Lord their God is with them, and the shout of a king is among them" (Num. 23.21, *RSV*). God's Reign is experienced in historical events.[4] The Psalmist speaks similarly:

> They shall speak of the glory of thy kingdom, and tell of thy power, to make known to the sons of men thy mighty deeds, and the glorious splendor of thy kingdom. (Ps. 145.11-12, *RSV*).

With power and mighty deeds God's rule is evident in the challenges and conflicts of human history. Frequently, God is addressed as king in the context of praise for deliverance from distress.

The Old Testament speaks not only of God's special kingship over Israel but also of a kingship over all creation. The "King, the Lord of hosts" in Isaiah's temple vision sits in the midst of a heavenly court, and the glory of God fills all of creation (Isa. 6.3, 5; cf. Ps. 103.19).[5] God's universal Reign derives from God's role as creator.

> For the Lord is a great God, and a great King above all gods. In his hand are the depths of the earth; the heights of the mountains are his also. The sea is his, for he made it; for his hands formed the dry land. (Ps. 95.3–5, *RSV*)

Thus all nations and peoples are under God's command (Jer. 10.10–12; cf. Ps. 22.28–29).

The Reign is timeless; yet there was an expectation in Israel of a fuller manifestation of God's glory.

> How beautiful upon the mountains are the feet of him who brings good tidings, who publishes peace, who brings good tidings of good, who publishes salvation, who says to Zion, "Your God reigns." (Isa. 52.7, *RSV*)

There was much in their personal and national experience that indicated that the fullness of God's Reign was not present in history. Suffering and disobedience were undeniable facts, and the people of God looked forward to a time when God would enter history in a much more powerful and certain way. Their hope was compounded of the "appeal of the ethical consciousness against things as they are and the incontrovertible assurance that God will act."[6] The Reign of God may be called the center of the whole Old Testament promise of salvation.[7]

What would this awaited Reign bring? An interior change in the people was expected: a new heart and a new spirit that they might obey God's law and be God's people (Ezek. 11.19–20). But there were also important social and political components. "As I live, says the Lord God, surely with a mighty hand and an outstretched arm, and with wrath poured out, I will be king over you" (Ezek. 20.33, *RSV*). This coming would bring both deliverance and judgment.

Justice would characterize God's Reign.

> The Lord reigns; let the earth rejoice; let the many coastlands be glad! Clouds and thick darkness are round about him; righteousness and justice are the foundations of his throne. (Ps. 97.1–2, *RSV;* cf. v. 6)

> Say among the nations, "The Lord reigns! Yea, the world is established, it shall never be moved; he will judge the peoples with equity." (Ps. 96.10, *RSV*)

After describing how God executes justice for the oppressed (Ps. 146.7–9; cf. p. 60), the Psalmist proclaims, "The Lord will reign for ever. . . . Praise the Lord!" (v. 10). The promise or expectation of a full manifestation of God's justice in the coming Reign of God is repeatedly given.[8] ". . . He comes to judge the earth. He will judge the world with righteousness, and the peoples with the truth" (Ps. 96.13, *RSV;* cf. 98.9).

Preparation for the arrival of the King had social and moral implications.

> A voice cries: "In the wilderness prepare the way of the Lord, make straight in the desert a highway for our God. Every valley shall be lifted up, and every mountain and hill be made low; the uneven ground shall become level, and the rough places a plain. And the glory of the Lord shall be revealed, and all flesh shall see it together, for the mouth of the Lord has spoken." (Isa. 40.3–5, *RSV*)

The straightening of the roads is a metaphor for establishing justice. The contrast is to the wicked who have "made their roads crooked"; "there is no justice in their paths" (Isa. 59.8, *RSV*). The passage then describes the compassion shown by the victorious monarch.

> Behold, the Lord God comes with might, and his arm rules for him; behold his reward is with him and his recompense before him. He will feed his flock like a shepherd, he will gather the lambs in his arms, he will carry them in his bosom, and gently lead those that are with young. (Isa. 40.10–11, *RSV*)

Zechariah hopes for the time when "the Lord will become king over all the earth" (Zech. 14.9); then there will be an agricultural utopia with no frost, no night, no drought, no mountains, no curse, and no danger (vv. 6–11).

Micah connects the hope of social tranquility and well-being with the coming Reign. After characterizing the evil in Israel as cannibalism (3.1–3) and prophesying the destruction of Jerusalem in judgment (3.12), the prophet speaks of the promise of "the latter days." Then God

> shall judge between many peoples, and shall decide for strong nations afar off; and they shall beat their swords into plow-shares, and their spears into pruning hooks; nation shall not lift up sword against nation, neither shall they learn war any more. . . . In that day, says the Lord, I will assemble the lame and gather those who have been driven away, and those whom I have afflicted; and the lame I will make the remnant; and those who were cast off, a strong nation; and the Lord will reign over them in Mount Zion from this time forth and for evermore. (Mic. 4.3, 6–7, *RSV*)

In this coming day the Lord will restore justice to the gate. The political and judicial system will again function justly (Isa. 1.26; 28.6; 32.1). The original relative equality in landholding will be restored (cf. pp. 68–69).

According to many prophecies, God would accomplish God's own purposes through an agent, later called "the Messiah." God's representative would lead the people in obedience under a new covenant of peace (Ezek. 37.24–28) and even die for their iniquities (Isa. 53, according to the traditional interpretation of the suffering servant in this chapter as an individual rather than the people collectively). He would also establish social justice.

> Behold my servant, whom I uphold, my chosen, in whom my
> soul delights; I have put my spirit upon him, he will bring forth
> justice to the nations. He will not cry or lift up his voice, or
> make it heard in the street; a bruised reed he will not break, and
> a dimly burning wick he will not quench; he will faithfully
> bring forth justice. He will not fail or be discouraged till he has
> established justice in the earth; and the coastlands wait for his
> law. (Isa. 42.1–4, *RSV*)

From the House of David would come a king whose rule would be
based on justice (Isa. 9.7), who would finally establish justice for
the poor of the earth (Isa. 11.4; cf. 16.5).

Toward the end of the Old Testament writings we find this
answer to the complaint "Where is the God of justice?" (Mal.
2.17): "Behold, I send my messenger to prepare the way before
me, and the Lord whom you seek will suddenly come to his temple; the messenger of the covenant in whom you delight, behold,
he is coming" (Mal. 3.1 *RSV*). With fire he would purge the people of their iniquity and social injustice (v. 5) so that their offer-
ings would again be acceptable to the Lord (vv. 2–5). This answer
finds an echo in the New Testament in John the Baptist's proclamation of the one who soon will come with a baptism of fire (Matt.
3.11; Luke 3.16; cf. Matt. 11.10 par).

At the time of Jesus, the notion of the Reign of God, although
it took various forms, pervaded Jewish expectations for the future.[9]
The hopes of the faithful remnant of Israel were voiced by Mary
and Anna and Simeon in Luke 1–2. Zechariah the father of John
the Baptist also prophesied that God's people, having been delivered
from the power of their enemies, would "without fear worship God
in holiness and in justice . . ." (Luke 1.74–75). Other writers of
this time share the three elements of this hope: 1. deliverance from
national enemies; 2. faithful worship of God; and 3. living in justice (*Psalms of Solomon* 17.26, 28 [60–45 B.C.] and the *Book of
Jubilees* 1.15–19 [*ca.* 120 B.C.]).

The Jewish apocalyptic literature envisioned a divine revolution that would create a society in union with its God and end
oppression forever; the vision compelled its belivers to conform

their lives and actions to the values embodied in their hope.[10] To a prediction of the time when a house would be built for the Great King (*1 Enoch* 91.13, *ca.* 175 B.C.), *1 Enoch* adds an appeal to love justice because this is the time for the destruction of injustice (94.1, *ca.* 85 B.C.). There follows a series of woes to be visited on the wealthy who have oppressed and plundered the just (especially 94.6–8; 95.6; 96.7; 97.8–98.3, 8; 102.9). The *Third Sibylline Oracle* (*ca.* 145 B.C.) states, "And then indeed he will raise up his kingdom for all ages over men." Justice will characterize this Reign: "Even wealth shall be righteous among men for this is the judgment and the rule of the mighty God" (3.767, 883–84 R. H. Charles; cf. 5.414–19 [A.D. 130]).

THE PRESENT JUSTICE OF THE REIGN

This Reign, seen from afar by the prophets, taught and lived by Jesus, with him began to enter history; it is both "the starting point and the goal of the church."[11] It is present, yet only in part. Günther Bornkamm warns of the peril of separating the statements made by Jesus about the future from those about the present. The presence of the Reign of God reveals the future as salvation and judgment, and the imminence of the future Reign reveals today as the day of decision and action.[12]

Jesus preached that the nearness of the full manifestation of God's Reign gives urgency to the present. As both promise and menace, "the victorious divine will and power [is] waiting at the door of the times."[13] The proclamation of the Reign is a call for repentance, a radical change of one's life: The time is full; the opportunity (*kairos*) is at its climax; the Reign of God has come near; repent! (Mark 1.15). The Reign brings both salvation and doom, and failure to recognize the time and the opportunity it offers results in judgment. Before his crucifixion Jesus wept over Jerusalem, for it did not recognize the time of its visitation (Luke 19.41–44; cf. 12.56; 13.1–5). A similar urgency is incumbent upon those who *do* repent: they must hold themselves in watchful readiness for the return of their Master (Luke 12.37). The fact that blessing or wrath lies in the future lends, rather than denies, crucial significance to the present moment.[14]

On the other hand, the things that are fulfilled in the present speak of the imminence of the remaining final acts of God. The salvation that now is evident gives assurance that the whole of which it is part will soon follow.[15] The mystery concerning the Reign of which Jesus spoke is that it begins before the Great Judgment and the end of the world.[16] To those who expected to be able to observe its coming as they would an astronomical phenomenon, Jesus replied, "Look, the Reign of God is in your midst" (Luke 17.21); it is already effective in the events that are related to Jesus.[17]

Various aspects of Jesus' teaching and actions reflected this present fulfilment. Before the coming of John the Baptist, the Reign had been the object of prophecy; since John, it had been present as a factor in history, even suffering violence. (The alternative reading of Matthew 11.12–13 is "exerting force.") The Reign is present, and it is that Reign of which the prophets spoke.

Jesus' personal authority signalled the time of fulfilment, both in his authoritative interpretation of the law and in his authority in forgiving sin (Mark 2.23–28; 2.1–12). The time of forgiveness had come.[18] The note of urgency in his preaching did not signify that time had run out, but rather that the time had come.

Jesus' ethical precepts are the ethics of the Reign, not ethics of preparation or of waiting for the Reign. They are the ethics of the present Reign of God, or new covenant ethics: "the righteousness of those living in the days of the new covenant and empowered and qualified by the reconciliation and redemption of that age."[19] Those who respond to Jesus are to live by the demands of the new age of justice that is breaking into history.

"Now" was a key word in early Protestantism and can serve as an illustration of the ethical significance of perceiving the presence of the Reign. "Justification was now to be apprehended; assurance of salvation was now to be received; the rule of Christ was now to become effective."[20] A sense of catastrophe but also of newness of life gave urgency to the idea of the Kingdom of God and deprived the feudal-hierarchical order of its halo. For the Puritans "the more the idea of the end and goal of life was brought into relation to their fundamental faith in sovereignty, the more it came to be an idea of the coming kingdom rather than of the other world."[21]

The conviction of the presence of the Reign of God was strengthened rather than crushed by the crucifixion of Jesus. By his resurrection and ascension, the apostles believed that God had made the crucified Jesus Lord (Acts 2.36). Christ *is* King. God's Reign is operative in the rule of Christ raised on high and is being realized in Christ's rule.[22] God has exalted him "that every tongue may confess that 'Jesus Christ is Lord' " (Phil. 2.9–11). The Book of Revelation, the saga of the battle between the demonic as manifested in human government and the Reign of God, begins by acclaiming Jesus as "the ruler of the kings of the earth" (1.5).

A dictum of the theorists of constitutional monarchy, according to Karl Mannheim, is "The king reigns but does not govern."[23] We can apply this statement (somewhat roughly) to our concern. Christ reigns but at present is governing only partially. The rebellion against God continues. God's purpose in the present age is to narrow the gap until Christ not only reigns but assumes complete control of the government of the world (cf. also pp. 95–96) so that all will join in the song of Revelation: "You have taken your great power and begun to reign" (Rev. 11.17). We live in a period between the small beginnings of the Reign and its triumphant and magnificent end. "The Reign of Heaven is like a mustard seed" which, when it is planted, is the smallest of seeds; but, when it grows, is the largest herb (Matt. 13.31–32). It is "like leaven which a woman takes and hides in a peck and a half of flour until the whole is leavened" (Matt. 13.33).

By holding together the presence and the future of the Reign, we eliminate a barrier which has kept many Christians from involvement in efforts for social justice. If the decisive battle of the Reign of God will not be won until after the Second Coming of Christ, if a cataclysmic intervention of God must come at the end of history before God assumes the full government of the world, can efforts to improve human institutions be part of the Christian mission? Why build, if the structure is to be torn down? Is not our task rather to help men and women come into the allegiance of faith which will ensure that they can share in the final blessings of God? Marx had precisely this attitude in mind when he called religion the opium of the people.

Our situation is like that of the first disciples of Jesus. We wait, as they did, in anticipation of his return. But according to his instructions our wait means renewed diligence, and not a slacking off, in carrying out the will of God (Matt. 24.44–51). The demand of God upon us now is intensified by anticipation of the future, and there is to be no narrowing of the scope of God's demands. The physical and social are integral to the Reign which is breaking in.

The awareness that we cannot build a perfect society in history must not deflect us from the obligation to work for a better society. We would not think of postponing personal righteousness—sexual purity, for example—on the grounds that perfection will not come until after the Second Coming. Rauschenbusch correctly stated that any argument mandating the postponement of social righteousness to a future era would in the same way justify the postponement of personal holiness.[24]

God is not asking us to build eternal structures but to accept our responsibility for God's creation. We are properly concerned about the health of our bodies even though we know the certainty of death. We should also be concerned for the health of our institutions despite their temporality. A similar comparison can be made with respect to evangelism, in the sense of winning allegiance to Jesus Christ. Our task is to bring the message of his love to every person, even if only a remnant will be believers at the Second Coming.

The miracles of Jesus. Luke depicts Jesus in an inaugural sermon in Nazareth stating the objectives of his ministry:

> The Spirit of the Lord is upon me. The Lord has anointed me for this purpose: The Lord has sent me to proclaim good news to the

poor, to proclaim release to captives and recovery of sight to the
blind, to set free those who are oppressed, to proclaim the acceptable year of the Lord. (Luke 4.18–19)

These tasks are stated in the terms of the Old Testament message
of justice (Isa. 61.1–2), and the Gospels show Jesus as in fact
giving sight to the blind. This literal fulfilment should warn us
against spiritualizing the references to justice in his ministry.

John the Baptist inquired whether Jesus was the Coming One.
When Jesus heard his question, he responded with an action: "He
healed many from diseases, suffering, and evil spirits and gra-
ciously gave the power of sight to many blind people." Jesus then
spoke: "Report to John what you saw and heard: blind people are
receiving sight; lame people are walking; lepers are being cleansed;
deaf people are hearing; dead people are being raised; and good
news is being proclaimed to poor people" (Luke 7.20–21). This
passage can hardly be spiritualized. Jesus performed the miracles
at the time he spoke the words. His actual deeds of compassion for
physical suffering are the evidence that he is the agent of God's
Reign.

In a key passage, Jesus argues that it is the arrival of the Reign
of God that has made possible the power that healed a man who
had been sightless, speechless, and demon possessed: "Since I by
the Spirit of God cast out demons, then the Reign of God has
come upon you" (Matt. 12.28). The Reign of God is present in
the physical world, not only in the hearts of those who receive
him. It is present in the relief of suffering of a physical body.

Healing and announcing the Reign are closely linked elsewhere. When Jesus sends out his disciples on their missions, which
are prototypical of the mission of the church, their instructions are
to "heal the sick and say, 'the Reign of God has come upon you' "
(Luke 9.9; 9.2; Matt. 10.7–8). This combination also characterized Jesus' own mission (Matt. 9.35).

What is the significance of the fact that each of these examples
from Jesus' ministry is a healing, rather than another aspect of the
Old Testament prophecy that he had applied to himself in Luke

4.18? To us healing would seem distinct from the more political acts of liberating prisoners and ending oppression. But to the Hebrews, physical healing and economic or political deliverance do not belong to separate spheres. Their juxtaposition in Isaiah 61.1 is not unique. In Psalm 146, for example, the opening of the eyes of the blind is made parallel to such divine actions as executing justice for the oppressed, setting prisoners free, and upholding the widow and fatherless (vv. 7–9). Thus it is appropriate for Matthew to view Jesus' acts of healing as the fulfilment of the prediction that the Servant of the Lord would establish justice (Matt. 12.18–21; Isa. 42.1–4; cf. p. 87). Malachi had promised that "the sun of *justice*" (ṣᵉdāqāh) would "rise with *healing* in his wings" (Mal. 4.2). Indeed, healing can be seen as a form of justice, because the body is a person's link with the world (cf. p. 117), and disease is one of the many forces by which it is assailed.

Jesus' ministry of justice was not confined to his healing. We should, however, note the restrictions to which his ministry was subject. His incarnation confined him to a specific place at a specific time in history. He was limited by the brevity of his public ministry. He was restricted by the obligations of his unique task of making atonement by his death for the people. Yet in compassion he used his special gifts and opportunities to relieve suffering. The nature of Jesus' healing ministry as serving physical and social needs has too often been overlooked when the miracles have been interpreted primarily as authenticating the gospel, rather than as bringing deliverance. But the Gospels frequently show Jesus' healing as motivated by simple compassion. In the accounts of seven of his miracles it is stated that he was moved by compassion; in five others he heals in response to a plea for compassion.[25]

Since the Reign is present in healing of the body, it cannot logically be excluded from dealing with other material factors which make people suffer. Augustine defined medicine as everything that either preserves or restores bodily health and included "food and drink, clothing and shelter, and every means of covering and protection to guard our bodies against injuries and mishaps from without as well as within."[26] General William Booth, founder of the Salvation Army, drew attention to the person whose *"circumstances are sick,* out of order, in danger of carrying him to utter destruction."[27] We may have different gifts (we may not have the gift of healing) and different opportunities from our Lord's, but in our way we too can respond in compassion to the whole spectrum of human suffering to be healed. "And he sent them to proclaim the Reign of God and to heal" (Luke 9.2).

The fight against Satan. The healing miracles of Jesus and his liberation of individuals from demonic oppression are both aspects of the same ministry. The Reign of God was present as he healed the sightless and speechless man and also as he cast out the demon who had possessed him (Matt. 12.22–26). The Reign is not an idea or a purely "spiritual" force. It is manifested as power in the physical affairs of people as they are hindered by demonic forces. God's victory is won in Jesus' actions overcoming the power of Satan and loosening his hold on creation.[28] The strong man has been conquered by one who is stronger; now his booty can be distributed (Luke 11.22).

The Reign of God frequently implies God's sovereignty over other rulers. In the Old Testament, God's universal power was contrasted to that of the eastern monarchs. At the time of Jesus, people saw a whole order of evil powers in opposition to God's Reign. In the first century A.D., *The Testament of Moses* looked to a time when "His Kingdom shall appear throughout all His creation, and then Satan shall be no more, and sorrow shall depart with him" (10.1, R. H. Charles; cf. *Test. Dan* 5.13–6.4). At Qumran, the Essene Community awaited God's triumph in which by a mighty hand God would defeat Satan and the angelic hosts of his rule. Then "the Reign will belong to the God of Israel" (1QM 1.15; 6.6). In the New Testament, the Reign of God combats the powers of the demonic and is contrasted to the power of the evil social order (cf. Luke 12.30–31; John 18.36; Col. 1.13; Rev. 11.15). "The true front on which the liberation of Christ takes place does not run between soul and body or between persons and structures, but between the powers of the world as it decays and collapses into ruin, and the powers of the Spirit and of the future."[29]

Our age comes between the initial triumph of Christ over the demonic powers, and his securing from them the final lordship over history. After mentioning the Second Coming of Christ, Paul states:

> Then will come the end, when he will hand over the Reign to the God and Father after he has destroyed each rule and each authority and power. For it is necessary for him to reign until he has placed all his enemies under his feet. Death, the last enemy, is in the process of being destroyed. (1 Cor. 15. 24–26)

Christ's Reign is associated with his battle with the evil power structures, described here as "rule, authority, and power." Paul describes death as the most powerful of these forces. The Reign of Christ will see the destruction of every power that is in opposition to the will of God. The Second Coming marks the final victory in the battle against the demonic. Christ's work here affects all of history, and not only the salvation of individuals.[30]

There is basic disagreement among interpreters of this passage as to whether the defeat of the demonic will come entirely at the end or whether Christ is carrying out this conquest now. The form of the verb used to speak of death being destroyed (*katargeitai*) is the present indicative, which indicates action in process. Since Paul is writing of the end (v. 24) and the last enemy, some take this present tense to be futuristic (e.g., in English, "I am coming" can refer to the future). But the normal use of the tense is present action now in process. Paul finds hope in the fact that the last events are under way. Christ's Reign ends when all the enemies are put in subordination to him, but the conquest of even the last of these is already in process. The present age is the time of the consolidation of Christ's Reign, as the enemies are being put under his feet and death is being destroyed, yet the final victory will come only with his triumphant return at the end of history. Until then, life is a battlefield of the divine and demonic, as Tillich correctly observed. Each event in which there is a victory over the demonic is to be seen in light of the outcome of history, when Christ will present to the Father a universe restored to its proper order.[31] This triumph of God is actual in our history to the extent that the destructive demonic forces are broken. If we limit the presence of the Reign to action within the church, we neglect this work of God upon the forces which govern social history.[32] Historical struggles are thus not irrelevant to the coming of God's full Reign. Like cool breezes before a refreshing summer storm, the small victories in which we share speak of the approaching outcome. The struggle against the demonic in general becomes concrete in the struggles against the oppression exerted by the power structures of our day. These can be discerned through a spiritual awareness of the existence of social evil and the injustices through which they work. Stalinism, capitalism, racism, nationalism, and tyranny over the human body and spirit on both the political right and the left are identifiable foci of such oppressive powers in our century.[33]

To what extent are we to participate in this struggle of the Reign against the demonic powers? We are involved by our basic allegiance to the Lordship of Christ over all of life and our consequent duty to resist the Devil (cf. pp. 18–19). Our involvement is in proportion to the measure of the injustice ranged against us, since as people of God we have a basic duty to execute justice (cf. "The Command To Do Justice" in Chapter 4).

Further, we have a share in Christ's mission. "As the Father sent me, so send I you" (John 20.21). His ministry is ours. We can start with the commission that he applied to himself in Nazareth (Luke 4.18; cf. pp. 91–92) and with the work that he shared with his earliest followers.

> The seventy-two returned with joy saying, "Lord even the demons are subjected to us at the mention of your name!" He said to them, "I watched Satan falling from heaven like lightning. Look, I have granted you the power to tread on snakes and scorpions and over every power of the Enemy; and no one will injure you." (Luke 10.17–19)

The disciples had been sent out to heal the sick and proclaim the approach of the Reign of God (Luke 10.9), as Jesus had done (Matt. 9.35). Satan fell as a result. The fall of Satan as a consequence of the witness of Christians is also praised in the Book of Revelation. This time it is their faithful testimony to the atonement, even in martyrdom, that causes the downfall of their accuser (Rev. 12.10–11; cf. 13.10).[34] The disciples also have power over snakes and scorpions (Luke 10.19). The hostility and bondage which have characterized the created world since the Fall (Gen. 3.13–15; cf. 3.17–18) were being overcome in their work. It is not surprising, therefore, for the fellow workers of Paul to be called "helpers [with him] in the work of the Reign of God" (Col. 4.11).[35]

Justice for God's Reign. The proclamation of the approach of the Reign of God brought with it an imperative for justice. When asked by the crowds what they should do in response to his preaching about the Reign, John the Baptist stressed the egalitarian theme of biblical justice and told them that "the one who has two tunics should share with the one who has none and the one who has food should do likewise" (Luke 3.10–11; cf. Luke 3.4; Is. 56.1). Jesus' demand that his disciples sell their property on behalf of the poor echoes the same theme (Luke 12.33; 14.33; Matt. 19.21 par.). The communitarian sharing of the early church is seen by Luke as the norm for a church that had been open to the outpouring of the Spirit at the end of the age (Acts 2.44–47; 4.32–35). It was appropriate for a community that sought to live according to the ethics of the Reign which it sought. Because the Reign comes with a claim that compels response, it was not possible to tolerate a situation in which some had much and others little or nothing at all.[36]

In both Luke and Matthew, Jesus is seen to associate his ministry from the beginning with the same downtrodden groups who were given priority in the justice of the Old Testament. At Nazareth, Jesus stated his goals to be the relief of oppression and proclamation of good news to the poor (Luke 4.18–19). In Matthew, Jesus' teaching begins with the Beatitudes, in which the blessings of the Reign are promised to groups similar to those of Luke 4. Particularly in the Lukan version, in which the blessings are accompanied by woes to be experienced by the rich and the plight of the weak is stated in unqualified terms, the Beatitudes are a radical expression of the principal of redress (Luke 6.20–26). This theme of social reversal is also reflected in the parables of Jesus (e.g., Luke 16.1–9; 16.19–31).

Jesus confronted a leadership consisting of the religious, economic, and political elite. His triumphal entry into Jerusalem and subsequent cleansing of the temple were a public demonstration, one of the most effective means of protest available in a peasant society. Control of the temple was the basis of both economic and religious power in Judea. Thus when Jesus symbolically seized that control, the Jerusalem aristocracy sought his death (Mk. 11.18). In his public denunciation of the leadership of the nation, he included their failure to execute justice (Matt. 23.23). By such actions he took up the role of social prophet.

John 18.36 has been understood by some Christians to dismiss the social and political aspects of the Reign of God. For some, no matter how persuasively the other side of the case may be stated elsewhere in Scripture, the question is settled once and for all by this proof text. Jesus says to Pilate,

> My Reign is not from this world [*cosmos*]. If my Reign were from this world, then my servants would fight in order that I might not be handed over to the Jews. But now my Reign is not from here.

The keys to understanding John 18.36 are the meaning of term *world* and the phrase *from* (or *of*) *this world*. What is the relationship between the fact that his Reign is not of this world, and the fact that his servants do not fight?

World or *order* (*cosmos*) has a variety of uses in the New Testament (cf. beginning of Chapter 1). Many readers understand *world* in this verse as the material world (a *spatial* interpretation). Jesus is understood to be saying that his Reign is "spiritual" or internal; it is seen as a matter of faith and personal relationship to God. His followers will not fight because his Reign has nothing to do with the material world.

But it is not for the reason that the world is material that it is opposed in the Johannine writings. This would imply that matter is evil or inferior and would allow no contact between God's rule and sensual reality. This Gnostic option was rejected by the church. John, in contrast, affirms the physical reality of Jesus' human body (John 1.14).

A second possibility would be to give a *temporal* interpretation to the world. *This* world is evil in contrast to the *next* world. The Reign of Jesus does not involve fighting becaue it does not relate to this age. The Bible, however, does not use *world* (*cosmos*) for the new time to come.[37] Other terminology is used to speak of the future age in contrast to the present. *The world* is transitory, but it is not an age. The word *now* in the last sentence might seem to lend support to the temporal interpretation: "But *now* my Reign is not from here." *Now* (*nun*), however, responds to the conditional clause, "if my Reign *were* of this world. . . ." It functions not temporally, but logically to show the real situation in contrast to the hypothetical condition: "But, as a matter of fact,[38] my Reign is not from here."

The best possibility is that *world* refers to the organization of society on principles in opposition to God's (an *ethical-religious* interpretation). For the very reason that Jesus' Reign has to do with social and political values, it cannot be of the evil social order. *This world* functions for John like *world* by itself.[39] Jesus says in one place, "I have come into *the* world (16.28); in another place he says, "I have come into *this* world (9.39). Satan is "the ruler of *this* world" (12.31) as well as "the ruler of *the* world" (14.30). *This world* is the world as it is estranged from its Creator and Lord.

Particularly telling is the phrase *from* or *of the world*. It literally means "out of (*ek*) the world." It speaks of one's source, the source of one's values. It is always used negatively by John.[40] Whenever the phrase is used with the verb *to be* (*einai*), it refers to evil values.

"Everything that is in the world—the desire of the flesh and the desire of the eyes and the boasting of wealth—is not of the Father but *is of the world*" (1 John 2.16). Therefore, not only the Reign, but also Jesus and his disciples "are not of the world" (John 15.19; 17.14, 16). Yet they are *in* Jerusalem and *in* the first century! Neither the spatial nor the temporal meanings of *the world* fit. The same phrase is used in 18.36. The Reign of Jesus was in society and in the present just as were Jesus and his followers, but because the *values* that were the basis of his kingship are distinct from those of the world, Jesus' servants do not fight. His Reign requires the saving death of its king and its origins lie in the Father's commission rather than in the political support of human beings (cf. John 10.18; 12.23, 27, 33; 18.37; and "The Exemplary Suffering of Jesus" in Chapter 9).

The Reign of God breaking into history brings a demand for justice that must affect the political outlook of those who seek this Reign. Its presence in history both relativizes and radicalizes the activity of building the human city.[41] In this respect the concept of the Kingdom of God has had a powerful impact, particularly in the Puritan tradition. The Kingdom of God represents a standard that is over and above any national culture or political or economic interest. By it all else is measured and to it all else must conform.[42] Calvin stated that the civil government "in some measure, begins the heavenly kingdom in us."[43] Calvinism insisted that God was king over every creature, and thus it refused to regard any part of human life as outside the need of restoration to the harmony of God's kingdom.[44] The political life of society may be used to reform the outward person and encourage moral virtue; so that while a government may not belong directly to Christ, it may apply to life the discipline that Christ desires.[45]

How then is the Reign of God present to us? "If the joyful news of the rule of God is proclaimed, if men humble themselves to do justice to its claims, if evil is overcome and men are made free for God, then the Rule of God has already become actual among them, then the Reign of God is 'in their midst.' "[46]

GOD'S PURPOSE IN HISTORY

Behind our personal redemption in Christ, the formation of the Christian community, the overcoming of injustice, and the subordination of the supernatural powers, Christian faith sees a divine purpose in history. Paul states that after the universe becomes subject to Christ, Christ himself will then become subject to his Father "so that God may be everything in everything" (1 Cor. 15.28). The same thought occurs in Philippians. In the exalted Lordship of Christ every tongue will confess that Jesus Christ is Lord "to the glory of God the Father" (Phil. 2.11). Beyond the victorious Lordship of Christ is the goal of the glory of God.[47] The ultimate purpose in history is the total sovereignty of God over all things. The hymnic materials in Colossians and Ephesians express this thought. It pleased God through Christ "to reconcile to himself all things . . . whether on earth or in heaven" (Col. 1.20, RSV; cf. Eph. 1.10). In the end, all the created world—people, supernatural powers, natural forces, and institutions—will be conformed to the will of God.

In this ultimate purpose we have a solidarity with the rest of the material world. The creation which fell with our Fall (Gen. 3.17; Rom. 8.20) retained within it a redemptive purpose. It was subjected to futility "in hope" (Rom. 8.20).[48] The creation will be set free from corruption at the time when our mortal bodies are redeemed from their temporality and weakness (Rom. 8.18–23).

Seen in eschatological perspective, the material world gains significance because it shares in the ultimate redemptive purpose. A privitization of the Gospel which refuses to take seriously the world with its sorrows and injustices is a sign that the eschatological dimension has been lost.[49] Christ "did not come in order to create a religion, but in order to accomplish God's purpose of placing all things under his government."[50]

Creation and salvation do not exist as distinct spheres of divine action. In the Old Testament, worship, ethics, politics, and nature are all closely related. God blesses the faithfulness of the people with prosperity and fertility. Their disobedience is punished through natural catastrophe.[51]

God's saving work is described as creation in two stages of the Exodus tradition. Mythic imagery associated with the creation (e.g., Ps. 89.10–11; 93.1–4; and in Canaanite texts) is utilized in a description of the Hebrews' escape from Egypt and crossing of the sea.

> When the waters saw thee, O God, when the waters saw thee, they were afraid, yea, the deep trembled. The clouds poured out water; the skies gave forth thunder; thy arrows flashed on every side. The crash of thy thunder was in the whirlwind; thy lightnings lighted up the world; the earth trembled and shook. Thy way was through the great waters; yet thy footprints were unseen. (Ps. 77.16–19, *RSV*)

Later God's future provision of salvation is pictured as a second Exodus, again using creation symbolism:

> Awake, as in days of old, the generations of long ago. Was it not thou that didst cut Rahab in pieces, that didst pierce the dragon? Was it not thou that . . . didst make the depths of the sea a way for the redeemed to pass over? And the ransomed of the Lord shall return, and come with singing to Zion. . . .(Isa. 51.9–11, *RSV*)

Thus the divine warrior of deliverance merges with the warrior of creation who defeats chaos.[52] God's coming deliverance of the people of God is seen as a new act of creation.[53]

> I form light and create darkness, I make weal and create woe, I am the Lord, who do all these things. Shower, O heavens, from above, and let the skies rain down righteousness; let the earth open, that salvation may sprout forth, and let it cause righteousness to spring up also; I the Lord have created it. (Isa. 45.7–8, *RSV*)

Divine actions are interrelated and God's purpose in history has a unity; creation and redemption are parts of one divine process, as justice is not separable from love. Thus human action against

misery and exploitation and the effort to build a just temporal city
are relevant to the divine work of redemption. In its particular
concern for redemption, the church is involved in all aspects of
human striving.[54]

The incarnation of Christ is also a link between creation and
redemption. The incarnation is the divine gift of God's own self to
the created world. The earthly form God chose was humanity, indeed the humanity of the oppressed. At his birth, God's Son was
wrapped in rags in a barn and visited by the lowly shepherds. In
his travelings he had no shelter for his head and he suffered the
most despised death.

The Holy Spirit in the church continues the saving work of
God. Our Lord ascends from the earth, but he leaves his Spirit
within history. The Spirit becomes incarnate in the church, which,
as the body of Christ (cf. Eph. 2.14–18), continues his incarnation. Christ's Spirit now dwells in a people whom he expected to
be among the hungry and imprisoned (Matt. 25.31–46; cf. 1 Cor.
1.26–28; Jas. 2.5). This church does the work that Jesus would
be doing if he were physically upon the earth. It is not the mystical body but the "working body of Christ."[55] God's Reign is
evident in the service of the crucified one, and it spreads wherever
the word about Christ is preached and acted upon.[56] The body of
Christ contributes to the cosmic task of reconciliation. After stating that Jesus has been exalted over all the supernatural powers
and has had all things placed under his feet, Ephesians says God
"appointed him as the supreme head for the church, which is his
body, which is the fullness of him who fills the universe in every
way" (Eph. 1.22–23). The church is the vessel of God's action to
fill all things with the Spirit of God and with power. This epistle
indicates that the church contributes in at least three ways. The
first is in overcoming the hostility between Jew and Gentile (2.11–
22). The second is through its growth in the love and knowledge
of Christ (3.19; 4.13). The third is by deeds of goodness, justice,
and truth, as well as by exposure of the works of darkness (2.10;
5.8–11; cf. Col. 1.6, 10). Schnackenburg notes that the conquest
of the world in Ephesians takes place in two ways: by the church's

growth in grace and by its mission. The two functions are intimately associated:

> By being built up in love, the Church, directed and nourished by its Lord and head, bears witness to the reign of Christ, the defeat of the powers and the return of man's world to God's order; and as, growing stronger, it proclaims all this to the world and summons men to accept Christ's rule, it widens its influence and sphere of action in the cosmos, it forces back the cosmic powers and takes their sphere of activity away from them.[57]

The Reign of God represents the promise and expectation of the conquest of all opposition to God in creation, both within individuals and within society as a whole. It is no longer the Reign that we seek if we serve a gospel which "haunts churches but never ventures out into the market and the stock exchange and the real estate office."[58] Neither is it the Reign if the neglect of its inner aspects results in empty and haunted churches.

The Reign is the Creator's constitutional order for every creature.[59]

> As he has for every man's life a plan, so has he for the common life a perfect social order into which he seeks to lead his children, that he may give them plenty and blessedness and abundance of peace as long as the moon endureth. Surely he has a way for men to live in society; he has a way of organizing industry; he has a way of life for the family, and for the school, and for the shop, and for the city, and for the state; he has a way for preventing poverty, and a way for helping and saving the poor and the sick and the sinful; and it is his way that we are to seek and point out and follow.[60]

As James Gustafson says, attention to the Reign of the sovereign God creates moral responsibility for all spheres of life. We cannot do everything "but we cannot arbitrarily decide that something is outside of the scope of Christian moral responsibility."[61]

"First of all seek the Reign and its justice"[62] (Matt. 6.33). This commitment to and longing for the triumph of God's will is the basis of the prayer, "Thy kingdom come, Thy will be done, On earth as it is in heaven" (Matt. 6.10, *RSV*). We are to choose our ultimate allegiance and then to be zealous in it. And we seek not only the Reign, but also the justice that belongs to it.

A KINGSHIP WHICH ARRIVES BY JOY

> The Reign of Heaven is like a treasure hidden in the field; the person who finds it, *because of joy* goes away and sells everything which he or she has and buys that field. (Matt. 13.44)

The Reign of God has broken into history with Jesus Christ, and the will of God no longer wears the aspect of a legal demand. The obligation now is caught up in our joyous response to the gracious work of Christ.[63] We can now be obedient to the rule of God through the special resources made available by Christ's coming: the power of the Holy Spirit and membership in the body of believers. We can carry out the requirements of the Law because with the Reign has come the new covenant by which God's law is written upon our hearts (Jer. 31.33).

This new covenant came into history through the atoning death of Christ, as he told his disciples at the Last Supper: "This cup is the new covenant in my blood which is shed for you" (Luke 22.20). His death was a necessary precondition for the completion of the Reign of God. The eschatological banquet of peace and joy can only come after his death is accomplished. "I will not drink again from this fruit of the vine until that day when I drink it in a new way with you in the Reign of my Father" (Matt. 26.29).[64] Through "the blood of his cross" Christ makes the peace which reconciles the universe (Col. 1.20). The cosmic reconciliation corresponds to the forgiveness of sin which the justified person shares in the new age ushered in by Christ.[65]

The resurrection continued the entry of God's Reign into history. It not only indicated God's acceptance of Christ's work on the cross, but was also an act of the new creation. The resurrection of his body was the "first fruits" for the resurrection of all who believe (1 Cor. 15.20; Rom. 8.21–23).

The Reign of God, breaking into history with its demand, also brought the Spirit, who makes the Reign present in joy (Rom. 14.17) and in power (Matt. 12.28f.; 1 Cor. 4.20). The gifts and powers of the Reign have been granted to the church (Matt. 21.43). It has tasted the powers of the age to come (Heb. 6.5). It is "surrounded and impelled by the revelation, the progress, the future of the kingdom of God. . . ."[66] The church is to be the community in which, through its behavior and its mission, the Reign of God becomes visible, serving as precursor and *avant-garde* of the society that will be the fulfilment of all hope. The Church is called to represent the Reign of God "between the times." It cannot, therefore, remain passive in the face of the evils of society.[67]

In reaction to the liberal preoccupation with the social aspects of the Reign, it has become fashionable in contemporary writings to state that Reign of God is not a social program and that people do not bring it in. But the very fact that it *is* God's Reign and is already present in grace means that our response cannot be passive. Roger Mehl states that what is involved is not *our* creating or building up the Reign since we are rather to expect it, but rather our service to *God* who is creating and building it up.[68] We receive the Reign as a gift but with it comes a demand and the power to meet that demand so that we can be channels of God's creation. The Reign of God is not a social program, but faithfulness to its demands for justice necessitates social programs and social struggle. The Reign, which shows up the relativity of such efforts, also provides the motivation and grace to carry them out.

Social action in service to God who is creating the Reign is not a matter of human arrogance. It is the obedient and joyful use of the powers that God has given us in Christ. It is faithfulness in the opportunities that God has opened up to us in God's long march through the history of the peoples, and powers, and institutions that form the kingdom which God will not give up.

II

Paths to Justice

Chapter 6

EVANGELISM

In the preceding pages we have seen that God has provided the means to achieve justice. God has made justice known through creative love and the revelation of the Word. Through the power available in the death and resurrection of the Son, God imparts the resources for carrying out God's will for justice in the world. We shall see, however, that those who would respond to God's provision and face the injustices of the world find that they must traverse many paths in the effort to make justice a historical reality. Each such path is important, but none is sufficient by itself. The first path to justice to be examined is evangelism.

THE IMPORTANCE OF EVANGELISM FOR SOCIAL CHANGE

I prefer to use the word *evangelism* to describe one central function of the church in the world, rather than its total work. Our terminology should preserve the distinctions among the different tasks of the church so that our labels do not delude us into thinking that by doing one task we are carrying out another as well.

Evangelism is the communication of the Gospel in a way that demands a decision from the hearer. The *content* is the Good News of the coming into history of God's Reign, centered on the death and resurrection of Jesus Christ, the Son of God. The *hope* of this communication is that the hearers will be converted—that they will give allegiance to God by accepting for themselves Christ's atoning work. The message is well summed up in Julius Schniewind's rendering of Matthew 4.17: "Turn to God for He has turned to you."[1]

While evangelism is extremely important for social responsibility, it is not synonymous with it. Evangelism is aimed at the basic allegiance of the person; it operates only through freedom, never by compulsion; it is addressed to the individual or to individuals in a group. To become a child of God through faith in Christ is an end in itself of utmost worth. While a great variety of nonverbal means can contribute to the communication of the Good News, the spoken and written word is essential, since the content is a past event, which ultimately must be communicated with language.

The biblical theology that discloses the provision and requirement of justice (cf. Part I) at the same time teaches the vital role of evangelism. The ability to be God's channel for justice is a gift of grace; conversion marks the beginning of a new life governed by God's grace, and conversion often comes as a result of that work of the Holy Spirit which is evangelism.

The contribution of conversion and consequently of evangelism to social change comes about not only through God's provision of gracious power to help others, but also through the satisfaction of the personal need for healing in the center of our being. Conversion is a redirection of life, characterized by a new allegiance at the center of the personality and by a new direction in social relationships.[2] As the self is delivered from itself and reoriented so that God is at its center,[3] the hampering hold of self-will is released and the person's latent creative and benevolent impulses are given free play. A break with the interests and values of the world accompanies a heightened awareness of moral responsibility. Paul stated that when one becomes a Christian "there is a new creation" (2 Cor. 5.17).

Conversion will have manifest ethical and social consequences. The coming of the Spirit will be visible in love and joy and kind-

ness and self-control (Gal. 5.22). John the Baptist, in his proclamation that the Reign of God was at hand, demanded "fruits worthy of repentance" (Luke 3.8). When asked what these fruits
would be, he referred to such concrete acts as the sharing of property and abstaining from injustice (vv. 10–14). Similarly, in the
Old Testament conversion was a turning (šûb) to God which was
manifested in love and justice: "You by the help of God return;
keep steadfast love and justice and have hope in your God" (Hos.
12.6). In the Gospels, Zacchaeus, the tax collector, provides a
striking picture of what conversion is meant to be. When he responded to Jesus in joy and resolved to distribute his wealth to the
poor and to those whom he had cheated, Jesus declared, "Today,
salvation has come to this house" (Luke 19.9).

Correspondingly, when revival and spiritual awakenings have
been widespread in a society, they have frequently resulted in
movements of social concern and reform. The best example in
America is the urban revivals in the 1850s. In a pioneering work,
Timothy Smith demonstrated the close relationship between the
revival and the movements for social service and legislative reform
which sprang up in this period.[4] Most significant was the movement to abolish slavery. In large measure an offshoot of the movement animated by evangelicalism in Great Britain, it spread to
America with the spread of evangelicalism.[5]

The order of society is fragile if its members are without the
personal resources contributed by evangelism and Christian nurture. Not all aspects of the personality are adequately touched by
external, societal change. Personal virtue is necessary for social
health, and conditioned social behavior cannot create it. Erich
Fromm, despite his great sympathy with Karl Marx, notes a dangerous error in the latter's

> neglect of the *moral* factor in man. Just because he assumed that
> all the goodness of man would assert itself automatically when
> the economic changes had been achieved, he did not see that a
> better society could not be brought into life by people who had
> not undergone a moral change within themselves. He paid no
> attention, at least not explicitly, to the necessity of a new moral

orientation, without which all political and economic changes
are futile.[6]

Evangelism contributes significantly to moral change in the
members of society; it is also a major factor in producing social
activists. People are God's channels of justice, as well as of proclamation. The coming of the Reign in the acceptance of the gift of
Christ provides workers for the growth of the Reign in historical
and political events.[7] As Elton Trueblood observes, we "cannot
reasonably expect to erect a constantly expanding structure of social
activism upon a constantly diminishing foundation of faith."[8]

Finally, any commitment to social action not accompanied by
commitment to evangelism, or otherwise failing to proclaim the
transcendent origins of our social claims, undercuts support within
the church for social justice. This failure allows those who suspect
that Christian social activism reflects a merely humanitarian interpretation of religion to remain content in applying faith only to
the personal life of the individual soul.[9]

THE LIMITS OF EVANGELISM FOR SOCIAL CHANGE

The only way? Some Christians not only would agree that the
change which comes through evangelism is crucial for changing
society, but would assert that it is the *only* way to achieve significant improvement. In any case, it is said, evangelism is *the* Christian path to justice. They would agree that Christians have a responsibility in society, but would insist that the way in which
Christians are to manifest it is by seeking individual conversions.

> The world has been seriously infected by the contamination
> of sin. Blisters of crime and war and divorce and immorality and
> disrespect for authority are breaking out everywhere. Every insti-
> tution of society has been damaged and disfigured by sin.
> Everybody has a solution to offer: get rid of unemployment,
> change the environment, rehabilitate the criminal, do away with
> racial and social and educational differences, soften the laws,
> shorten the work week, build one great common world.
> Sadly, such "cures" not only fail to bring relief and health;

they also distract from the one cure that will work—the cure
from within, a changed heart.[10]

In this understanding, evangelism equals the mission of the
church; only as the persons who make up society are changed
through conversion are social institutions and the life of society
changed. The advocates of this position either discourage other
means of change as distracting, secular, ignorant, or disobedient,
or they never get around to specifying how the converted person
will change society apart from "being good" and being faithful in
evangelism.

To view evangelism and the process of conversion as the only
Christian way of furthering justice is to neglect the full imperative
of biblical justice, which includes the central command to execute
justice both in the structures of society and in direct service to the
needy. Other unbiblical elements present within this view are optimism, individualism, and a Stoic view of the body.

Optimism. The position that conversion is all that is needed for
social change is based on an optimism which is surprising in light
of the fact that those who hold this position generally consider
themselves to be pessimistic about human nature and history. Optimism is evident, however, in an overestimation both of the number of conversions occurring and of the moral renewal of those
converted. Such optimism must assume that large masses of the
population will be born again so that beneficial social changes can
occur. The Bible provides no grounds for thinking that such numbers of conversions will take place. On the contrary, Jesus asked,
"When the Son of Man comes, will he then find faith on the
earth?" (Luke 18.8). Christ comes again when the Gospel is *proclaimed* in every nation, not after mass conversions in every nation
(Mark 13.10). Luther, in arguing for the role of power and authority in society, stated that we cannot rely solely on the inner
working of the Holy Spirit to assure external peace and welfare.
To do so would mean first filling "the world with real Christians.
. . . This you will never accomplish; for the world and the masses
are and always will be unchristian."[11]

If Christian conversion is the only means to achieve it, then significant social change is unlikely; one must either be very optimistic regarding evangelism or very pessimistic regarding the implementation of justice. This pessimism often begets passivism.

Reliance upon conversion also requires an optimism regarding Christian character. What we may think people *should* be when converted is one thing; what they actually are is another matter, thus Luther's reference to "real Christians." Bible Belt conversions resulted in no general change with respect to racial segregation nor did northern Fundamentalist conversions result in more just relationships between the classes of the industrial structure. In addition, the convert as such has no greater knowledge of the principles governing the life and death of societies; conversion does not make us wise in any particular area of knowledge.[12]

Optimism is further reflected in expectations concerning the ability of the average Christian to cope with his or her social environment. Such optimism may be expressed about the life of the industrial worker:

> While modern industry, at worst, may distort and thwart one's spiritual sonship during working hours, it cannot really make a machine of one who is a son of God. . . . Even monotony can be justified in the ministry of God and of humanity; it stems from a constructive activity that has no better alternative.[13]

Some have taught that if one is born again, one will not be spiritually or emotionally affected by social and economic forces destructive to others in the same situation. But many Christians who perform assembly line tasks do feel thay they are machines in their working life, alienated from their true humanity in their labor. In addition, they question whether producing needless or destructive items for a wasteful or a militaristic society is a legitimate form of God's ministry or a service to humanity. Their anxiety and frustration have an adverse effect upon their understanding of themselves as God's children, as well as upon their functions as parents, spouses, and church members. If we encourage such people to ignore the reality of the anti-spiritual and dehumanizing forces af-

flicting them, we cause Christianity to function as an opiate, sup-
pressing the impulse for constructive change. If they deny the
oppressive conditions of their employment, that will not change
the economic system. Even if such a denial were a virtue, these
workers could not change the impact of the system on others by
this personal goodness. An element of dualism is apparent in this
view of the Christian in an oppressive situtation. The spiritual reality of the sufferings of the body and psyche is denied. This is not
the biblical view of the body or of suffering.

Stoic view of the body. Reliance upon evangelism alone to
bring relief to our social problems is often accompanied by the idea
that conversion transforms a person in such a way that change of
the social environment becomes unnecessary. The way to deal with
physical and psychological conditions is to have the spiritual resources to keep the situation from affecting one's attitudes rather
than to attempt to change it. This Stoic approach carries the implication that bodily conditions can be ignored if one is spiritually
strong. If conditions are dehumanizing, should they not be objects
of our concern? Christianity does provide comfort for situations
that cannot be altered, but it does not deny the reality of the
suffering in them.

Statements about the proper relationship between a person and
a hostile social environment are often based on the behavior possible for "the real Christian," the behavior of the strong few. But,
as John Bennett observed, "it is not enough for the world to be a
gymnasium for saints." It is more important that the world be a
good school or a hospital for the rest of us.[14]

Our attitude toward suffering and our concern about the environment reflect our understanding of the nature of the body. According to Scripture the person is a unity. The suffering of the
body affects the whole person. Failure to grasp this truth fully has
caused many to devalue social concern.

In both Paul and the Old Testament, anthropological concepts
such as body or soul do not refer to distinct parts of a person, like
individual members or organs. They are terms, referring to ways

in which the person as a whole functions.[15] Almost all of them can be used as equivalents of "I":

> My *flesh* trembles for fear of thee, and *I* am afraid of thy judgments. (Ps. 119.120, *RSV*)

The phrase *"your bodies* are members of Christ" (1 Cor. 6.15) can be rendered as "you are the body of Christ and individually members" (1 Cor. 12.27). The manner in which this language deals with functions of the whole person rather than with isolated components may be seen in the statement "how beautiful upon the mountains are the feet of him who brings good tidings" (Isa. 52.7, *RSV*); the beauty is not in the graceful form of the feet but the messenger's swift movement.[16] In Hebrew poetry the images are frequently interchangeable:

> My *soul* longs, yea, faints for the courts of the Lord; my *heart* and *flesh* sing for joy to the living God. (Ps. 84.2, *RSV*)

If flesh and Spirit in the New Testament appear to be a dualism, it is because they are taken from a Hellenistic context. But *flesh* describes the whole person, and therefore does not refer to an inferior, material part of the individual. As Augustine stated, flesh means "the man himself." Many of the sins attributed to the flesh are not physical but mental or social, e.g., hatred, jealousy, strife.[17] Whereas in Greek philosophy flesh has only a physical reference, in Scripture it has psychical aspects as well. It has a will (John 1.13); it reasons (Rom. 8.6–7); and it has a mind (Col. 2.18).[18]

Flesh also has a social aspect, describing us in relationship and solidarity with others. In the Old Testament it refers to that which binds people together, from marriage (Gen. 2.24) to family (Gen. 37.27) to tribe (Lev. 25.49).[19] In the New Testament flesh represents social status and relationships: reputation for wisdom (1 Cor. 1.26); mastery over slaves (Col. 3.22); and status ascription (Gal. 6.12). Thus for Onesimus to be a brother "in the flesh and in the Lord" to Philemon (Phlm. 16), means that he is to be a brother in the social sphere as well as in the Christian fellowship.[20] Flesh reveals our social nature, in both its good and its corrupted aspects. In a negative context, flesh has a meaning close to that of the evil social order, the *cosmos*. A phrase like " wise according to the flesh" (1 Cor. 1.26) differs little from "wise according to the world" (cf. 1 Cor. 1.20: "the wisdom of the world"). Flesh then is "the sphere of human weakness in which the individual shares," as opposed to the sphere that is according to the Spirit.[21] It represents the person in his or her human fraility, subdued by the values of the evil social order and controlled by the evil powers. Thus when flesh is used with a verb, e.g., "to walk according to the flesh," it means that the person in one way or another is making his or her goal something in this world.[22] But the reference is to the person as a whole. "When we were in the flesh," says Paul (Rom. 7.5), referring to the time before he and his followers became Christians. Obviously, they were no more disembodied than prior to their conversion. Rather the role of each as a whole person was now different.[23] No longer were they functioning "according to the human standard" (1 Cor. 3.3); they now functioned as people who live according to the Spirit.

Body for Paul designates the person insofar as one is part of the world and communicates with the world. It represents the person insofar as something can be done to one, can happen to one,[24] or as one can act on something else (Rom. 8.13). It is the person in relation with his or her environment. The person does not *have* a body, but rather *is* a body in this usage.

This concept of the body is perhaps best seen in connection with death. "We groan and long to put on our dwelling from heaven inasmuch as, after having put it on, we will not appear naked" (2 Cor. 5.2–3). Death is nakedness. The person as body has been lost, which makes Berdyaev's description of death comprehensible: "To die is to experience absolute solitude, to sever all connection with the world. Death implies the disruption of a whole sphere of Being, the termination of all relationships and contacts—in a word, complete isolation."[25]

"Christians do not await release from their bodies, but the release of their bodies."[26] The body is essential to the person; to be fully a person one must have bodily existence. In ancient Hebrew thought there was no non-bodily existence after earthly life; one continued in Sheol in a physical but shadowy form. In Paul's teaching, the perishing physical body of one who trusts in Christ is the seed of an imperishable body in the next life (1 Cor. 15.42–44, 53–54). The resurrected person retains personal identity; he or she remains a body.[27] The continuity appears even more clearly elsewhere, in reference to the empty tomb and the nail prints in the body of the risen Christ, and in Paul's statement that God "will give life also to your *mortal bodies*" (Rom. 8.11). In the Christian hope of the resurrection of the body may be seen the value both of the body and of the individual's relation to the surrounding world.

What then in a person is saved from sin? We cannot isolate one part of the person as the locus of salvation. Salvation is of the whole person. We do not share the Greek view of the body as a prison or a tomb. The body is not something to be sloughed off (as seems to be implied in speech about "saving the soul"); it is to be resurrected as the last phase of salvation. The work of God does not end with conversion, i.e., with the person as soul, *soul* being understood as the person in relationship to God. The person as body also is included in God's saving work.

When the Bible says that Jesus came "to save his people from their sins" (Matt. 1.21), it means that he will deliver them from the political and social consequences of their sins as well as root out the sin itself. God's saving concern cannot be restricted. Salvation extends to the whole of creation (Rom. 8.18–23; cf. "God's Purpose in History" in Chapter 5). The creation waits to be set free from corruption at the time when our bodies will redeemed. For Paul the body is not the sign of our independence but is an element of solidarity.[28] The body is part of nature, and the hope of its redemption is one with the hope of all creation.[29] A person who is free from guilt but whose body is still subject to injury is not fully redeemed. "We groan to ourselves as we wait for adoption, the redemption of our bodies" (Rom. 8.23). For Paul there is no definitive salvation without bodily resurrection.[30]

Our concern, then, must be with the whole person—with the body as well as the soul. We cannot deal with the soul in evangelism and leave aside the bodily needs of the person. Action to free a person from the forces of evil, corruption, and death is not irrelevant to the total process of salvation.

The body is the person's link with society, and with the uses and misuses of power. When buffeted by external forces, the whole person is affected adversely. This biblical understanding of the mind-body unity has been reinforced by modern psychology. Concern for people's salvation should arise from genuine and informed love for them as whole persons and must take into account the relationship between the person and his or her total environment.

Individualism. Those who would offer evangelism as the only Christian method of social change need not necessarily have a Stoic view of the body. They may see a relationship between the inner dimension and the social dimension of the person and maintain that, when one is changed inwardly, one is affected in one's social relationships, and consequently society is changed. The difficulty with this position is that it sees influence flowing in only one direction. This places undue emphasis on the character of the individual to the neglect of the structures of society.

Those who have been raised in Western culture with its heritage of individualism have difficulty in grasping the biblical perspective of the person in society. Only recently has this ancient biblical understanding been recovered by contemporary sociology and psychology. The Bible's view of the person as flesh and as body promotes an understanding of the individual as living in solidarity with the social group to which he or she belongs. The biblical social imperative involves an understanding of the importance of the community. It was to a community that the life-giving Law and Covenant were given. The New Covenant is proclaimed by a new community, to which people are called. According to biblical doctrine, the person is truly human only as a member of a group.[31]

> I am like a vulture of the wilderness, like an owl of the waste
> places; I lie awake, I am like a lonely bird on the housetop. (Ps.
> 102.6–7, *RSV*).

This cry of the individual abandoned by society reflects the dependence, in biblical thought, of the individual on community. The
desire for solitude has no part in the biblical idea of happiness.
Separation from society is a dreaded fate. Social isolation implies
wretchedness and affliction (cf. Ps. 25.6). The sentence of expul-
sion from the community was so serious that it could not be pro-
nounced by local judges but only by the central court (Deut.
17.12).[32]

Reliance upon individual change ignores the objective reality
of social life and social evil. As we have seen, one cannot deal with
the problems posed by capitalism merely by getting enough good
people into the system; a loving father is not of necessity a just
industrialist. The well-being of society depends not only on the
personal virtue of those in power (and out of power) but also in
the nature of the social and economic system in which they work.
Our society often regards drive or ambition as a virtue that will
cause one to get ahead, and some argue that a lack of drive is the
reason many people remain poor. Some years ago a study by the
New York State Commission against Discrimination showed that
black children had more aspiration than whites from the same income level, but less opportunity to fulfill their hopes.[33] Their personal "virtue" was thwarted by the nature of the social structure.
The structures have an autonomous character which is distinct
from that of the individuals within the structure and aspects of
which the Bible describes as demonic.

There are no psychological Robinson Crusoes;[34] our personalities do not develop in isolation from social influence. We come
naked, crying, and completely helpless into the three worlds of
Karl Popper's definition: the first is the world of nature, the physical world; the second is the world of the mind; and the third is
the world of human culture. The third world is the realm of ab-
stractions the reality or power of which cannot be denied. They

include kinship relations, forms of social organization, and government, law, custom, learning, religion, and language. The Bible
itself belongs to this world. The power of the third world over the
other worlds can be illustrated by what it has done to the first
world of nature through the application of nuclear theory.[35]

Human personality develops through the process of encounter
in culture. We become aware of our own existence as we experience
ourselves and see the results of our activity in the attitudes and
responses of those with whom we are in close reciprocal relationship. We see ourselves reflected in the attitudes, first of persons
with whom we have close primary relationships, particularly our
parents, and later of the subgroups of society to which we are
attached. The consistent behavior of others makes us aware of ourselves, at the same time revealing the ethos of the society of which
they and we are members.[36] Our self emerges in the midst of a
social process and becomes a part of it.

Thus the third world, which we encounter even in our earliest
development, is not merely human culture in general. Socialization
always takes place in a very specific social situation, with distinct
class and subcultural characteristics. Just as we speak the language
of our group, we think in the manner in which our group thinks.
The words and meaning that are at our disposal reflect the angle
and the context of the thinking of the group from which we de-
rived them. In a culture with a strong sense of private property,
for example, the child will find that if one states that something
is one's property, one will get a response stressing respect for the
property of others. From the attitudes of others the concept of "my
property" becomes established in the child. We inherit patterns of
thought that are determined by the alignment and the tensions of
the forces of social life.[37]

We do not choose those who are responsible for our socialization; yet society influences our basic attitudes and ethical thinking,
passing on to us as we come to maturity not only its strengths but
also its evils.

In the process of socialization of course the individual has an
influence on society. Our distinctive, creative adjustments to soci-

ety force society in turn to change. Healthy individuals have a capacity to transcend their social environment. Moreover, they respond not only to society but also to God, as a transcendent referent beyond society.[38] But the individual is never free from the influence of society. Our creativity exists in the context of the existing order. Change comes out of the struggle of the individual with forces of the third world.[39]

Rollo May has stated that it is a truism that mental health and a healthy social order are intimately interdependent.

> Such diseases of society as unemployment, economic insecurity of all sorts, fear of war and the social upheaval that follows war have a tremendous bearing upon the adjustment of individuals concerned. Spasmodic unemployment with its consequent continuous burden of insecurity increases the personality tensions with a severity the importance of which cannot be exaggerated.[40]

Concern for the conversion and spiritual nurture of the person caught in that situation does not fulfill the full Christian responsibility. The structure must be confronted directly. Paths to justice other than evangelism must also be followed. Responsibility for the social environment and its structures is tied in with our highest responsibility for the souls of people. William Booth stated:

> While recognizing that the primary responsibility must always rest upon the individual, we may fairly insist that society, which by its habits, its customs, and its laws, has greased the slope down which these poor creatures slide to perdition, shall seriously take in hand their salvation.[41]

THE INTERDEPENDENCE OF EVANGELISM AND SOCIAL ACTION

Evangelism and the implementation of justice are really inseparable in Christian conduct and in the goal of God's work in history. Both tasks are subordinated to that of making real the sovereignty of God in every outpost of creation. Both arise spontaneously out of love for our fellow human beings who are hurt, who need us, and whose need we feel within us. When Jesus "saw the crowds, he had compassion for them" and sent out his disciples to proclaim *and* to heal (Matt. 9.36; 10.7–8). John Stott states that the Great Commission to make disciples does not explain, exhaust, or supersede the Great Commandment of love for the neighbor; rather it adds a new and urgent dimension to love.[42] For this reason, when one has met either the need for material help or for commitment to Jesus Christ, "there must be deep restlessness of the Christian's spirit" until one has met the dimension of need yet unfulfilled.[43] To the crisis of individual meaning and the crisis of society, our response must be that of Peter: "What I have I give unto you" (Acts 3.6). Neither in view of the basis of our mission nor of its goal may our hands remain unstained if they withhold a justice that could have been achieved, or the message of redeeming hope that could have been shared.

Social ministry and evangelical witness exist side by side in Scripture without conflict or subordination. Paul states that because of the church's contribution, the poor saints in Jerusalem "will praise God for the obedient way in which you confess the gospel of Christ and for the generosity of your sharing to them and to all" (2 Cor. 9.13). Care for the material needs of others leads to the praise of God; it is an obedient subjection to the requirements of the gospel.

Witness is hurt when social action is absent. "Our life-style, our attitudes, our concern for the sick and the suffering, the underprivileged and the hungry, either confirm or deny the message of salvation, of wholeness, which we proclaim."[44] Frequently the public posture of the Church and its witnesses has constituted a denial. This failure has given rise to persistent and damaging criticism of evangelistic Christianity in particular. When our faith is not made relevant to the immediate problems of social justice, our witness is dismissed as a hypocritical luxury with which imperiled people can hardly identify.[45] If we allow Christian faith to be viewed as pertinent only in the private sphere of life, we subject to suspicion its claim of integrating every area of life.[46]

Witness is helped when social action is present. If the absence of genuine justice presents a stumbling block to the world, its presence can make people attentive to the presentation of the gospel. Jesus said that our good works would lead people to glorify God (Matt. 5.16). The Hellenistic moralist Plutarch observed, "Whenever the populace see that those whom they respect and consider great show zeal toward the divine by being generous and liberal, they feel a strong conviction and belief that the godhead is great and holy."[47]

Actions are certainly important in our day of mass communications. The spectator attitude has robbed the preaching of the Word of some of its verbal power. As they sit before a television set people become unaccustomed to respond in depth.[48] Especially in the inner city, where experience has engendered a skeptical attitude toward promises and claims, the verbal message of the gospel needs credentials of active compassion and justice.

On of the greatest barriers to evangelism is the failure of Christians to have significant relationships with non-Christians. Social action frequently places the Christian in the midst of non-believers in a situation in which the question of one's motivation comes to the fore. A common struggle for justice establishes vital links and a kinship that facilitates evangelism.[49] A seminarian,[50] studying the power structure of a community, in an interview with a selectman found himself questioned as to why a Christian, particularly a seminarian, would be engaged in such a study. The student wrote in a report:

> For the next two hours I was beset with a barrage of questions and was able under the empowerment of the Holy Spirit to present from the Old Testament to the New the ethical demands of Scripture and God's concern with human society and its shape. This person was literally brought to tears as he exclaimed, "I have never heard the message of the Bible presented in this way." I have been invited to return to talk over community politics and my "unusual" concept of biblical faith. His concern is now not only focused upon society but his own individual lack.

This opportunity might never have arisen without social involvement. The fear that social involvement will draw believers away from evangelistic efforts misses the fact that social involvement gets them into the world, where evangelism must take place.

Social involvement can open doors for a church. David Moberg writes,

> When a church engages in social action and social services, community leaders and agency representatives become aware of its existence. They become favorably disposed toward it, are more likely to listen when its leaders speak to public issues, will refer people with spiritual problems to its ministries, may turn to the Christian for help in times of personal need, and are more likely to open their minds to give favorable consideration to the claims of Christ in their own lives.[51]

But will not social involvement hurt evangelism by offending people with its specific commitments to justice? Jimmy Allen was chided for a strong statement on racial injustice: "When you as a Baptist preacher get into that kind of controversy, you cut off my chance as a Baptist to win my neighbor who has racial prejudice." Allen's response is appropriate. "Evangelism is not tricking people into signing the policy and then letting them read the small print."[52] Evangelism is the proclamation that God's Reign has broken into history; the nature of the rule of God cannot be removed from the proclamation. As Paul stated, "If I were to please people, I would not be a slave of Christ" (Gal. 1.10).[53] The founder of the "Brazil for Christ" Pentecostal movement, Manoel de Mello, declares, "The Gospel cannot be proclaimed with half-truths, but only with the whole truth. . . . The Gospel cannot be proclaimed fully without denouncing injustices committed by the powerful."[54] Jesus and John the Baptist are then appropriate models for evangelism. Social involvement does not hurt evangelism, although it may hurt certain narrowly conceived attempts at making disciples.

Social action is needed to protect the fruits of witness. Since the person as a whole is affected by his or her environment and since conversion is neither a total transformation nor a separation of the Christian from the world, we must take responsibility for the environment of the young Christians under our care. Thomas Guthrie, a Scottish pioneer of the "ragged schools," said:

> So long as religion stands by silent and unprotesting against the temptation with which men, greedy of gain, and Governments, greedy of revenue, surround the wretched victims of this basest vice . . . , it appears to me utter mockery for her to go with the word of God in her hand, teaching them to say, "Lead us not into temptation."[55]

Guthrie is talking about alcohol; his logic applies to many other concerns. In our priestly responsibility for the nurture of Christians we cannot ignore the surroundings which for six days may be turning a person's whole personality away from what is shown to him or her on the seventh.[56] William Booth spoke of environments in which "vice has an enormous advantage over virtue," whose influence could be summarized as "atheism made easy."[57]

PIGEONHOLING THE COMMANDS OF GOD

It is dangerous to give priority to any one of God's basic tasks for the people of God. Many of such emphases reflect not a priority in Scripture but the bent of one's personal piety, or the choice of one's favorite portion of Scripture.

When Jesus was asked to assign priorities, his answer differed markedly from those frequently heard. "What is the greatest commandment? . . . You shall love the Lord your God. . . . You shall love your neighbor. . . . There is no commandment greater *than these*" (Mark 12.28–31). Victor Furnish notes that the two commandments *together* are set over against all other requirements of the Law. When in Matthew's account (Matt. 22.39), Jesus says the second is like (*homoios*) the first, this means that the second is equal to the first in importance.[58] Luke does not describe them as "first" or "second"; the priority is the double commandment of love.[59]

> It is time for evangelicals to refuse to use sentences that begin with "the primary task of the Church is . . ." regardless of

whether the sentence ends with *evangelism* or *Bible teaching* or
"social concerns." They are all integral, necessary aspects of the
Church's task.[60]

In rejecting the designation of primary and secondary tasks, René
Padilla states that "in order to be obedient to the Lord the church
should never do anything that is not essential; therefore nothing
that the church does in obedience to its Lord is unessential."[61]
This observation is pragmatically as well as normatively true.
Christians will really exert themselves only for what they regard as
essential. Moreover neither the work of evangelism nor the implementation of justice is ever finished; if one is given precedence,
there never will be time for the other. But the effort to assign
priority to evangelism or to social responsibility belies their true
fusion "into *one* conceptual framework and *one* incarnational ministry."[62] When it is said that something is not primary for the
church, this is an excuse for giving it only token attention. James
Daane has put it bluntly: Those who claim that "the primary task
of the church is to preach the gospel" do not really believe that
the church has either spare time or a secondary task.[63] Instead of
classifying the tasks that God gives to us as primary and secondary,
we should respond with the humility of wholehearted obedience.
"We are unprofitable servants. What we ought to do we have
done" (Luke 17.10).

The biblical concern is for the totality of creation. Therefore,
in addition to utilizing the special gifts of the Spirit given to each
of us, we are all to be active in witness and in working for justice.
When the church neglects one part of this concern, the other part
loses vitality and is endangered. Concern for inner personal commitment to God is part of the concern for the reconciliation of all
creation. Political and social concern for the created world is motivated by God's grace within the individual. As servants of God,
we must make both tasks our own if we would be true to either.

Chapter 7

THE CHURCH AS COUNTER-COMMUNITY

The primary social structure through which the gospel works to change other structures is that of the Christian community.[1]

This statement is startling, but no more so that Jesus' words to his disciples: "You are the light of the world" (Matt. 5.14). Neglect of Christian community would place the mission of the church in jeopardy.

THE SIGNIFICANCE OF THE CHURCH IN GOD'S STRATEGY

When Jesus said that salvation had come to the house of Zacchaeus, the "lost" tax collector, he added, "For he also is a son of Abraham" (Luke 19.9). Jesus' work of salvation is the preparation of a people dedicated to God, a people to whom Zacchaeus, having strayed, is here restored. We share together the life-giving promise as a people who are by faith members of the family of Abraham and heirs of God's favor (Rom. 4; Gal. 3). The Epistle of the Hebrews depicts the church as the people of God journeying toward a goal promised by God. Only in association with the whole people of God is there life for the individual. Outside of this company there is only lonely and hopeless wandering in the wilderness.[2]

The new life of the individual "in Christ" (cf. 2 Cor. 5.17) is at the same time life in a new society founded "in Christ

Jesus." A separation of the individual and social aspects is not possible; the personal union with Christ also involves incorporation in the collective Christian society.[3]

Our participation in the Spirit as individuals brings us into community with all who share that "fellowship in the Spirit" (Phil. 2.1).[4] For this reason the term *saint* is never used in the singular in the New Testament. One is a saint in connection with one's relatedness to others in Jesus Christ.[5]

The individual act of faith by which we are born anew takes place in the context of the church, which proclaims the gospel, nurtures the converts, and shares the eternal blessings for which it was chosen by God (Eph. 1.3–4, 11–12; Rom. 8.28–30). Since the church is the context for conversion, all that has been said about the social significance of conversion (cf. "The Importance of Evangelism for Social Change" in Chapter 6) is equally relevant to the social importance of the church.

Since the Bible shows our basic need for and dependence on community, it is not surprising that God's salvation calls us into a community. The importance of the church for salvation is not only that it is an instrument of God for our conversion, but also that what we are converted to is a new realm of social existence which God is calling into being (cf. p. 26).

The church, then, must be understood in relation to the Reign of God, the eschatological order now appearing in history. The church is not in itself the Reign of God, but the Reign is both its starting point and its goal. As a new society founded in God's love and grace, the church is the community in which the Reign of God becomes visible in history. The church is the *avant-garde* of the Reign, demonstrating and serving the demand and promise of God for human society (cf. pp. 88, 106). *It is both the presence of God's grace and God's instrument.* It is the partial realization of Christ's goal in history and also carries forth his purposes toward the world.[6] At the Last Supper Jesus indicated that it was with his followers that God was making the promised new covenant. In covenant the church is a "purposive social-group" representing the new order that God intends.[7]

Ephesians puts forward this view of the church, on a cosmic scale. As "the fullness of him who fills the universe in every way" (Eph. 1.22–23), the church is the instrument of Christ's work to place all things under the sovereignty of God. As Christ's body, it is the continuation of the incarnation; it is the agent of Christ for reconciliation. This reconciliation is partially realized within the church (cf. pp. 103–4). In the war against the evil supernatural powers, the church is the beachhead established by the resurrection triumph of Jesus (cf. p. 19).

The role of the church in God's mission in the world compels us to attach the utmost importance to the community of believers of which we are a part.

THE CHURCH IS COMMUNITY

In recent years many Christians have sought a form of Christian community in which members would be in closer relationship, and which would involve greater actualization of the values of the Christian life. One such seeker has said, "It's sad that we even need to use the word 'Community.' 'Church' should suffice."[8] These intentional Christian communities are not of a different order from the church. They should not in effect serve as a new monastic movement governed by a higher standard of values than the rest of the church, whom they would thus represent as surrogates in fulfilling the command of Jesus. What they seek should be sought by every body of believers.

I am not suggesting that the churches should necessarily adopt such institutional forms of these communities as communal living. Some of the forms, if mandated, could be inimical to Christian mission in the world. The maintenance of a radical fellowship of Christian love often requires such an expenditure of energy and emotion that intentions for outreach in the community go unfulfilled. Furthermore, it has been observed that too large a number of relationships on an intimate and primary level can provide an overrich social and emotional life, making it difficult to establish new friendships outside the compact community.[9] The form of the church will depend on the situation and the needs and strengths of the persons involved. Since the church is mission as well as fellowship and worship, the need for contact with the world must be taken into consideration along with the internal growth of the community. Some churches, such as the Church of the Saviour in Washington, D.C., have met this dual need by using groups organized around tasks as the locus for fellowship without neglecting within these groups the requirement for a depth of sharing and growth beyond the mission enterprise alone.[10]

The church is itself a society. It is not a task force whose members' mutual social contacts stem only from the common task itself. It is not a periodic encounter of otherwise unrelated individuals. Moreover, the relationships among its members, the ways of dealing with their differences and needs, and the patterns of leadership and decision making[11] constitute a discrete societal structure within the larger society. Thus the church can embody the patterns for shared life that God desires for all of human society.

Because the church is a manifestation of the Reign of God, the norms that guide it must exemplify the highest vision of human community. It cannot leave to another group the effort to live wholly according to the teachings of Jesus. In the Pauline letters a direct consequence for the ethical life of the church is drawn from the fact that, as "the fullness of him who fills everything in everything" (Eph. 1.22–23), it is the instrument of Christ's work. When "Christ is everything and in everything," then all external distinctions of status cease to exist:

> Put on the new nature [literally, the new human being] . . .
> where there is here neither Greek nor Jew, circumcised nor un-
> circumcised, Barbarian, Scythian [the savage par excellence],
> slave, free person, but Christ is everything and in everything.
> (Col. 3.9–11)

The unique character of this new nature derives from the fact that, when the body of Christ (v. 15) truly acts as Christ's body, it is

totally ruled by him. The "new human being," which closes the
rift between Jew and Gentile, is also described in Ephesians 2.14–
16:

> For he is our peace, who made both elements [Jew and Gentile,
> vv. 11–12] one, by tearing down the dividing wall, that is, the
> enmity, and in his flesh invalidating the law of commandments
> consisting in ordinances, in order to create in himself one new
> person out of the two so that peace shall come, and to reconcile
> in one body both persons to God through the cross, thus putting
> the enmity to death.

"The apostle can . . . only be understood to be saying that the
one physical body of Christ which bled on the cross for the two
previously divided groups of mankind and which established reconciliation, then becomes after the resurrection in a new way
through the Spirit the one 'Body of Christ' which is the
Church."[12] In three passages Paul states that the putting on of
Christ, the putting on of the new human being, or the creation of
the new human being, abolishes status distinctions in the church:
Colossians 3.9–11; Ephesians 2.14–16; and Galatians 3.27–28 (cf.
Gal. 6.15 ["new creation"]).

If the church is that society which has "put on Christ" and in
so doing has abolished status distinctions, there are direct consequences for human relationships within it, which should exemplify
the new order that the church is called to be. Colossians 3 continues:

> *Therefore*, as chosen and loved saints of God, put on a merciful
> heart, kindness, humility, gentleness, patience, bearing with one
> another and forgiving each other if anyone has a complaint
> against any other; . . . and in addition to all these put on love,
> which is the bond of completeness. And be thankful. Let the
> word of Christ dwell in you richly in all wisdom, teaching and
> admonishing each other, in grateful response with songs of
> praise, hymns, and spiritual songs singing in your hearts to God.
> . . . (Col. 3.12–16)

Such a community, embodying the presence of God's Reign, submits itself in uncompromising faithfulness to its new covenant ethics (cf. p. 89).

The church, then, is a counter-community: alternative norms and values are organized into a social grouping.[13] The difference between the church and the world is "the exceptionally normal quality of humanness to which the community is committed."[14] For the church to have a corrective impact on culture it must maintain a separate and distinct identity from the surrounding society and any new society that it may help to create.[15] Mission is consistent with separation as long as it is kept in mind that the motivation for that separation *is* mission, and not separation for its own sake (cf. p. 20). "The only way to really retain true spiritual values is to quicken them with the divine imperative of witnessing to the world."[16] This dynamic nonconformity finds its base in Scripture (rather than in the culture of two generations ago) and those who live by it will be enabled to give moral and spiritual direction to the world.[17]

The practicality of this vision of the church may be questioned by those in struggling churches whose total efforts are needed to support flagging faith and keep the doors open for a witness in the community. Is the church to be primarily the fellowship of the strong or a hospital for the sick? Paul's churches often seemed to be the latter. The point I would make here is that, while these maintenance efforts are used by God, we must not be content with this level of Christian community. The vision of what the church is meant to be can provide the hope and the courage to draw us out of ourselves in the openness that the Holy Spirit so often has given and used in the history of the church.

Genuine Christian community contributes to social change in three ways. The first is through various forms of social action and service. The second is the impact its nonconforming life has on the surrounding community. Third and most important is the support it gives to the individual involved in mission.

SUPPORT OF THE CHRISTIAN IN MISSION

As social beings, we are strongly influenced by our society in the formation of our personalities and the maintenance of our values; yet we have seen that this social order is unredeemed and basically hostile to God and God's standards (cf. beginning of Chapter 1 and "Individualism" in Chapter 6). Therefore, since in conversion our system of values is transformed and in mission we are to set forth the new order which God has for society, we require the support of a community that expresses this new order in its life. Christian community is the social context for the supernatural transforming work of the Holy Spirit.

If we are to reject significant aspects of the cultural context, we must be able to react against the approval of the very community that previously has been crucial to us. This calls for a higher form of community, which can "out-vote" the influence of the former community. A new process of socialization is needed. As "newborn infants" in Christ, we must have as our spiritual parents and peers persons with whom we can identify and who exemplify the type of person we are to become.[18] Such relationships are important for developing, mastering, and maintaining Christian attitudes and values. Political convictions that grow out of our faith, for example, are most likely to be sustained if those in our immediate social grouping support them.[19] Such support is all the more important when the viewpoint is not only a minority opinion in society but also runs against class and social interests. Growth in one's Christian life is strongly dependent upon the growth and maturity of others in Christian community.

Christ has given to his body, the church, gifts for carrying out the work of his Reign. These spiritual gifts include a social ministry: giving to the poor (2 Cor. 8.7; cf. pp. 32–33), and service, sharing, giving aid, and acts of mercy (Rom. 12.7–8). Since the church is granted these gifts, it is responsible for their nurture and support. Involved in social mission, weakened by encounters with power, pressured to compromise, heartsick from weeping with those who weep, frustrated by the struggle against human inertia, we find in the community which sent us forth the renewal of life and vision. There strength to continue must be found. In mutual searching of the Word of God and in prayer, we gain perspective on our task and are able to make responsible decisions. Since we are fulfilled in love and companionship in this community, we do not pursue mission to satisfy our own social needs; we are freed to work on behalf of the needs of others and to relate openly to them.[20] We go forth backed and empowered by the prayers of our community.

"What we are together is what we shall be for others."[21]

THE WITNESS OF COMMUNITY LIFE

A city on a hill. The presence of the church as a visible sign of the Reign of God produces social change in the surrounding society. Two movements in the Christian community help to effect such change. The first is withdrawal of support from practices contrary to the inbreaking of the Reign. The second is is the example a community creates when its social relationships are characterized by the new human person that God is creating. The two are interrelated. The nonconformity is based upon and points to the vision of a new order: "The radical No can be a valid witness to the Yes because implied in the No is often a radical Yes."[22]

A society that places a high value on conformity views the people of God as a band of deserters, who ignore the social order as in Exodus they rise up and depart in search of the city whose founder and maker is God (cf. Heb. 11.8–9, 22).[23] The society perceives this moral independence as undermining its social system and challenging its authority.[24] An integrated community in a segregated society raises questions about assumptions otherwise easily left unexamined. Such a refusal to cooperate with entrenched legal and cultural practices may act as a rallying cry to other sensitive citizens.[25]

A Christian community is a voluntary society, freely chosen by its members and not hampered by the responsibilities of maintaining community-wide institutions or the temptations of great eco-

nomic or political power. It is free to create experimental institutional forms whose usefulness can be appreciated in the greater
community and adopted by analogy. Existing alongside structures
in society that are oppressive, the Christian community can serve,
in the words of Arthur Gish, as a parabolic community and parallel
structure.

> The parallel structure serves three basic functions. First it un-
> masks the moral bankruptcy and contradictions of the society
> around it. . . . Second, it points to a new reality. It indicates
> new possibilities. . . . It means raising new alternatives, asking
> questions that are not being asked, and challenging commonly
> held assumptions. Third, it helps create new alternatives. . . .
> The parallel structure is free to try new approaches, to do the
> unthinkable. Out of the experimentation with new forms, the
> radical community can show concretely to the larger society not
> only what can be done, but what in fact is already being done.[26]

In an area of Georgia where 40 percent of the homes were declared
"unsafe, structurally unsound, or too run-down to be repaired economically," Koinonia Partners built and sold sixty homes at cost
to neighbors in need. It demonstrated to its community that
Southern rural black and white families do not need to be con-
signed to substandard housing but could have new homes for a
down payment of $700 and payments of less than $60 a month for
twenty years.[27] The existence of the new exposes the needlessness
of the misery of the old. A tested and proven model is provided
for the efforts of others.

John Howard Yoder suggests that a Christian community by
"a sort of moral osmosis" over the years can raise the general moral
level in the secular world around it. Its influence works upon those
who receive religious education in their youth but may not become
adult members, in the example of the diligent lives of individual
Christians, and through customs that continue even after their religious roots are forgotten.[28]

Finally, the Christian activist pressuring for justice in society
has a greater legitimacy because of his or her association with a
community which is itself demonstrably working in good conscience on the same issues.[29]

The potency of the church's exemplification of the new order should not be used to justify a lessened commitment to pressure for justice, or other forms of social ministry within the secular society. The following statements can be misconstrued to yield such an argument:

> The church is not directly God's *agent* for the realization of the kingdom, but rather it is God's harbinger of the kingdom by being the *fellowship* in which the reality of the kingdom is manifest.[30]

> The church's value to the world is not so much in what she does for the world as in what she *is* in the world. . . . Over the long run, the greatest service which the church can perform in and for the world is to *be* the household of faith which, by its example, demonstrates a better way of life.[31]

As we have seen, the Scriptures do present the church as the agent of God's Reign (pp. 96–97, 103–4, 106). On the other hand, the biblical evidence is slim for the ability of the Christian fellowship of love within the church to produce, by itself, positive changes in the social environment. The acts of love that lead to individual conversion and the glorification of God[32] are not restricted to deeds within the community but include what the church does for the world (1 Pet. 3.1–2, 16; 2.12; Matt. 5.16).

The traditional biblical image of the social influence of the presence of Christian community is found in Jesus' statement "You are the light of the world. A city set upon a mountain cannot be hidden" (Matt. 5.14). The Christian community as a city shedding light in the world seems a fitting picture of the social impact of the church as an alternative social reality.

It must be remembered, however, that *light* in Scripture represents a positive, aggressive force combatting darkness. In Isaiah the great light seen in Galilee is associated with the breaking of the rod of oppression in bloody battle and the establishment of justice (Isa. 9.2, 4–5, 7). The light to the nations (Isa. 42.6) is the servant who brings forth justice (v. 1; cf. v. 4). In these passages the light is a force for justice, an image of triumph and

dignity.[33] Kings prostrate themselves (Isa. 49.7) before the light
to the nations (v. 6; cf. 60.1–3, 12). Matthew's Gospel was written for a church in close dialogue with the Jewish synagogue.
"Light of the Gentiles" appears to have been a view of itself held
by Israel at this time (cf. Rom. 2.19). Rudolf Schnackenburg argues that in the Matthaean context this lofty title for Israel is
applied to the disciples, and so represents the church.[34] But the
church is raised to this dignity through faithful service to God in
ministry and suffering. It is through helpful deeds that the light
shines (Matt. 5.16), as the light to the nations in Isaiah 42 comes
through the Servant who opens the eyes of the blind and releases
prisoners (v.7). And this light before whom kings prostrate themselves was once despised (Isa. 49.7).

With the metaphors of the light and the city upon the mountain, Jesus reminds a hesitant church of the dignity of its mission
and its destiny and thus encourages it to boldness and rigor in its
task. Matthew 5.14 functions much as does Luke 12.32: "Do not
be afraid, little flock, for the Father has considered it good to give
you the Reign!" The imagery of light brings the tasks of service
and justice to the foreground.

A surprising optimism underlies the argument that the example of a new social order in the church will capture the attention
of the world and so produce significant results. It is optimistic to
suppose that demonstration and witness of the life of the Reign
will be noticed, much less copied by the world. It is surprising
because advocates of this position are often extremely pessimistic
about the level of morality in the systems and institutions of the
world, which are controlled by the powers. Yet they must depend
upon the possession by members of the secular community of personal virtues such that they will be attracted by the example and
in numbers sufficient to create new social structures. The position
thus seems to reveal a tendency toward pessimism regarding institutions and optimism regarding individuals.

The historic Anabaptist model of the church was theologically
sounder than the above position, because it did not assert that the
existence of an intentional community would lead to changes in

other structures of the society[35]—thus avoiding the implicit optimism regarding human nature or history. When the church is defined in terms of social change, some theological assumptions are affected. The Anabaptists believed that any such change would have to result from the conversion of individuals to the church, but they had little confidence that this would happen on a mass scale.[36] To suggest today that significant social change can be effected through the proliferation of Christian communities is analogous to expecting social change from evangelism alone (cf. "The Only Way?" in Chapter 5).

What appears to be a theologial defect, however, may actually be a failure to detail thoroughly this theory of change. How does the threat to the establishment posed by nonconformity result in change? Some advocates appear to attribute to the disconformity of Christian community effects which more properly belong to forms of social non-cooperation more public and more disruptive, or which withhold from the greater community more crucial resources (cf. Chapter 8). The relationship of the theory of counter-community to the general theory of nonviolent direct action needs more elaboration, as does the understanding of power.

The creation of an alternative community has validity in itself, but is inadequate to express fully the biblical images of executing justice in the gate and breaking every yoke. The demonstration of Christian community is a facet of social change, but as the single expression of social justice it is inadequate.

There is no such things as "the very presence" of Christian community, as distinct from what Christians are to do in the world, and the notion involves us in an unnecessary either/or choice. There is no "presence" or "existence" of Christian community without mission. The church is not to be absorbed into mission but neither is it to be divorced from its tasks in the world. Neither mission nor church is to be subordinate to the other; both are essential in the great work of the Reign of God.[37] The call of Jesus to discipleship was a call to a task. It came first as a call to be fishers of people (Mark 1.17). The Twelve were chosen to be *with* Jesus and that he might *send* them to proclaim the Good

News and to cast out demons (Mark 3.14–15). Then in the period
before the Spirit came to the church at Pentecost, the risen Lord
commissioned his apostles for service in the world.[38] We do not
have to choose between "the very existence" of Christian community and the mandates that God has given to it. Indeed we cannot
and must not make such a choice.

The battle for change must be fought on a variety of fronts;
the necessity of one campaign does not negate that of another.[39]
Innovation should not be advocated without reference to the fact
that ideas which threaten the established order will not be adopted
without a power struggle. It may be true, as Gish asserts, that
"the modern ideas of hospitals, schools and universities, mental
care, public health, and training for the blind have come out of
the church." But to add that "hospitals began not because Christians petitioned the government for new structures"[40] sets the
reader up for unnecessary conflict; although hospitals did not *begin*
as a result of petition, the battle for public health, education, and
mental care was in fact a long political effort. The two methods of
change are compatible. Many who participated in the educational
innovation of "ragged schools" and Sunday schools for the poor in
the slums of nineteenth century Great Britain, for example, were
at the same time putting a great deal of pressure on the government for badly needed reforms. Lord Shaftesbury is among the best
known of such reformers.

In these areas as well, we must avoid the presumption of allot-
ting priorities to aspects of God's gifts and tasks. When we speak
of community and church or of carrying out justice and creation of
community, it is not for us to consult our personal predilections
and pronounce which is the greatest, the primary, or the most
powerful force for social change. Instead, we need a new boldness
in affirming both Christian community and the tasks of the Christian in the world, and new creativity in carrying them out together. Both are given to us by God. Both flourish or fail together.
We are the presence *and* the agents of the Reign of God. Jesus
prepared his apostles to be his church, but he also prepared his
church to be apostolic. As apostles, they were the agents of the

one who sent them. [41] Their power was not their own but that of the Spirit of God whose Reign they represented. They were a community, and they had work to do in the world. They were a small and seemingly insignificant group, but they were called the Light of the World.

Chapter 8

STRATEGIC NONCOOPERATION

Three statements well express the biblical teaching on the relationship of the believer to the institutions of society: "Do not be conformed to this age" (Rom. 12.2); "be subordinate to 'every fundamental social institution' "[1] (1 Pet. 2.13); "establish justice in the gate" (Amos 5.15). There is a distinct tension among these imperatives. One is to submit, yet one is not to be conformed to the world with its institutions; and one has the additional positive duty to carry out justice within them. The command to submit reflects God's intention that the basic structures of society be instruments of good for his creation. The command to nonconformity is a recognition of the organization of social life in opposition to God. The command to establish justice places in the hands of God's servants the responsibility for recovering God's purposes for human society.

Strategic noncooperation seeks justice through selective, socially potent forms of nonconformity. Although it is brought to bear when the fallen nature of society denies normal channels of political decision-making to those who work for justice, it is carried out under the self-discipline of respect for the order of society. In recent times, civil disobedience has been the best known form of strategic noncooperation.

THE THEORY OF SELECTIVE NONCOOPERATION

The political theory of strategic noncooperation stems from the fact that social organizations must have the consent of their members to the exercise of power over them by persons in certain roles. We call this "legitimized power" or "authority." A foreman in a factory can give orders without making threats and a police officer can make an arrest without using force, because others accept the power vested in their roles. The government, the key agency of decision making and control in the society, must rely upon continual support from many sectors of that society.

The theory of strategic noncooperation asserts that if power is voluntarily granted it can be voluntarily removed. Institutions with immense power can falter if those who customarily cooperate decline to do so. The sixteenth-century French essayist Étienne de La Boétie stated that the tyrant is the same as everyone else in society "except for the advantage you give to him to destroy you."[2] Gene Sharp describes the effects of massive political noncooperation:

> Political power disintegrates when the people withdraw their obedience and support. Yet the ruler's military equipment may remain intact, his soldiers uninjured, the cities unscathed, the factories and transport systems in full operational capacity, and the government buildings undamaged. But everything is changed. The human assistance which created and supported the regime's political power has been withdrawn. Therefore, its power has disintegrated.[3]

Most forms of noncooperative action are local and specific, as for example the boycott of a municipal bus system which discriminates against blacks.

When an institution is involved in injustice, noncooperation can be a form of protest to draw public attention to the fact and threaten the institution's ability to function under the cover of a presumed goodness.[4] The form of noncooperation may be only the violation of convention or disruption in the expected pattern. In May 1963, normal business transactions in down-town Birmingham, Alabama, were interrupted by three thousand black children going through the stores singing "Ain't gonna let nobody turn me 'round" and "I'm on my way to freedom land."[5] A startling departure from "business as usual" was combined with a message of protest.

Other forms of noncooperation are more aggressive. Sit-ins to protest racial discrimination not only refuse cooperation with legal ordinances supporting discrimination, they also interfere with the normal process of business by politicizing its transaction, breaking the normal pattern of consumption, and thwarting the desires of customers and operators. The conflict between pickers and grape growers in California involved not only employee noncooperation in the form of strikes but customer noncooperation in the form of grape boycotts in several cities across the nation.

When noncooperation is widespread and daring, the targeted institution is placed in an awkward position. If it ignores the opposition, it appears helpless in the face of defiance, and risks its spread. If the opposition is repressed, the power of the institution may be weakened by adverse public reaction or the hardening and enlarging of the protest movement.[6]

The attraction of strategic noncooperation is that it provides nonviolent corrective actions outside the normal working of the political system based on a realistic analysis of power and self-interest. It exercises power by making the existing situation, including the specific injustice involved, less attractive than the alternatives. The loss of prestige, the nuisance of contending with the resisters, the difficulty in carrying out normal functions, the internal division as the movement picks up allies in the institution's own ranks, all help to determine the outcome. Noncooperation, as in the boycott and picketing of a business, can bring new considerations of order and profits into the debate.[7]

Practical considerations make nonviolence important for this strategy.[8] The demoralization of the "target" is crucial. Those engaged in noncooperative actions must present to the public a moral position superior to that of the institution they oppose. Their nonviolent posture often serves to confirm their claims regarding justice; their position will almost always be undercut in the eyes of the public by the use of violence or the destruction of property.

Christian community can make an important contribution to this strategy. The refusal to cooperate requires solidarity. Group action is important to prevent the target institution from dealing with the resisters one by one.[9] Groups serve to crystallize sentiment, embody morale, and mobilize for action. A Christian counter-community can also provide a lifestyle of self-discipline and sacrifice.[10] The right to organize group action (freedom of association) accordingly is fundamental to effective communication of ideas (freedom of speech).[11]

Strategic noncooperation does not require conventional economic or political strength. The United Farm Workers estimate that a consumer boycott needs the participation of only 2 to 3 percent of the population to succeed, and 10 percent participation would critically affect a producer within a few days. Studies of the black movement for civil rights in the South showed that conventional appeals were effective for this minority group only when used in combination with political protest actions and economic sanctions.[12] Direct action makes a cause a public issue and forces a response from the wielders of political and legal power.[13]

One of the most significant forms of noncooperation is civil disobedience. Here the purpose is to hinder the execution of a law and make its legitimacy a public issue, and thus such an act raises the question of the Scriptural injunctions to submit to governing authorities.

SUBORDINATION TO GOVERNMENT IN SCRIPTURE

The statement "be subordinate to 'every fundamental social institution' " is applied to the state in 1 Peter: "whether to the king as the ruler or to the governors as sent by him . . ." (1 Pet. 2.13). A similar but longer passage in Romans 13 states, "Let every person be subordinate to the ruling authorities. . . . One who resists the authorities sets oneself against the ordinance of

God" (Rom. 13.1–2). Civil disobedience would appear incompatible with faithfulness to these passages.

In interpreting these passages, as always with Scripture, we must try to discern the intention of the authors. With what questions were they dealing? Were they concerned with anything like the modern idea of civil disobedience, which is motivated by a concern for a higher standard of justice than a particular law and by the quest for the implementation of justice? Or were they dealing with something quite different?

Recently, two contexts have been proposed for Romans 13 that suggest that Paul was condemning disobedience, even if it be motivated by moral principle or a sense of justice. If either proposal is valid, the injunction might appropriately apply to modern movements of civil disobedience.

Marcus Borg proposes as background an event that took place in Rome in the decade preceding the composition of the letter. A Roman historian, Suetonius (early second century A.D.), reported of the emperor Claudius (A.D. 41–54) that "since the Jews constantly made disturbances at the instigation of Chrestus, he expelled them from Rome" (*Claudius* 25.4). Borg argues that the messianic anti-Roman agitation occurring then in Palestine had spread to Rome. By "Chrestus" (a rendering for *Christus* which has other documentation in Rome) Suetonius might be referring to a messianic pretender who sought to lead the Jews to rebel against Rome. Since at the time of Epistle to the Romans the turmoil continued in Palestine, the Roman Jewish community could have again been stirred up. The Christians had close contacts with the Jewish community, and Borg suggests that Paul is warning them against participation in such an insurrection.[14]

In another article Johannes Friedrich, Wolfgang Pöhlmann, and Peter Stuhlmacher suggest a different background for the chapter. They cite the historian Tacitus, who wrote *ca.* A.D. 80–115, and mentioned tax protests under Nero in A.D. 58 (*Annals* 13.50–51; cf. Suetonius, *Nero* 10). Noting the unusual emphasis on taxes in Romans 13 (cf. vv. 6–7), they believe that, when Romans was written in A.D. 56, the tax issue was alive and Paul wanted to avoid a repetition of the disturbances of the Jews under Claudius.[15]

However, there are compelling arguments against both of these suggestions. Tacitus does not give evidence of any form of insubordination or anti-government resistance. He writes that Nero instituted tax reform in response to "frequent requests" (*flagitationes*) by the people, who complained about extortion on the part of the tax collectors. These petitions should not be seen as a new phenomenon. (Suetonius does not even mention complaints.) Complaints about corruption in the collection of the customs tax went back to the days of the Republic. The reform is rather presented as an example of the spirit of clemency which inspired the early reign of Nero.[16] Indeed, the popularity of Nero's reign during this period makes an insurrection unlikely, particularly since a climate of unrest would necessarily have extended back at least two years (from the tax protests in 58 to the time of the writing of Romans in 56). His domestic problems did not begin until the 60s. The early administration of Nero was thoughtful and enlightened. The senate had an increased role in administration and policy, and there were popular measures in support of public welfare and morale.[17]

Romans 13 does not mention the specific tax which was involved in Nero's reform, the import duty (*portoria*); instead, the tax which is emphasized is the tribute (*phoros*, v. 6 and listed first in v. 7). The singling out of taxation in an argument for accountability to government does not need special explanation. Payment of taxes represents allegiance and acceptance of rule. The tribute, a tax paid by a subject people to the imperial state, particularly symbolizes formal allegiance.

There are equal difficulties in Borg's suggestion of a resistance movement spreading from Palestine to Rome. On sociological grounds one would not expect the uprising of Palestinian Jewish peasants to be quickly reproduced in an urban situation. Furthermore, the title *christus* would not indicate such activity; Josephus, our source of information for these movements, nowhere applies this title to the figures leading the uprising. Even if there were evidence that Claudius had in fact expelled the Jews for anti-

Roman nationalistic agitation in sympathy with Palestine, there is still little evidence of later disturbances among the Roman Jews related to the Palestinian upheavals. Even during the Jewish Wars (A.D. 66–73 and 132–135), the Jewish community in Rome remained calm, causing no embarrassment to the government.[18]

The fact that "today there is a growing number of scholars who do not see the situation at Rome as the primary occasion for Romans"[19] creates further difficulties, although not decisive ones, for these arguments. Professor Robert Karris has summarized the recent literature interpreting Paul's ethical teaching in Romans 12–15 as expressing his mature reflections upon problems encountered in his earlier missionary work, particularly as reflected in 1 Corinthians.[20] Paul's emphasis on *tribute,* a tax on subject peoples and not collected in the capital, is difficult to understand if he has in mind a specific situation in Rome. Paul is dealing with a general problem of Christians in the Roman Empire.

The historical issue behind 1 Peter 2 and Romans 13 is actually the question of Christian freedom. Particularly in the Pauline churches, there were Christians who overemphasized and misused their freedom in connection with their spiritual gifts, whether present possession of the powers and privileges of the age to come, or a mystical participation in the perfection of knowledge and moral purity that freed them from material reality. As a result, they sought to cast off the duties of their roles in society, in the form of moral codes, marriage, slavery,[21] or labor. It would not be surprising if secular civil authority should also be disregarded by those who in their spiritual powers "reigned as kings" (1 Cor. 4.8). 1 Peter indicates that it is the emphasis on Christian freedom which necessitates the admonition concerning subordination to the state: "[Subordinate yourselves] as free persons and not using your *freedom* as a covering for vice, but as slaves of God" (1 Pet. 2.16). The author recognizes that the Christian freedom of those who live as aliens upon the earth (1 Pet. 1.1) is their motivation for denying the authority of the state, but he informs those so tempted that their interpretation is contrary to the calling of the slaves of God. Those owned by God must bear their share of community responsibility; they are not exempt from such responsibility.

E. G. Selwyn notes the similarity of this teaching in 1 Peter to Romans 6.18–22.[22] In Romans 6 Paul asks the question "Are we to sin because we are not under Law but under grace?" (6.15). To those who might misinterpret the implications of Christian freedom Paul has to demonstrate that although the Mosaic law is not the basis of salvation, this does not mean that the Law itself was not good (ch. 7), or that we are free to participate in the immorality forbidden by the law (ch. 6). We are set free from slavery to sin in order that we may become slaves of God and God's righteousness (6.18–25).

Romans 13 has also been taken as an argument against spiritual "enthusiasts" parallel to Paul's arguments elsewhere on marriage and slavery.[23] Earlier in Romans Paul established the continuing integrity of the Mosaic law, and in Romans 13 he asserts the integrity of the civil law. The chart illustrates his argument.

Freedom	Law	Affirmation of Law
Grace Spirit	Mosaic Law	Law is good (ch. 7) Power given to fulfill it (ch. 8)
	Civil Law	Government is good Obligation to be subordinate

The writers of both Romans and 1 Peter assume for the sake of their argument that the government is good, that it is in accord with the will of God. They do not deal with the exceptions, where it is obviously not; the position they were refuting called into question the very principle of secular government, as symbolized particularly by the payment of taxes. In contrast, they present the state as indispensable to the support of a morally good order in human society. Both authors restate a formula known in the Graeco-Roman world for nine centuries: the government is to praise or honor those who do good and to dishonor or punish those who do evil (Rom. 13.3–4; 1 Pet. 2.14).[24] Paul further describes government as the "servant of God for *good*" (*to agathon,* Rom.

13.4). Both authors assume that the acts of government conform to the highest ethical and religious standards. "Therefore one must be subject . . . for the sake of conscience" (Rom. 13.5); "Be subject for the sake of the Lord" (1 Pet. 2.13).[25] And the occasion it provided for vice is the reason for the rejection of the antinomian attitude (Rom. 13.4; 1 Pet. 2.16).

The passages demonstrate that public authority has a claim upon us. Order, law, and even coercion have a legitimate purpose which we must accept. Yet the passages do not establish the validity of the assertion "Because one does have an obligation to obey the law, one ought not ever disobey the law."[26]

Romans 13.1–7 and 1 Peter 2.13–17 do, in fact, imply a limit to government. The authority of God, under which government functions, provides the basis for judging specific acts of governments. Further, those purposes of government raised in the argument can serve as a yardstick for evaluating laws and the conduct of governments. Yoder states, "We can judge and measure the extent to which a government is accomplishing its ministry, by asking . . . whether it persistently . . . attends to the rewarding of good and evil according to their merits; to be 'minister to you for good' is a criterion, not a description."[27]

If the ruler is sent by God, one might acknowledge the ruler's wrong-doing without viewing the injustice as one for the subjects to correct.[28] But these passages go further, authorizing obedience on the grounds of the critical discernment of what is duty and what serves the Lord. From the fact that conscience is to be a motivating force in obeying government a basis may be inferred for disobeying government when its actions are not in conformity with the voice of informed conscience. "God does not dissolve into his own immanence. . . ." If our civil responsibility stands under our recognition of God's supreme authority, then "Christian obedience comes to an end at the point where further service becomes impossible—and only there."[29]

Other biblical passages indicate that the relationship of the Christian to government includes more than obedience. In the Gospels Jesus says, "Pay back to Caesar the things which are Cae-

sar's and to God the things which are God's" (Matt. 22.21 par.).
Jesus is here responding to an effort to trap him into speaking
against loyalty to the state. His opponents assumed that Jesus was
disposed to reject authority, because of his teaching about the
Reign of God: "We know that you teach the way of God in truth
and that you look at the appearance of no one" (v. 16). They suspected that he lacked reverence for the ruler's authority. Jesus' response affirmed obligations to the government but placed them
within limits. Arguing that use of the imperial coinage system
indicated participation in an administration which expressed and
acknowledged Roman authority, Jesus stated that his questioners
should perform the obligations resulting from their involvement.
But then he introduced a concept that qualified and limited what
he had just said: "And pay your obligations to God" (since you
also participate in God's transcendent administration; cf. v. 16).

Bornkamm correctly asserts that the emphasis in Jesus' teaching is on this second part of the response.[30] The state is placed
within limits and made subject to criticism. There is a duty to
God apart from that to Caesar. Such a concept was novel in that
day, when religious and political claims were combined in one
system. Jesus' statement shows that the state was no longer to be
regarded as intrinsically sacred. Moral and religious claims existing
apart from the state can be drawn upon for criticism of the state.

Denial of the possibility of civil disobedience is contrary to
Jesus' answer; it implies that the authority of the state is absolute
and that all its laws belong to "the way of God." Or, if it is
acknowledged that laws can be unjust, then the relevance of injustice to "the way of God" is denied, since the laws are still to be
obeyed in any case. But the Bible, more than any other ancient
document, exposes government as frequently acting in disobedience to God, and it reveals God's will that such injustices be corrected.

The relationship of the apostles to the local Jewish authorities
in the Book of Acts is consistent with this interpretation of Jesus'
teaching. Peter and the apostles say, "It is necessary to obey God
rather than persons" (Acts 5.29). They had been ordered not to

teach in the name of Jesus (v. 28). They were resisting the authority of the Sanhedrin, which had responsibility for internal legal affairs delegated to them by the Roman officials. The high priest, who in turn was subject to the Roman procurator, served as its president and convener.[31] The terminology in Acts reveals the political nature of this local council. It is called "the Sanhedrin, that is to say [epexegetical *kai*] all the senate [*gerousia*] of the sons of Israel" (Acts 5.21). Peter addressed it as "the rulers [*archontes;* cf. Rom. 13.3] of the people" (Acts 4.9). The Sanhedrin, which the apostles openly disobeyed, accepting the consequences, was nevertheless an authority in the terms of Romans 13 and 1 Peter 2. The Old Testament also provides examples of disobedience to human governments by the people of God. The Book of Daniel emphasizes God as the King of Kings. When Shadrach, Meshach, and Abednego refused to worship the golden image of King Nebuchadnezzar (ch. 2) and Daniel violated the ordinance against praying to any god for thirty days (ch. 6), they showed, in the words of Charles Ryrie, that "subjection to the law of God takes priority in a believer's life over obedience to the laws of man."[32]

One traditional response at this point is first to note that the apostles in Acts had been involved in witnessing and then to draw the conclusion that a ruling prohibiting witnessing (or worship, as in Daniel) is the only law that a Christian may disobey. But what is the criterion for such an arbitrary distinction? Romans 13 and 1 Peter 2 make no such exception. Is God's will in conflict with the state only with regard to Christian proselytizing and worship? This view reflects a narrowly defined doctrine of sin. In the prophetic confrontation with the state in the Old Testament, social and economic matters were a point of contention between God and human governments. Elijah, Amos, Jeremiah, and others resisted the will of kings in their quest for justice and suffered the consequences; they belong to "the prophets, who by faith . . . carried out justice" and "suffered chains and imprisonment" (Heb. 11.32–33, 36). Such a prophet was Moses, who saw that justice was done (*ekdikēsis poiein,* Acts 7.24, 37; cf. Bauer[5], 238). He repeatedly sought the normal legal redress, the permission of the king, to deal with the plight of the people. Pharaoh withdrew his earlier consent for the people to leave, as such a monarch was free to do. But with Pharaoh in pursuit, the people of Israel "went forth defiantly" (Exod. 14.8, *RSV;* literally, "with a high hand" [$b^e y\bar{a}d$ $r\bar{a}m\bar{a}h$]), still within his jurisdiction, disobeying his edict. The concern behind this action was not simply freedom of worship but deliverance from physical, economic, and social mistreatment (Exod. 3.7–8; Acts 7.34). Earlier the Hebrew midwives had violated the command of the king by sparing the newborn sons of Israel, and they were honored by God for their disobedience (Exod. 1.15–21). Our duty is not only to preach the gospel, but also to live it.

Christians through the centuries have often resisted political laws deemed in violation of duty to God. The ancient church suffered persecution for disobeying decrees requiring participation in emperor worship. This early defiance of laws was not forgotten when the Christian church became part of the political establishment and individual Christians were confronted by unconscionable laws enacted by other Christians, often in the name of the church itself. Civil disobedience became the first principle of Christian jurisprudence.[33]

In light of this tradition, it is not surprising that fifteen years before Thoreau's imprisonment for refusing to pay his poll tax, Christian missionaries among the Cherokees were arguing for civil disobedience on biblical grounds. A Georgian law stated that the Cherokees must give up their claim of sovereignty over their land (1829), and to restrain their missionary advocates it ordered the missionaries either to acknowledge this law and obtain a license to preach or leave the state. The Rev. Samuel A. Worcester and Dr. Elizur Butler defied the law and went to jail. The missionaries argued that the Cherokees needed the support of the missionaries in their efforts to retain their rights, and that they themselves were bound to uphold the cause of justice for the oppressed. Worcester argued that he was not acting from political expediency but from "clear moral obligation—a question of right or wrong—of keeping or violating the commands of God. . . ."[34]

Civil disobedience has also been a path toward change among Third World Christians. For example, in the community of Oro in Nigeria, Christian women protested an order of the chief and some of his subordinates levying burial ceremonial fees on relatives of the deceased that would be a strain on the poor and would be used by the officials for themselves. The women complained, called meetings, demonstrated several times, and later boycotted the market center. Such a boycott customarily takes place only when the chief dies. To take this action while the chief was still alive implied that they desired his death. Their request was quickly granted.[35]

THE ETHICS OF CONFLICTING DUTIES

We possess normative values that we regard as absolute. We consider them binding upon us at all times and in all cultural situations. They are primarily presented to us in Scripture, but they also arise in rational reflection upon historical experience with Scriptural norms. Thus basic human rights are always and everywhere the same, without exception. One method of dealing with the unalterable character of our basic values, while dealing realistically with situations in which they cannot be observed, is the concept of *prima facie duties.*

Prima facie means "on first appearance." A prima facie duty derives from moral rules that hold true whenever the factors which they govern appear in a situation. They are not culturally bound, yet other moral considerations may intervene so that finally they may not be the actual duty in the situation. Our basic ethical norms are expressed in relationships with particular people. The people around me stand in relation to me, wife to husband, child to parent, friend to friend, creditor to debtor, citizen to citizen, unbeliever to witness, etc. Each of these relationships forms the basis of fundamental duty, such as fidelity, justice, or noninjury to others. The Ten Commandments enumerate several such duties. If we make a promise to someone, we put ourselves into a relation with that person which creates a basic duty to that person. We can call these prima facie duties.[36] They may be said to embody absolute or universal values.

We are surrounded by people in various relationships who represent a multiplicity of duties. Sometimes we must choose among duties to various individuals. "Most moral problems arise in situations where there is a 'conflict of duties,' that is, where one moral principle pulls one way and another pulls the other way."[37] "Every moral problem of the slightest interest is a problem about who is to get hurt."[38] Ross suggests that every act has countless effects and will have some adverse effects (however trivial) and probably some beneficial effects. Even if only indirectly, these effects involve prima facie duties which are met or not met.[39] The fact that the reader is spending his or her time in studies rather than in some form of ministry or service means that there are claims which are presently unmet. In deciding among these claims, we must consider three types of duty: prima facie, secondary, and actual duty. The *actual* duty is the right decision for the given situation. The *prima facie* duty is the same as the actual duty unless there is an overriding moral consideration in the form of another prima facie duty. A *secondary* duty, such as a claim of custom, etiquette, efficiency, or utility, cannot be the actual duty if there is a prima facie duty in the situation. One could not shoot another person or tell a slanderous lie in order to deliver the mail on time. A prima facie duty allows no exceptions. It has a claim upon us even in a situation in which we cannot fulfill it. It must always be taken into account. The prima facie duty is duty—other things being equal. The actual duty is duty—all things considered.

Why bring in this new terminology instead of speaking of absolute values? The purpose is to use language which accurately reflects the fact that in practice even permanently binding values cannot always be the actual duty, while preserving "the absoluteness of the general principles of morality."[40] The term *absolute* or *universal* disguises the actual process of ethical decision making.

The Scriptures contain many instances of moral conflicts. Norman Geisler calls God's command to Abraham to kill Isaac the classic example of such a conflict and also cites the tension in the

Gospels between following Jesus and filial responsibilities or between the Sabbath regulations and the hunger of the disciples.[41]
In such situations prima facie duties are not always actual duties.
The command of God prohibiting divorce is accordingly modified
in the case of adultery or of the desire for divorce on the part of an
unbelieving spouse.[42]

Similarly, we do not hold a househoulder morally culpable for
leaving the home lighted when on vacation to deceive burglars into
thinking that someone is at home. Or if a mother sees a murderer
in pursuit of her child, most people would believe that she has a
right to mislead the murderer by any means in her power.[43] In
both cases there are overriding duties and claims.

Many ethical arguments are simplistic because they look at
only one characteristic of the act in question. For example, let us
take the act of abortion and consider the variety of claims upon a
woman who is considering this action. We are not concerned at
this point with her actual duty, but with the complexity of the
situation. In an abortion there is the claim of the human fetus (and
there are differing medical, religious, and philosophical opinions
as to when the fetus is to be regarded as a person), the life of the
mother, the claim of the mother to control her own body, the
mental health of the mother, the stability of her marriage, the
future physical and emotional condition of the fetus when it is
born, and the other children of the mother and their economic and
psychological needs.

As we have stated, every act involves a multiplicity of claims,
not all of which can be met. The claims that are met in a particular
action are the *right-making characteristics*[44] of the action. Claims
which are not met are *wrong-making characteristics* of the action.
These characteristics are right-making or wrong-making according
to whether they would be right or wrong if they were the only
factors involved. Right actions are those which have the greatest
balance of prima facie rightness over their prima facie wrongness.[45]
It is, of course, not a matter of counting up duties met and not
met, since even prima facie duties differ qualitatively according to
basic moral claims as well as degree of involvement in the specific

action. The harm of another person is always a wrong-making characteristic, but not every act which includes this characteristic is necessarily wrong for that reason. We grant the state the authority to coerce, to put people in jail. We do this not because liberty and personal dignity are not duties which must always be considered but because having a community which preserves many values including liberty and personal dignity outweighs some particular claims of liberty and dignity. The latter remain as wrong-making characteristics of the right actual duty of preserving community.

Let us suppose that you have a reputation for never showing up on time. You have agreed to conduct a service at a church, and the pastor, knowing your weakness on this point, makes you solemnly promise that you will be at the service on time. You leave in plenty of time to get to the service, but as you are driving along, you see that there has been an accident and someone is injured and in need of help. What do you do? The right choice for this situation may be clear, but at this point our concern is how to regard the alternative not taken. No matter what you decide, your action will have a wrong-making characteristic representing the claim which is not met. Doing the actual duty of helping the injured person still has the wrong-making characteristic of not keeping your word. Promise keeping is a prima facie duty. It is always there even when it cannot be fulfilled.

Harvey Seifert approaches the dilemma of decision-making from another angle. We are responsible to a total system of values. Because of the limitations of nature and our imperfect human situation, it is usually not possible to realize all values at the same time in a given situation. Ethical norms become goals to be approximated as closely as possible under existing circumstances.[46] Again we must be reminded that all norms are not equal in their claims upon us, and a stronger claim cannot be surrendered for a weaker one.

The advantage of this approach to ethical decision-making is that it allows a person to approach complicated situations honestly and realistically, recognizing that responsible involvement often means a choice among values and duties, so that one valid claim must sometimes be denied in order to fulfill a stronger one. This method allows one to think and act without paralyzing guilt or shame.

Another advantage of this method is the recognition that the duties which are not met remain as valid claims upon us. Thus we shall sometimes act with a sense of sorrow fitting to the difficult choices which we have to make. This regret is not equivalent to guilt because we know that we must choose and act; [47] seeking the Lord's guidance in our choices, we know that he accepts and understands the integrity of the choice of the right duty (Rom. 14.23). The consciousness of unmet claims should make us self-critical of our choices. We must act; we must make commitments; we cannot wait for perfect understanding or crystal clear choices between good and evil. Yet we are aware of the high possibility of error when choosing one claim over another, and we must review our choices in order to discern error and the intrusions of selfishness.

When one says, "The ends do not justify the means," one holds that even though the purposes of the act in question have a preponderance of right-making characteristics, we are not justified in dispensing with consideration of wrong-making characteristics in the means to reach those ends. Our evaluation of the act must include the duties involved in the means as well as in the ends. It is possible that, in the total evaluation, the right-making characteristics in the act may outweigh wrong-making characteristics which lie in the means. The wrong-making characteristics in the means continue to exist, yet the actual duty may be to go ahead despite these reservations. We may not like to use coercion, such as the threat of a fine or prison, to make a slumlord act more responsibly, but it may be necessary in order to meet the higher claims of justice for the tenants.

In considering what our actual duty is in a situation of ethical conflict, we must first isolate and evaluate the different duties that are involved. We then must try to determine which claims have more weight. Is one claim prima facie while another is secondary?

Are the prima facie claims of one alternative of greater weight than those of another? Ethicists have rightly refrained from the impossible and counterproductive task of providing a recipe for making decisions in all situations. Certain priorities can be identified, however. For example, persons are more valuable than things (one does not shoot a boy stealing tomatoes), and Infinite Person is more valuable than finite person(s).[48] In many conflicts the concept of justice will come into play. Here the special claims upon us of parent, spouse, child, fellow citizen, etc. have weight to the degree that they indicate dependence upon us, and if there is not a significantly greater good which could be done to a person who does not have this special claim. Justice has priority over efficiency, but justice which also promotes secondary principles such as efficiency and stability is preferable to the same justice without them.[49] As was stated above (p. 80), the greater the extent to which an ethical claim is related to what is basic to life, dignity, and minimal inclusion in community, the higher its priority.

One may also refer to one's concept of the good, whether it is conceived in terms of the relief of suffering or the realization of self-potential. (Other considerations of the good include pleasure, power, and knowledge.) An evaluation of ethical action would then include an analysis of which alternative would produce more highly valued consequences. When there is a conflict among basic claims, we should not, however, simply invoke the principle of what will result in the most good, since that in effect leads to the adoption of the utilitarian principle, i.e., consideration of the quantity of good rather than the nature of the duties involved.[50] What brings about the most good is only one factor. Ross gives the following illustration. If I have made a promise to a person that will do him or her 1000 units of good (assuming for the sake of the argument that such measurements are possible), while in breaking the promise I could do 1001 units of good for a different person, I would not be justified in breaking the promise.[51]

Although we cannot prepare specific answers for unforeseeable future conflicts among values, our best preparation, over and above a clear knowledge of the nature of our duties, is to foster in our-

selves those traits of character "that will sustain us in the hour of
decision when we are choosing between conflicting principles of
prima facie duty or trying to revise our working rules of actual
duty."[52] If the church is to assist in this work of the grace of God
within us, it must not only instruct us in the knowledge of ethics,
but also shepherd us in personal growth.

The words of Peter to the Sanhedrin were literally, according
to Acts, "to obey God is more of an obligation than to obey persons" (Acts 5:29). One of our prima facie duties is obedience to
government. This is our obligation unless it is overridden by
stronger prima facie claims. The character of such an act of civil
disobedience is conditioned by the realization that the obligation
to government continues as an unmet claim and a wrong-making
characteristic of the act.

CIVIL DISOBEDIENCE AS SUBORDINATION

Civil disobedience accords with the major characteristics of the
biblical teaching on the relationship of the believer to society. It
is nonconformity with the world as in conflict with the new life
under God. It is undertaken in order to establish justice. But in
its classical form it also expresses subordination to government.

Civil disobedience, as it has been defined in modern times, is
a limited tactic. It is based on the principles which regulate civil
life.[53] In principle it recognizes the prima facie claim of governmental authority, and in method it appeals to moral sympathy in
the general populace. Civil disobedience seeks to bring law and
morality into greater congruence, and this congruence underlies
respect for law.[54] Those who employ civil disobedience act within
the framework of acceptance of the legitimacy of a particular system of law. The action taken implies that the system is generally
worthy of support. Such an act respects rather than defies the authority of the government, and thus legitimate civil disobedience
entails certain qualifications. (This does not mean that other forms
of disobedience or resistance are never ethically valid. The nature
of the action contemplated may be incompatible with the restric-

tions of civil disobedience. For example transportation of slaves through the Underground Railroad obviously could not be a public act.[55] Or in a highly repressive political regime, such as in Nazi Germany, the chances of success may be negligible and the cost too high for it to be worthwhile to engage in public disobedience and accept the penalty.)[56]

QUALIFICATIONS OF CIVIL DISOBEDIENCE[57]

1. The law opposed is immoral. Because of the prima facie duty of subordination to government, the first characteristic of genuine civil disobedience is that the law to be protested must be in conflict with a higher prima facie claim. The law stands in contrast to what is basic to life, dignity, and social harmony—indeed to the very purpose of law. The law violates values fundamental to personal morality and allegiance to God.

It must be recognized that subordination to government makes it impossible to avoid totally involvement in every instance of injustice. No social institution is entirely free from evil, and participation in any existing society involves compromise with the ideal of the Reign of God.[58]

The thought of Thomas Aquinas on obedience to civil law is relevant to contemporary considerations of civil disobedience. He wrote that laws can be unjust in two ways. A law is unjust if it is unfair or unconstitutional. It may be beyond the scope of the power which has been granted to the authority. For example, a law may not interfere with matters which depend on "interior movements of the will" (conscience), are essential for life, or are voluntary and private, such as contracting marriage or a vow of chastity. We would say that such a law interferes with basic liberty. A law is unfair if the ruler acts for personal interests, rather than for the common good, which is the legitimate basis for law and the possession of power. Laws are also unfair when they lay burdens unevenly on the governed. A law which violated the civil rights of a minority, we might say today, could be disobeyed because it fails to provide equal protection and thus distributes justice unevenly. Because these laws are not legitimate, says Aquinas, they are acts of violence rather than true laws. He quotes Augustine, "A law that is not just, goes for no law at all." Such a law is therefore not binding on the conscience; it has no power of obligation although one might go the second mile and obey it to avoid scandal or turmoil.

The second way in which Aquinas says that a law may be unjust is that it may be in conflict with the good itself, with God. This would include anything which is against the divine law. An oppressive law may contradict God's commands of justice for the oppressed or love for the neighbor. Aquinas states that such a law is not lawful at all. It *must* be resisted. One is obliged to disobey.[59] Accordingly, laws directly contrary to one's basic moral integrity and conscience should not be obeyed.[60] They are not legitimate; they do not exemplify the authority spoken of in Romans 13.

If it is a sin not to respect legitimate law and order, it also is a sin to fail to oppose unjust law and order. Disobeying unjust law has always been part of the struggle for justice. Rauschenbusch stated:

> Law is unspeakably precious. Order is the daughter of heaven. Yet in practice law and order are on the side of those in possession. The men who are out can get in only through the disturbance of the order now prevailing. Those who in the past cried for law and order at any cost have throttled many a new born child of justice.[61]

Similarly, Booth wrote;

> Some men go to a gaol because they are better than their neighbors, most men because they are worse. Martyrs, patriots, reformers of all kinds belong to the first category. No great cause has ever achieved a triumph before it has furnished a certain quota to the prison population. The repeal of an unjust law is seldom carried until a certain number of those who are labouring for the reform have experienced in their own persons the hardships of fine and imprisonment.[62]

To protest an unjust law, one may have to disobey a different one. How does one oppose a voter qualification law when one does not have a vote? How does one protest the absence of a law by disobeying it? The law actually disobeyed should not be a law that protects or provides for a value with a higher moral claim than the one opposed. One would not destroy property to protest discrimination in the mail service, a service which is a subsidiary good. One chooses the least important law which will allow an effective protest.[63] The effectiveness of the protest will usually depend on the relevance of the substituted law to the one protested.

It is important to reiterate that civil disobedience is a matter of *moral* dissent. Unacceptable motivations include self-interest, prejudice, unexamined emotional reaction, and unconfirmed factual claims.[64] One supports one's judgment with reference to moral principles—to a higher law. This criterion of civil disobedience, as well as those which follow, refutes the argument that civil disobedience is no different from any other type of law breaking.

2. *Every possible nondisobedient recourse has been exhausted.* Because civil disobedience affirms obligation to the legal system, one must first vigorously attempt to change the law through the means of change that the system provides. Some would apply this qualification legalistically to stifle any civil disobedience. However, there are situations in which the political processes are flagrantly inefficient, and there are times when immediate action is necessary. The meanings of "exhaust" and "possible" will be tempered by the context.[65]

3. *The protest is not clandestine.* The clearest sign of the affirmation of legal authority in civil disobedience is the fact that it is carried out in full view of the agents of law enforcement and of the public. This indicates that one is not trying to benefit from disobedience or subvert the system. Openness is required not only for the sake of principle but also for the strategy of appeal to public opinion. There should be a clear statement of the purpose of the act, and one should relate one's actions to one's goals in such a way

that this relationship will be clear to the outside observer.[66] For the same reasons the act should be nonviolent (cf. pp. 144–45).

4. *There is a likelihood of success.* Michael Bayles distinguishes between two types of civil disobedience. In the first, *personal civil disobedience,* obedience is incompatible with one's moral integrity. One acts solely for the sake of conscience, not for social change. Here the criterion of likelihood of success is inapplicable. The second type is *social civil disobedience,* in which the purpose is to change or protest a law.[67] Since we are considering strategies for social change, we are primarily concerned with this type. Because the violation of the duty to submit to governmental authority is a grave act, one does not seek change through civil disobedience without some assurances that one's purpose is attainable. Consideration should also be given to the proportion between the good that may probably be accomplished and the probable evil effects accompanying the good. The latter might include disrespect for the law, violence, social conflict, as well as the disadvantages of the punishment that could follow.[68]

5. *There is a willingness to accept the penalty.* Because civil disobedience is carried out in the context of support for the legal system as a whole, the participant in civil disobedience does not try to evade arrest, trial, or the penalty which the legal system may assign to him or her. The rule of law means indictment of all persons whom it is reasonable to believe have violated the law, and acceptance of the rule of law includes a commitment to the equal enforcement of the law. Therefore, respect for the system means accepting the application of legal punishment to oneself.[69]

This criterion is closely connected with the openness of the act. One does not flee prosecution or sentence. One does not try to hide one's act. By accepting the penalty, one reaffirms one's membership in the community. By accepting the penalty, one also admits that one's judgment is fallible. One might be wrong and society right after all.[70]

This criterion does not mean that one does not use all the means of defense available through the law. Using the legal system is one aspect of affirming it. In addition, the court process often provides the public and legal attention which the act of disobedience sought.

   Civil disobedience contributes to the legal order. No constitutional process is so perfect that it avoids injustice entirely. Civil disobedience, stepping into the breaches of constitutional order, gives justice a second chance.[71] If it were not for the possibility of civil disobedience, departures from justice would have less chance of being corrected. Pressure for justice and resentment against injustice could be ignored and continue to build up until there was a threat of violence and revolt. Without the disturbance of civil disobedience,

> the legal system and the social order can become a stagnant haven of injustice, a harbinger of violence or of revolutionary action. When other checks and balances in the society and the government do not function adequately, civil disobedience can step into the breach and promote the fundamental values of a just democratic society.[72]

Thus civil disobedience can truly be a way of paying our obligations of respect and honor to the political system (Rom. 13.7).

   The method of civil disobedience is strategic noncooperation (cf. pp. 143–45). Civil disobedience aims at changing law. Real change of laws and customs is a long process, but the first step is to alter public opinion and to stir people to action. Civil disobedience may be considered effective when it contributes to either or both of these ends.

   Civil disobedience shares the limitations of other forms of strategic noncooperation. It is a criticism of the social system but inadequate by itself for the positive achievement of justice.[73] It is not an alternative to political action within the system but a component of such action.[74] Strategic noncooperation is most effective when it can feed back into the constitutional system. For example, in the successful black civil rights struggle, the protests and boycotts were accompanied by the intervention of federal power. Civil disobedience contributed to the racial integration of public schools, but it had little effect until there was a federal decision, which in turn required the cooperation of a whole network of individuals and public agencies.[75] Because civil disobedience exists in the framework of a government the authority and legitimacy of which it supports, it accepts its place beside other aspects of the political activity of that system.

Civil disobedience is not the normal path to justice, but the situations which demand it in a world hostile to God are not uncommon, and they often involve the most crucial issues of justice.

Chapter 9

AFTER ALL ELSE—THEN ARMS?

> Think of them laughing, singing
>> loving their people
>>> and
>> all people who put love
>>> before power
>> then
> put love with power
>> which is necessary
>>> to destroy power without love.[1]

We have seen that, because evil is embodied in powerful social structures, our response to the claims of love must take the form of determined resistance against injustice. Love for the powerless cannot be separated from the struggle against power. Are there social and political conflicts in which justice requires the use of arms?

Evil can infest the institutions of a society to the point of subverting their true purpose, which is to maintain the welfare of all the people. At the same time, this evil discloses the fact that those who benefit from social perversion also control the government, thereby preventing significant amelioration. In such societies, the terms *reform* and *development* often connote mere changes in appearance, and do not touch the reality of the problems. At the same time, radical change through strategic noncooperation and other forms of nonviolent action may prove impossible, because of the diffused nature of the targets, the absence of an established democratic context, and the lack of commitment to nonviolence among the masses, or on the parts of significant numbers of the advocates for change. In the face of massive and concentrated oppression, the justification of recourse to arms becomes a serious ethical question.

The claim of justice is prior to that of peace, because there can be no genuine peace without justice. The false cry of "Peace, peace," against which Jeremiah railed, came in circumstances of social injustice (Jer. 6.13–14; cf. v. 12; Zech. 8.16). Final peace follows upon final justice: "The effect of justice will be peace" (Isa. 32.17).

Many leading contemporary advocates of nonviolence agree that without some form of power governments cannot maintain order nor can activists secure justice. The question remains, however, whether the use of force to secure the common good can properly embrace the use of instruments that inflict personal injury and death.

Even if justice is only obtainable through the use of arms, it does not necessarily follow that such use is therefore ethically warranted. Certain acts cannot be justified by the common good. If the inhabitants of a city were to preserve their lives by handing over their children (or even one child) to an invader to be killed, the worth of the continued existence so obtained would be negated by the crime against innocent human life that secured it. The same can be said about the currently popular lifeboat analogy according to which, when there are not enough provisions for all, some must be sacrificed so that all do not perish. But it would in fact be better for all to die than for some to maintain their existence on a subhuman level (if these are indeed the only two alternatives). Do we find support in biblical values for the claim that the taking of life cannot be justified by any duty or good, including the overthrow of violence and tyranny?

ORDER AND REVOLUTION

By *revolution,* we mean a change in the external structure of a society involving both a redistribution of power and a revision of the form and direction of the institutions of that society. A group with a different power base from another quarter of the society takes

control. The change is sudden, rather than gradual, or evolutionary. A revolution need not be violent in the sense of directly in-
tending the physical injury or death of its opponents. (Whether
violence includes acts against property is contestable.) But revolutions frequently involve the use of armed force, and this is the fact
that now challenges us. Thus, for the purposes of this discussion
the following definition of revolution will apply: "an internal war
directed toward changing a government's policies, rules and organizations and transforming the social and economic structures."[2]

The ethical problems inherent in this act of revolution are
complex. One is confronted with not only a seeming conflict with
the prima facie claim of public authority, but also a conflict with
the prima facie claim of personal security, the duty not to injure
physically or take the life of another person.

We laid groundwork for dealing with the conflict between revolution and political allegiance in the last chapter, in the discussion of civil disobedience. Now, however, we are faced with a
broader conflict, between the duty of justice and respect for a
whole system of law, when that system is characterized by the
same immorality perceived in a particular law in the case of civil
disobedience. Now the whole system is opposed, as in basic violation of God's intention for the political order. The government
itself is rejected, as failing to provide basic security, welfare, and
justice for a significant portion of the populace. As Ernst Käsemann states in reflecting upon Romans 13, one can participate in
a revolution as an authentic act of service to God

> only . . . when the possessors of political power are threatening
> and destroying in a radical way those ties which hold together a
> political community as a whole in bonds of mutual service
> . . . when every concrete act of service within the individual's
> province takes on the character of participation in a common
> self-destruction.

Käsemann cites as an example the Third Reich of the Nazis, at
least after Stalingrad.[3]

In other words, revolutionary disobedience is warranted when

the possessors of political power by their every act reveal themselves not to be an authority sent by God as God's servant for the
good of the people (cf. Rom. 13.4). Despite their claims, they are
not legitimate rulers and are not owed the duty of obedience.

There are a number of examples in Scripture of movements
overthrowing governments become illegitimate by opposing the
will of God. In the Book of Judges one savior after another is sent
by God to deliver the people of Israel from the hand of oppressive
rule. Even in the period of national independence in the Divided
Kingdom, the Lord sent prophets to anoint civilians as kings with
instructions to destroy the existing rulers (2 Kgs. 9.6–7). While
today one cannot claim such direct revelation of the divine will,
such episodes indicate at least in principle the opposition of God
to those who would seem to be "the powers that be." The problem
for us is to discern when those who hold political power have
moved off the base of legitimacy.

One must consider the need for government and the duty of
respect for authority with great seriousness, but the greater ethical
conflict associated with armed revolution is centered on the question of violence.

THE NEW TESTAMENT AND VIOLENCE

If the question of a just use of arms is to be dealt with on a biblical
foundation, we must include the teaching and example of Jesus.
Most Christian ethicists who approach this issue assume that the
Gospels present Jesus as teaching nonviolence, although they may
differ on how his teachings relate to contemporary society. In this
section we will challenge the assumption that the teaching and
example of Jesus have direct application to the concept of violence
as it functions in Christian political deliberation.

Since Christian love seeks the well-being of the other person
and expresses itself in provisions which preserve the minimal conditions of life together, it would be expected that love prohibits
inflicting physical injury on or taking the life of another person.
This aspect of love (from the New Testament perspective, Rom.

13.9–10) is found in the Ten Commandments: "You shall not murder" (Exod. 20.6). But this Sixth Commandment is a prohibition of the *unjust* taking of life. It is not an absolute proscription of life taking. The term used in Exodus 20.6 is the term for *murder* (*rāṣaḥ*), rather than the comprehensive term for *killing* (*hārag*).[4] There is still a place for such action by the community, as seen in several provisions in the Law. That the Old Covenant contains only a relative prohibition of killing is recognized by those who advocate a nonviolent interpretation of biblical ethics; they argue that the reservations in the Sixth Commandment have been overcome by Jesus' teaching, whose interpretation is decisive.[5] The question then becomes in what way Jesus has extended the command against murder to a total prohibition of killing. We will examine the key passages used by those who have made specific Scriptural arguments for nonviolence.

Turn the other cheek. In commenting on the law of *talio*, "an eye for an eye," in which the sufferer had the legal recourse of demanding satisfaction from the aggressor even to the administration of the same injury,[6] Jesus used examples that have little to do with violence directly, but could logically be seen to limit several forms of violence (Matt. 5.38–42).[7] None of these forms of violence, however, are pertinent to the classical Christian defense of certain uses of arms.

Jesus states that a slap on the right cheek may not be returned (Matt. 5.39). But a slap on the cheek should not be interpreted as an image of violence. Robert Tannehill has shown that in these verses Jesus used a type of imagery in which in each case a concrete example shocks his hearers into a new moral awareness. The hearer knows that because the instance is *extreme,* it includes all similar relevant cases up to and including the literal sense.[8] A slap on the cheek cannot be considered an extreme case of physical injury. Rather, in the culture of Palestine a slap on the cheek, apparently with the back of the hand, was an extreme form of insult.[9] In the freedom of love, Jesus expects his followers to have no need to even the score, even against an extremity of scorn and contempt that would normally severely damage pride. A similar teaching in Romans 12.17–21 speaks against vengeance in more general terms: "Do not render to anyone evil for evil" (v. 17). Vengeance provides the context for Paul's often quoted statement "Do not be overcome by evil, but overcome evil with good" (v. 21, *RSV*).

In the Sermon on the Mount, Jesus deals with situations in which not only does one not resist what may be an unjust claim against oneself, but one goes beyond, to give more than is demanded. Exhorting his followers not to defend themselves in court against wrong,[10] not to respond to insult with pride or revenge, to allow even the protection of their garments to be taken away (Matt. 5.40), Jesus asks of them actions expressive of a freedom from anxiety and self-protection that can only be understood in terms of the total trust in the providence of their Heavenly Protector (cf. Matt. 6.25–34) enjoined in his teaching elsewhere. If these injunctions regarding response to unjust actions against oneself are applied to more complex social relations, the consistent thrust is to prohibit *any* attempt to resist injustice, much less the employment of violence in such resistance. A social ethic extrapolated from these injunctions would exclude both violent *and* nonviolent resistance. Yet such utter passivity is rejected even by many who believe these teachings to enjoin total nonviolence.

Even though the passage does not treat the question of violence per se, it (with Romans 12) certainly rules out any use of violence for the purpose of vengeance, retaliation, or protection of one's property; such actions are proscribed. To argue further that the examples used by Jesus implicitly prohibit protecting oneself from violence, is to argue from the lesser to the extreme; Jesus' argument was from the extreme to the lesser. Nevertheless, in the light of these passages it is questionable whether one could use force to defend oneself against violence without offending the spirit of "freedom from the self-protective consciousness"[11] and utter trust upon God that Jesus calls forth. The passage does not deal with the question of self-protection against violence, but the call to total trust in the care of God would seem to exclude even that.

But these applications of the teachings of Jesus still do not speak to the crucial questions regarding the use of arms. The traditional Christian rationale for armed force does not permit arms for the sake of vengeance or retaliation. As we shall see in the next section, the classical argument did not permit force even to save one's own life from an aggressor. Each of the cases of Matthew 5.38–42 is *bilateral*, concerned with the relationship between the subject and one other person. The situation for which arms were permitted was *multilateral*,[12] in which the subject's duty is not only to a second person but also to a *third* person (or party) for whom one bears responsibility.

Does the injunction against resistance in self-defense cover the different question of resistance to injustice done to a third party? The passage is not applicable to this crucial question, which includes the role of the state; one cannot answer the multilateral question with bilateral injunctions alone. The evidence of Jesus' commitment to justice, however, (e.g., Luke 4.18–19; Mark 12.40; Matt. 23.23–25)—indeed the whole tradition of biblical justice—indicates that bilateral nonresistance does not extend to one's responsibilities *for others,* but we do not have instructions as to whether resistance to the injustices suffered by others is or is not to include the use of arms.

Jesus and the absent Zealots. Several scholars have interpreted the temptation of Jesus by Satan in the wilderness as including the temptation to advance his Messiahship by means of violence. Showing Jesus all the kingdoms of the earth and claiming that they were under his power, Satan said they would be Jesus' to rule if Jesus would worship him (Matt. 4.8–10; Luke 4.5–8). Jesus' refusal to yield to this temptation has been seen as a rejection of the use of the sword.[13] With this refusal, Jesus rejected the Zealot option.[14]

The interpretative key to the temptation narrative in Q appears to be the fact that each of Jesus' answers to Satan is drawn from the same section of Scripture, Deuteronomy 6–8.[15] Jesus experienced testings similar to those of the people of Israel, who were also led by God into the wilderness, to be tested as God's "sons"

(Deut. 8.2, 5), and he strengthened himself by reflecting upon these Scriptures. Through his hunger and their dependence upon the manna bread, trust in the word of God was learned (Deut. 8.2–3; Matt. 4.4 par.). In the contexts of the temptation to leap from the temple and the demand for water, Jesus and the people learned not to violate the relationship of patient trust by forcing God to provide protection (Deut. 6.16; Matt. 4.7 par). Finally, neither the lands which God promises to put under the Son nor those given to the people of God must become a cause of distraction from utter loyalty to God, leading to the worship of false gods associated with them (Deut. 6.10–13; Matt. 4.10 par.).

Declared Son of God in his baptism, Jesus is now tested in his filial trust and loyalty to God. The temptations do not involve "ways of being a king."[16] What Jesus might do for others does not enter into the temptation narrative. Rather it is a matter of what he might wrongly attempt to do for himself. Like Israel, Jesus is tested in his devotion and trust in God.

All reference or allusion to violence is absent from the passage. If worship of Satan is rewarded with kingdoms, this does not mean that Jesus would also be expected to fight for them.[17] Satan claimed that the kingdoms were under his control and his to give (Luke 4.6). Jesus' answer "You shall worship the Lord your God" is not concerned with violence or politics but rather focuses on the matter of allegiance.

How can violence be introduced into the exegesis of this account? The answer lies in a so-called Zealot option which was supposedly constantly before Jesus. The interpretation of the passage has been influenced by an understanding of the Zealots as a powerful revolutionary force within Judaism in the days of Jesus—a movement so significant that Jesus surely had to confront it in his teaching and ministry. If Jesus were to take control of the kingdoms of the world, this would mean overthrowing Roman rule. Acceptance of Satan's offer would thus associate him with the anti-Roman politics of the Zealots. Since the Zealots were violent, Jesus would thus also be accepting a violent course. Setting aside the question of the validity of this logic, the picture of the Zealots as an unavoidable option in this context is now under question. Recent studies on the Zealots have shed new light on the chronology and the diversity of the revolutionary movements of first-century Judaism.

The Zealots have been thought to have been a major party in Judaism, formed in A.D. 6 in the turmoil following the death of Herod and continuing through the Roman War and the fall of Jerusalem in 70. New studies of Josephus indicate, however, that the Zealots did not in fact become a party until 66–67 or 67–68.[18] Even during the war, the resistance against Rome was carried on by several diverse groups, not by a distinct movement unified in ideological motivation (Josephus, *Jewish War* 7.253–74).

The evidence of Josephus[19] supports the assertion of Tacitus regarding Palestine that "under Tiberius [A.D. 14–37] all was quiet" (*Histories* 5.9–10).[20] The idea that the Zealots were the fourth major party of Judaism in the 1st century down through the Roman War is based on Josephus's statement that Judas of Galilee (A.D. 6) started a fourth philosophy and planted the roots of the subsequent troubles (*Antiquities* 18.9). But Josephus's own treatment of the subsequent history does not indicate that he meant by this more than that Judas and his forces set a destructive example which gained currency in the two decades before A.D. 70. He connects none of the major political and religious disturbances after A.D. 6 and before the 50s with the party of Judas.[21] If the Fourth Philosophy of Judas of Galilee was indeed continued by the Sicarii (terrorists in Jerusalem who stabbed their victims with a curved dagger, Latin *sica*), it must have disappeared or lain dormant after the turbulance of Herod's death until the rise of the Sicarii movement in the 50s. The various independent prophets who led the masses with promises of deliverance did not begin their activities until the mid-40s. The last flurry of insurrectionist activity had been in the generation previous to that of Jesus' ministry and not even the beginning signs of the deterioration which led to the Roman War would occur until more than a decade after his crucifixion.

The incidents of confrontation between the Jews and the Romans which did take place between A.D. 6 and the late 40s, according to David Rhoads in his recent history of violence in this period, support rather than contradict the claim for a low level of revolutionary activity during the period around the ministry of Jesus. These confrontations were provoked by Pilate's troops carrying standards bearing Roman images into Jerusalem (and possibly a separate incident involved hanging votive shields inscribed with the emperor's name in the palace in Jerusalem), Pilate's confiscation of temple funds to finance an aqueduct, and the placing of a statue of Caligula in the temple. In each of the situations the Jewish response was an understandable spontaneous reaction to an extreme violation of their religious sensitivities. In general the confrontation was nonviolent, and where it was not it was a case of an angry crowd rather than an armed uprising. The participants were from all groups of the society and there is no indication of instigation from a particular party. The limited extent of the protest and the apparent readiness to return to peaceful citizenship when the incident was past support the picture of a relative tranquility in relations with Rome at this time.[22] Of course a smoldering resentment against the foreign Gentile rulers must have existed, but it was only a part of the larger picture of conflict and social hatred between the landless and the landed, the country and the city, and the sects and the temple.[23]

It is in the context of this social unrest that the indications of civil strife and violence in the Gospels are to be understood. If the external evidence showed an established resistance movement in existence at the time, some of the material might reasonably be seen as referring to that phenomenon. But the Gospel instances alone are insufficient to establish the existence of such a movement. The reference to Pilate's mingling the blood of the Galileans with their sacrifices (Luke 13.1), according to Josef Blinzler's careful analysis, cannot be connected to the Zealots and apparently was too incidental to merit Josephus's attention. Blinzler suggests that it was a short and swift police action initiated by Pilate against a small group of insubordinate Galilean pilgrims who had provoked the Roman soldiers at the temple with a leer or gesture.[24] Such an event would indicate a long-standing resentment against the Romans, but the narrow reference of the incident does not point to an extended movement. Barabbas, who was released instead of Jesus at the request of the people, is called (John 18.40) a *lēstēs* (*robber*), a term Josephus uses of the later insurgents. Professor Richard Horsley's argument that we should take Josephus at his word and understand these figures in the framework of the widespread phenomenon of peasant banditry is sociologically compelling.[25] Accordingly, the imprisonment of Barrabas, charged with sedition and murder in a significant social uprising (Mark 15.7; Luke 23.19), reflects the severe social tensions of the time but not necessarily the existence of an anti-Roman revolutionary party. The charge under which Jesus was delivered to Pilate, that he stirred up the people (Luke 23.5), must be treated seriously; but the Gospel context indicates that the charge was based on actions of Jesus, centered on the temple, which were perceived as threatening to the Jerusalem hierarchy and not directed against the Romans.

With this in mind, we can see that the fact that one of Jesus' disciples was called "the Zealot" (Luke 6.15) has little political significance in the sense of national liberation. In the time of Jesus this title could not mean membership in a revolutionary party since such a party with that name was not founded until thirty-five years later. Rather, at this time *zealot* (*zēlōtēs*) referred to those individuals, modelled after Phinehas and Elijah (e.g., 1 Macc. 2.24, 26, 58; 4 Macc. 18.12), whose zeal to defend the Law was so great that they were willing to use violence if necessary; their principle opponents were not foreign occupying forces but Jewish apostates. In the New Testament we find zealots (Acts 17.5), who in attacking the Christians in Thessalonica even identified themselves with the interests of Rome in the prosecution (v. 7). Paul, in speaking of his former role as a persecutor of the church (Gal. 1.13), states, "I was a *zēlōtēs* for the traditions of my forefathers" (v. 14). If during Jesus' ministry an apostle was named "Zealot" because of his background, it would have been extremism for the Law, not revolutionary activity.[26] One should note, finally, that

Galilee, the center of Jesus' ministry, did not have a Roman military occupation at this time. Herod Antipas toed the line, and there does not appear to have been an organization of guerrilla soldiers during his reign.[27] The evidence does not support the existence of a Jewish party of resistance in the 30s A.D. of such significance that Jesus would certainly have had to take a position with respect to it and which can be identified by reading between the lines of the Gospel account.

The exemplary suffering of Jesus. The strongest New Testament case for nonviolence for many of its defenders is drawn from the event that is at the heart of the New Testament ethos—the death of Christ. Christ did not use violence to protect his life but allowed himself to be killed. He dealt with his enemies by dying for them. And his sufferings are presented as exemplary for us. Therefore, it is argued, we are also to be nonviolent, particularly in the situation where it is most difficult—before our enemies.

The passage which most explicitly uses Christ's sufferings as a model for Christians in their conduct is 1 Peter 2.18–25.[28] The passage deals with the behavior of slaves with respect to their masters (v. 18), with special attention to situations where suffering is inflicted upon them. The main point of the passage is that they should follow the example of Jesus in being sure that they have done no wrong to deserve punishment (vv. 19–22). But verse 23 goes further in applying Jesus' suffering as a model (v. 21) for their conduct in the midst of suffering: "Who although he was reviled, did not revile in return, who when he suffered, did not threaten; instead, he placed himself in the hands (*paradidonai*) of the one who judges justly."

This verse (v. 23) recalls Matthew 5.38–42. One does not return the evil of one's accusers or tormentors. While the idea of not reviling or not threatening in response to suffering does not necessarily imply waiving any form of self-defense, it is consistent with the spirit of handing oneself over to God, mentioned in the last part of the verse. As he seems to have commanded in Matthew 5.39,[29] Jesus himself, according to Matthew, did not answer the false testimony against him (Matt. 26.62–63). The Petrine passage is not as radical an exhortation to nonresistance as the Matthew 5 passage, but it is grounded in the basic principle of taking the suffering Christ as one's pattern.

How does this imitation of Christ apply to the question of violence? In Jesus' example, we find a refusal to consider retaliation to verbal and physical abuse, even to the point of the loss of one's life. This would seem to imply nonresistance to injustice to oneself. The point, however, would be nonresistance, not nonviolence as such. If a principle of nonviolence can be drawn from the passage, it must derive from a broader principle of not resisting injustice. Nonviolent resistance then would be as equally excluded by 1 Peter 2 as violent resistance.

But this interpretation must be questioned because once again it applies bilateral materials, i.e., the behavior of Jesus in relation to his executors, to situations structurally different, in particular, to the multilateral situation presented by action in defense of a third party. If I preserve the life of an aggressor by allowing that person to kill *me,* I may be following the model of Jesus' death on behalf of his enemies (Rom. 5.6).[30] The model does not, however, apply to the dilemma that is created when such surrender would allow the aggressor to kill someone under my protection.

Is the death of Jesus presented as an alternative to violence? The Gospels indeed portray Jesus as dying without using violence, but do they see his death resulting from an intentional rejection of violence? The mere absence of the use of force by Jesus does not necessarily mean that force is disapproved of in principle. The hermeneutical principle that whatever is not made normative is therefore wrong is not satisfactory. The silence may only indicate that the question was not present in the minds of the authors.

Jesus may be described as choosing death over the use of force in Matthew 26.53, where the Matthaean account has Jesus say that he could call upon twelve legions of angels but will not. The purpose of calling such angels would be to do effectively what Peter was attempting to do ineptly: to protect him from arrest and death. Why did Jesus choose not to call upon such angels? The reason for Jesus' choice is not an ethical principle of nonviolence over violence (if so, it would rather be a choice of *nonresistance* over violence since Jesus did not resist in any form). The prudential proverb given to Peter that "all who take the sword will die by the sword" (v. 52) does not illuminate Jesus' choice, because he did in fact choose a violent death. Jesus states in the next verse (26.54) that the reason for his not calling upon angels was "that the Scripture might be fulfilled that it might be so [that he die]." If one is to deal with the passage at the level of Matthew's presentation (and the saying about the legions of angels would then also be on this level),[31] Jesus' death must be interpreted in terms of the unique divine intention of his death as a sacrifice (Matt. 20.28 par.; 26.28 par).

That Jesus surrenders to death because it is his destiny in God's plan of salvation, rather than in obedience to a principle of nonviolence, is also seen in the other text in which the consideration of arms is raised in the context of the Passion. In John 18.36[32] Jesus states that if his Reign acknowledged the values of the world, then his supporters would fight, but that the values which control his Reign are different.

The uniqueness of the kingship of Jesus is the reason his servants do not fight. How is his kingship unique? Jesus discloses its character in the following verse (v. 37):

> Then Pilate said to him, "So, then you are a king?" Jesus answered, "You yourself are saying that I am a king. For this purpose I have been born and for this purpose I have come into the world that I should bear witness to the truth."

Jesus' kingship is unique in its origin: "for this purpose I *have come into the world."* He is one who has come into the world from God. The basis of his kingship does not lie in any human support but in the will of God who has sent him. In addition, his kingship is distinct in its purpose: *"that I should bear witness to the truth."* That Jesus' reign is not of this world does not mean that is has no contact with material, temporal, or political reality; such a conclusion misses the Johannine conception of *cosmos* as an ethical-religious concept rather than a temporal one (cf. "Justice for God's Reign" in Chapter 5). His Reign involves material and political reality, but it has an ultimate purpose which goes beyond any human kingship. The truth to which Jesus witnesses in his kingship is knowledge of the only true God and of the sending of God's Son; this knowledge leads to glorification of the Father and the Son and conveys eternal life (cf. John 17.1–3). Jesus' witness to this truth is uniquely and most clearly made through his death. In his death the Son and the Father are known and glorified. Through his death all people are drawn to him (John 12.23, 28, 32).

Accordingly death is chosen, even sought, by Jesus. The Gospel of John emphasizes Jesus' choice of death by showing him to be in control of the situation at his capture and trial. For example, John, in contrast to the other Gospels, has a force (*speira,* normally a cohort of six hundred) of hundreds of troops pouring into the garden, yet Jesus orders them to let his disciples go and is obeyed (18.8); the disciples do not flee as in the Synoptic Gospels.[33] And the dialogues with Pilate show that it is Jesus who is in command—that it is Pilate and Jesus' accusers who are truly on trial. Pilate, powerless and driven by circumstances into doing what he would have liked to avoid, is told that he would have no authority to kill Jesus if it had not been given to him from above (19.11). Jesus is in control, and he chooses death. His servants do not fight, not because Jesus chooses nonviolence, but because he chooses death. To the violence of the cutting off the ear of the slave of the high priest, Jesus responds not with an admonition about violence but with an affirmation of his choice of death: "Shall I not drink the cup which the Father has given me?" (18.11, *RSV*). Jesus' servants do not fight, not because violence is the wrong means, but because it has the wrong end: to prevent Jesus' death. Earthly kings cannot die and reign. Jesus must die to reign; that is what his kingship is about.

Fighting has the wrong end in light of Jesus' purpose; it also is irrelevant in terms of Jesus' origins. The authority of Jesus' kingship is based on his coming from God and God's commission to him. It is a kingship that is not based on human effort or support. With respect to the legitimation of his rule, in another cultural context Jesus could have said, "My government is not of this world; therefore my followers do not support me by the ballot." The passage leaves unexamined the methods by which human governments, which cannot and indeed must not claim such an origin or mission, are (or are not) to be established or defended; that question is not touched upon in the passage.

There is a theme in the Gospel of John that does relate Jesus' death to ethical conduct. Here the meaning of his death is love (cf. 13.1), a pattern of conduct that his disciples are to follow: as Christ in love had died for his friends so they now are to love one another (15.12–14; 1 John 3.16 makes the connection: "he gave up his life for us, and we ought to give up our lives for our brothers and sisters"). This ethical exhortation to loving self-sacrifice as the proper application of Jesus' death does not appear, however, in the passages that present his death as willed by God for the sake of human salvation. There is a clear demarcation in John between the two treatments of Jesus' death, the ethical and the theocentric.[34] The dialogue with Pilate in John 18.28–19.16, in which the reference to arms is found, belongs to the latter type, as we have seen; the interpretation of the death as love calling forth love is not present. The passages which interpret Jesus' death in terms of love do not mention arms and do not speak to the question of whether situations could arise in which arms should be taken up, not to save our own life, but as a form of giving up our life for our brothers and sisters.

But what would be the implications if we accepted the suggestion that in rejecting the angels in the Garden, Jesus was rejecting an "apocalyptic holy war" to bring in God's Reign?[35] Or what would be the implications for current revolution or warfare, if Jesus *had* chosen that option (or had chosen such an option in the wilderness temptation)? Holy warfare, in which Yahweh as the Divine Warrior directly leads the chosen people, who prepare themselves for war as a religious ritual, is not like other warfare. Accordingly, efforts to cite the Old Testament holy war as a precedent for ordinary warfare have rightly been rejected. For the very same reasons, a choice by Jesus of holy war would not constitute a general sanction for wars by earthly rulers. Since his acceptance would not have supported the principle of the *use* of arms, neither would his rejection support the general *rejection* of arms.

Jean Lasserre, whose *War and the Gospel* was described by John Yoder as "the most adequate theological presentation of Christian pacifism,"[36] has written, "The New Testament never speaks of the principle of military service, nor of the problems raised by the Christian's submission to this service, for the good reason that the problem did not then arise."[37] This explanation may quite well be correct, but this does not alter the fact that the question of arms is simply not discussed, nor is the simple case of which the state's use of arms is a much more complex instance: the armed defense of one's neighbor from violence.

The absence of such discussion in no way negates the possibility that nonviolence might prove to be the only legitimate Christian position, when the full implications of biblical values have been understood. But this must be established through other means than exegesis and exposition of particular passages. If the case for nonviolence must be built on the general structure of biblical values, this will require reflection upon the historical and philosophical implications of biblical principles as applied to situations concerning which the Gospels are silent. Only by such reflection can one arrive at valid conclusions about the use of arms; it is not enough merely to point to the teaching and life of Jesus or to call for obedience to canonical Scripture.[38]

REFLECTIONS ON LOVE AND ARMED FORCE

Continuation of responsibilities of love. When one turns from the ethical situation involving the relationship between oneself and one other party, to the situation that concerns relationships to many distinct parties, one comes to an area in which the various duties of love often can conflict. The multilateral situation may consist of two or more bilateral obligations which cannot be met at the same time. The actual duty may be different from what is called forth by a prima facie duty that is involved (cf. "The Ethics of Conflicting Duties" in Chapter 8). One who acts either as a leader of a state, or as a leader against the state, must make choices in a very complex multilateral situation. In such a position one is responsible to many other people, and one's obligations may differ from what would obtain if it were a case of just oneself and another person. For example, individuals are commanded not to "avenge (*ekdikein*) themselves" (Rom. 12.19), while the ruler is "an avenging (*ekdikos*) servant of God for wrath upon the doer of evil" (Rom. 13.4).[39] What is not permitted to individuals is authorized for the state.

We are not faced with a dualistic ethic: there is not one ethical standard for private and intimate life and a different one for commercial and political life. The same criteria of judgment apply to both situations, but the latter is more complex. Love for the evildoer will always prohibit the ruler from retaliating for the sake of his or her own self-interest; love for others in the community, however, will call on the ruler to punish the evildoer. The ruler cannot refuse the requirements of love for the citizens of the community on the basis of what would otherwise be required in his or her own personal relationship to an evildoer; the requirements of that bilateral relationship do still obtain, however.

To the extent that Jesus' teaching affects the question of the use of violence, it applies to all in the society, whatever their position. The use of force to protect one's pride, property, or other self-interest is ruled out. Arms cannot be used against any person or group on the grounds that they are an "enemy." When the state kills without justification it is guilty of murder, just as an individual would be. Accordingly, the state's use of arms cannot be justified by analogy to a principle of individual self-defense, for self-defense is forbidden by Jesus. As Paul Ramsey has noted, the classic formulators of criteria for a just war—Augustine, Aquinas, Luther—forbade the use of force to save one's own life; and they did not base their theories of just war on the principle of self-defense.[40]

When love requires arms. When one encounters a hostile force that threatens not one's own life and security but those of others of God's children, the obligation of Christian love may necessitate the use of armed force. In most cases, love for the neighbor in community means abnegation of force. In this situation, however, it may mean risking one's own life and security on behalf of others. Here the question is not whether one is ready to suffer unjustly at the hands of the neighbor, but whether one is willing to suffer so that injustice to the neighbor can be prevented.

At this point there is a conflict of duties, in which one must choose between force sufficient to stop the perpetrator of injustice and protect the security of innocent people, on one side, and the claim of the aggressor for security from personal injury, on the other. Christian love, motivated by the distinctive biblical concern for the weak and needy, will act with the minimal force sufficient to protect the innocent and helpless from the agent of an unjust and hostile force.[41]

The gravity of the taking of human life cannot be overstated. The Christian will never take human life, the Christian will be nonviolent—unless the requirements of love in the situation *demand* otherwise. We are not speaking of compromising duty. We are speaking of a situation where the claims upon the person make the bearing of arms a *duty* as the expression of Christian values. Against possible misuse of this exception, one should remember Yoder's observation that even having accepted this theory one will actually follow a pragmatic pacifism because this argument would condemn most wars and most causes for war.[42]

Yoder raises the pertinent question of in what way the death of the aggressor even if it prevents evil can be considered an expression of Christian love toward the aggressor. Is not the argument for violence based on the assumption that "the life of the aggressor is worth less than that of the attacked"?[43] The problem raised for a love ethic by this question is not limited to the question of violence. Yoder's question applies in principle to all instances of distributive justice. In answering, one can assert, first of all, that the aggressor is not repelled because the aggressor belongs to an unpopular group or has undesirable personal characteristics. The aggressor is repelled solely because of the aggression and the unavoidable choice that it presents.

Second, in a situation involving justice one must choose in favor of one claim over another (cf. pp. 53–54), but this does not mean that the choice is not motivated by Christian love. What if two persons ask for my cloak but only one actually needs it? Is Christian love relevant to the choice? Does love have anything to say in a choice between the welfare of tenants and the economic interests of a slumlord? Is it inconsistent to enact a law to compell or restrain the slumlord, to use the sanction of jail or a fine to back up the law, to use arms, if necessary, to enforce it? Love has a biblical content to aid us in such choices. Biblical justice enjoins the defense of the oppressed against the perpetrator of injustice. That this may sometimes mean the use of arms makes the choice more difficult, but it is not inconsistent with the other expressions of love in justice.

Justice and arms. Widespread injustice in the institutions of a society can cause physical injury and death comparable in scope to that caused by the use of military force. It is in such a society that the question of justified revolution is most pertinent. We are discussing the type of society in which 2 percent of the population might own 60 percent of the land while 40 percent of rural families are landless. It is one in which 90 percent of the workers might be malnourished and 40 percent of them suffer from a parasitic illness. The life expectancy of the upper classes can be twice as high as that of the lower classes. Every year in which change is delayed, thousands of people die of hunger or curable illness.[44] The physical damage caused by injustices built into many such societies is compounded by violence committed by those in power against any who resist the injustice. Murder, torture, rape, and subhuman prison conditions add to the toll. In such situations the claim for social justice is similar to the claim of defense against aggression: a demand for a public order which assures the minimal conditions of security and well-being for its citizens.

From the biblical perspective, violence is a subcategory of injustice. Violence here is not simply physical abuse or even the taking of life but killing or injury arising from injustice. The force condemned is that which is employed by the economically strong for the victimization of the weak, or, secondarily, it is excessive brutality, cruelty, and murder of innocents.[45]

In the Old Testament, *violence* (*ḥāmās*) is frequently linked with oppression (Amos 3.10) and injustice (Job 19.7).[46] The victims are aliens, orphans, widows (Jer. 22.3), and the needy and the poor (Ps. 72.12–14). The perpetrators are the rich and powerful (Ezek. 7.11, 19, 23–34). *Violence* is also frequently coupled with false testimony in the context of oppression (Ps. 55.9–11); social repression occurs both in the use of force and by means of false testimony in court. Violence is physical force in company with malice, deceit, and economic oppression. The physical force that puts down this injustice is not condemned as violence but is allowed to those in authority, whether judges (Judg. 6.1–6; 7.19–25) or kings (Isa. 11.4). Force is condemned when it serves social injustice, but legitimate armed force to overcome injustice is approved.

In this biblical perspective, the sanctity of life and person is not a claim which clearly and always outweighs any other claim. Physical brutality is an injustice closely associated with a comprehensive range of other injustices. Neither one's own biological survival nor that of a perpetrator of injustice is a supreme value, standing above all other considerations. Force is assigned a value in accordance with the more basic concepts of justice.

> Happier were the victims of the sword than the victims of hunger, who pined away, stricken by want of the fruits of the field. (Lam. 4.9, *RSV*)

In certain situations, which we will now briefly consider, armed revolution becomes a duty, with the claims of order and physical well-being yielding to the stronger claims of the oppressed.

Justified revolution. It has been understood, at least since the time of the early Calvinists, that the classical Christian criteria for justifying and limiting warfare apply also to revolution. Paul Ram-

sey has stated that the only way Christians can speak of allowable
revolutionary violence is in terms of a "just revolution."[47] The just
war theory states the conditions and limitations of the justifiable
use of force in terms of moral criteria, which include concerns both
of duty and consequences. The theory takes cognizance of the tension between the obligation to do no harm to one's neighbor on
the one hand, and the obligation to protect and lay down one's life
for one's neighbor on the other. Under exceptional circumstances
it justifies the use of force to protect the innocent and to vindicate
justice.[48] We shall summarize the main points of this theory in
order to construct the hypothetical situation in which armed revolution would be obligatory.

1. The cause must be just. The motivation for revolution must
be the attainment of a relative degree of justice with realizable
peace and order,[49] in the overthrow of a regime whose perversion of
justice has made manifest the illegitimacy of its claim of authority.
The claims of the oppressed neighbor for relief of gross injustices
which threaten life itself must outweigh the claims for public order
and physical security of those who would defend the aggression of
the ruling powers. The controlling motivations of the revolutionaries must not be pride, private interest, personal retaliation,
hatred, greed, or vindictiveness. Karl Marx spoke of "the war of
the enslaved against their enslavers" as "the only justifiable war in
history."[50] Often the revolutionary use of arms will be precipitated
by an attack of the regime's soldiers on groups engaged in nonviolent resistance. The injustice shows its violence in the direct and
intentional agression against life, and the choice between life and
life becomes unavoidable. The moral imperative is then comparable
to repelling an international aggressor in the just war theory.

2. The last resort. Before there can be a resort to revolution,
efforts to change the laws and conduct of the oppressive regime
through parliamentary and nonviolent means must have been
crushed beyond hope. Even then, however, the use of arms is not
justified by this fact alone. All conditions of the theory must be
met before action is justified.

3. By a lawful public authority. This criterion for a just war may seem inapplicable to a revolution because the premise of revolution is that, since the purposes of a state are not being met, the agents of the state are not lawful public authorities; the question of legitimacy is fundamental to revolution. In the Calvinist tradition the concept of revolution developed side by side with the concept of democracy. Given a covenantal concept of civil society, it can be argued that when a government exceeds its bounds and passes into tyranny, the authority to rule reverts to the people from whom it originates. The requirements for a revolution then would include evidence of broad support among the populace.

The revolution is on firmer ground if the sovereignty of the people is expressed in the formation of a parallel government.[51] Such an organization makes clear that the movement's intentions are not anarchic, provides a focal point for the people's allegiance, indicates to some degree what the nature of the hoped-for new order will be, and eases the transition to a new government. By giving their allegiance to the parallel government, individuals can ease their consciences regarding the subordination to authority required in Romans 13.

4. Reasonable hope of victory. This provision by itself could never justify a revolution, but its absence is thoroughly damaging. A strong chance of success is of the utmost importance; it is demanded by the seriousness of the denied claims of order and personal safety. Lives have too frequently been needlessly lost in blind and futile revolutionary attempts. A revolt against Rome in the time of Jesus and the early Church would not have been a just revolution, as was seen in the Jews' tragic experience in A.D. 66–70.

5. A due proportion between the good that may probably be accomplished and the probable evil effect. This criterion is related to the criteria of justice and the hope of victory. Again, by itself it cannot justify revolutionary action. But the movement also cannot be justified unless a realistic assessment of the probable consequences yields a preponderance of good over evil. In practical terms it means that the revolutionary movement should possess forms of power other than military force sufficient to ensure success with minimal violence. This certainly includes support by the mass of the people.

6. *Rightly conducted through the use of right means.* The duty of using force to protect the innocent from an aggressor cannot justify the use of force against any who are not directly engaged in or immediately cooperating with a force to be resisted. Only military personnel and their political commanders can logically be included in this category. Any lethal force which is directed against noncombatants is therefore murder.[52] Any terrorist violence against civilians is ruled out. The observer can judge the character of the proposed new order by the respect which the revolutionary forces show for human life. Without such respect the movement confounds its basic purpose, which is to secure the dignity of human life.[53]

Torture of anyone, whether military or civilian, cannot be justified. Torture can only be inflicted on a captive, who thus by definition cannot be an aggressor, but rather is weak and helpless. Torture can constitute a greater assault on the dignity of human life even than killing. Torture is one of the surest indications of the denial of justice by a regime. Any revolutionary movement that engages in it reveals the superficiality of its alleged commitment to justice. "One cannot dehumanize the oppressors without ultimately dehumanizing oneself, and aborting the possibilities of the liberation movement into an exchange of roles of oppressor and oppressed."[54]

The importance of Christian reserve. The teachings and Spirit of Jesus are indispensable to revolutions in preserving them from their own excesses. Many revolutions have been successful militarily only to suffer a much greater defeat when the new order of justice was thwarted because the revolutionaries took their cause, or worse themselves, seriously to the point of idolatry. From such overinvolvement, the Christian is restrained by three factors: 1. the concern to meet all claims engendered by the obligation of universal love; 2. the awareness of evil within oneself and others; and 3. the knowledge that revolutionary goals, like all political goals, are neither ultimate nor total. There are many paths to justice, including daily taking up our cross and following Jesus. A role in armed revolution can only be "agonized participation." The conflict can never be joyous.

Christians will demand of a revolutionary movement an awareness of the extraordinary temptations of post-revolutionary power and the preparation of checks on that power and provision for the protection of minorities. We have access to a power which can transform "self-justifying self-destruction" into the "displacement of the love of power by the power of love."[55] We should have the capacity to accept death or failure, if it comes,[56] rather than grasping at excessive power to avoid facing the reality of defeat. Our self-knowledge should forestall the projection of evil and failure upon the enemy so as to avoid criticism of ourselves and our movement.[57] Finally, this Christian reserve should provide a sense of the need for continual change, an awareness that no revolution can produce a static and final good state, and an expectation that a new system must ever be in the process of being established.[58]

Chapter 10

CREATIVE REFORM THROUGH POLITICS

THE IMPORTANCE OF GOVERNMENT

In the Bible the government, more than any other human agency, is given responsibility for justice. The first task of government is to ensure the basic rights of living in community. In this way love promotes the good of every person.

God has granted specific powers to individuals and institutions within society, which serve as instruments of God's sovereignty for the benefit of human life and as barriers against tyranny, chaos, and disorder.[1] One of these agents of power to which special authority is given is the government. Power created by God for good is perverted by the selfishness of individuals and groups that struggle for power over one another; in this context the state is authorized by God to "bear the sword" (Rom. 13.4). Force may be used to protect the innocent and punish those who prey upon them. Likewise, it is God's instrument for the maintenance of order[2] and the securing of justice in society (Rom. 13; 1 Pet. 2).

The ruler is the servant of God for the good of the people (Rom. 13.4). The content of this good (*to agathon*) needs to be understood in light of the Hellenistic Jewish understanding of the ruler as father and shepherd of the people and the Old Testament view of the king as the one who feeds the people in justice by seeking the lost, bringing back the strayed, binding up the crippled, strengthening the weak, and watching over the fat and strong (Ezek. 34.3–4, 15–16, 23–24). Throughout the ancient Near East, justice was a royal function. Thus God, in the context of the divine attribute of justice, could be addressed as a king.

> Mighty King, lover of justice, thou hast established equity, thou has executed justice and righteousness to Jacob. (Ps. 99.4, *RSV*)

The ideal earthly ruler is characterized as one who carries out justice and in particular defends the cause of the oppressed (Ps. 72.1–4). Even pagan monarchs are commanded to exercise such justice (Dan. 4.27). The state, when it is obedient to God, advances the welfare of its citizens through laws which contribute to "freedom and brotherhood";[3] if the state is disobedient, it voids its God-given responsibility and threatens the welfare of its citizens. Attention to the activity of government thus follows from Christian concern for welfare and justice.[4] Calvin reflected the biblical perspective when he taught that civil rulers should "exhibit a kind of image of the Divine Providence, guardianship, goodness, benevolence, and justice."[5]

The far-reaching institutionalized benevolence characteristic of biblical justice, with its connection to the ruler, stands in contrast to a historical theme in American political thought in which the power of the state figures primarily a threat to freedom. Accordingly, some would restrict the activities of the state to maintaining security of the borders and to such limited functions as the enforcement of contracts and protection against physical violence, theft, and fraud. Christian realism about the tendency toward evil in individuals and in groups will question the practicability of leaving significant areas of social relations without a higher authority. Biblical thought is quite aware of oppressive forces against which the government must act. In an industrial society such forces appear in groups holding concentrated economic and social power and in environmental factors such as disease and hunger. Here justice often requires an expanded role for the state. Objections to civil rights legislation on grounds of "states' rights," or objections to taxation for support of basic social programs, bring to mind Bishop Francis McConnell's observation about "the absurdity of raising small problems of coercion when the necessity of providing against a more general coercion is upon us."[6]

Although the state continues as servant of God, it belongs to the fallen order of society. Unjust laws and corruption in government participate in the reality of social evil. The government, like other spheres of social life, is the scene of the struggle between the fallen worldly powers and the authority of God for the control of the human community. Two value systems are in conflict. We are to "battle for God's intention" over the powers and "against their corruption."[7] This charge has a political dimension. We either passively acquiesce in the activity of the government, even though that activity is contrary to God's will, or we refuse political subjection to the powers by struggling for justice "in the gate," as the Scriptures command (Amos 5.15; cf. Zech. 8.16).

The political task receives a new dynamic with the Reign of God breaking into history. The new social order that God is creating intermingles with and acts upon and against the old order, which it will someday replace. Such a theological motif enabled the Puritans to become the first group in history to understand that one could intentionally and organizationally make changes in one's community.[8] The Puritans combined their passion for the sovereignty of God over all of life with the conviction that the fruits of conversion were relevant to the reconstruction of the social order. Against the traditional conservative view that intentional changes interfere with the natural order of things, the Puritans perceived history as a degeneration, arrested only by the intervention of God. Historical precedent does not prevent required change; Scripture and reason are sufficient. God, not history, is sovereign. Consequently, Thomas Case could proclaim, "Reform the university . . . reform the cities . . . the countries . . . the ordinances . . . the worship of God. . . . Every plant that my heavenly Father hath not planted shall be rooted up."[9]

Some contemporary Christians allow the necessity of the government's authority, yet argue that they cannot be involved in that process because the Christian is under a higher ethical standard with which the coercive role of the state is incompatible. For some, the basic text excluding Christian participation in politics is Mark 10.42–43 (Matt. 20.25–26/Luke 22.25–26):

> You know that those who are supposed to rule over the Gentiles lord it over them, and their great men exercise authority over them. But it shall not be so among you; but whoever would be great among you must be your servant. (*RSV*)

One interpretation of this text can be that there is something basic to the Christian ethic which is contrary to the meaning of the state, and that the purpose of the state is to lord it over others, to tyrannize.

Jesus refers his teaching in this passage to relationships among the disciples ("among you," repeated twice). The things here observed of secular government are not to characterize the voluntary Christian community. While Jesus does not suggest the application of this teaching to the conduct of the state, the standard for the Christian community will create a critical awareness in evaluating analogous functions in the political community.

But what is actually said about the state? The rendering "lord it over" is a misinterpretation. The Greek term (*katakyrieuein*) is not an intensive usage; it carries no suggestion of arrogance or oppression but simply means "to rule over, to be lord over." [10] It is not true that the passage equates political coercion with tyranny or the abuse of power. Jesus is referring to the fact that there is a hierarchy of authority in the state which is not to be repeated within the Christian community.

As it appears in Luke, this saying has an added point: "Their authorities are called 'benefactors' " (Luke 22.25). The term *benefactor* (*euergetēs*) was an honorific title given in gratitude to a human or divine benefactor. It was a sought-after title of very high status. A grateful recipient of benefaction who bestowed this title acknowledged his or her inferior position by so doing. The term belongs to a status system which, though highly developed in the Greek and Roman world, is nonetheless not an essential or universal aspect of the state. This extension of status went so far that such terms as *benefactor* served as central expressions of the "bene-

factor cult," through which a community honored its human benefactors with sacrifices and other religious honors otherwise re-
served for divine benefactors.[11] It is noteworthy that the
designation which in the Lukan account is associated with the fact
of rule connotes status, rather than use of force. In the Christian
community there must not be such distinctions of rank.

The contexts supplied for this saying of Jesus by the Gospels
support the contention that the teaching primarily concerns status,
rather than authority. In the Markan tradition, the context is the
request of James and John to receive positions of highest honor in
Christ's coming rule (Mark 10.35–41/Matt. 20.20–24). The saying refers specifically to the one who desires to be great (*megas*) or
first (*prōtos*), both terms of rank and dignity (Mark 10.43–44/Matt.
20.26–27).[12] The desire for status is condemned.

The Lukan account places this saying at a later point in the
ministry of Jesus. The context is simply a dispute among the disciples about who would be the greatest (*megas,* Luke 22.24). They
are told that the ruler or leader (*ho hēgoumenos*) will appear as the
servant (Luke 22.26); the function of authority exists in the community, but carries with it no superiority in status.

In both these accounts, Jesus alludes to the rulers of the Gentiles in order to condemn not the power of authority as such, but
rather the pride of seeking to be elevated above others. It is not
the fact of rule that is proscribed, but the personal misuse of authority. The function of authority is an acceptable inequality insofar as it is of service to everyone, but it does not carry any implication of superior dignity or worth.

These passages, when applied by analogy to the political community, will not prevent the Christian from participating in the
decision-making processes of government. They should, however,
sensitize one to the temptations of political power for personal
pride and superiority.

The other means to justice—evangelism, the Christian community, strategic noncooperation, and even revolution—are completed by legislation. Political reform is a normal path to social
change; only in the breakdown of this process must recourse be

had to the use of nonviolent coercion or, most exceptionally, to justified armed revolution.

THE LIMITS OF POLITICS

Many who at first appear particularly hostile to the legislation of social change are, upon further examination, seen to oppose not political reform itself but, one, an excessive dependence upon reform, or, two, the use of excessive power in reform.

With respect to the first concern, they are rightly critical of such heavy reliance upon political and economic means to deal with social evil that political action becomes the principal thrust of the church in society. While seeking external controls to resolve social problems, we may come to neglect other aspects of Christian mission. Creative reform must be only one in a spectrum of means to justice.

Not only is a preoccupation with reforming the legal structure of society unfaithful to the full responsibility of Christian life and mission, but as a consequence it also fails to nurture the vital forces that can make genuine reform a historical reality. In a democratic society the institutions of government can improve but little on the general morality and values of the community at large.[13] The effectiveness of a law depends in large part upon the ability of voluntary associations, such as religious and educational institutions, to lead and mold public opinion.[14] The person in office, much of whose energy is spent on the maintenance of society and on staying in office, needs the creative support of those out of government, who are free from these obligations.[15] The Christian drive for social righteousness needs to be present in both spheres.

The legislative and judicial processes promoting social justice, though vitally important, are only the tip of the iceberg. A just and humane society can exist only because its people possess such qualities as self-respect and self-acceptance, tolerance, mutual respect, unselfishness, honesty, the sense of right and duty, the desire for equal treatment, and fidelity to law. Law itself is more than a system of regulations; it embodies many of these same qualities, which constitute the indispensable foundation of every legal order. It is important that the content of legal regulations *encourage* the growth of these values. The *creation* of these values, however, must come about through associations distinct from the state; the formation of these values should not, and indeed cannot, be subject to governmental control. Inattention to these ethical, even religious, dimensions of order can deprive justice of its capacity to survive. Politics alone will not suffice to elicit or instill such values. Evangelism and Christian community do contribute to the process, even when only indirectly through a leavening effect in society.[16]

The abuse of power in reform movements has also been rightly protested. Although the advance of justice requires support from political authority, Christians must always be mindful that, as Reinhold Niebuhr warned, power easily becomes the tool of the will-to-power, the sinful need to have power over others. The very corruptions which make the use of power necessary for achieving justice may infect the reformers themselves.

It is essential, in the attempt to combat evil and to advance righteousness by means of legislation, to distinguish between those actions which impose necessary restrictions on others in order to further the welfare of the neighbor, and those actions which stem from a will-to-power and the desire to dominate others. The goal must not be to gain power for oneself in the interest of attaining one's own objectives, but rather to empower others.[17]

Christian efforts for just legislation will find expression in democratic processes rather than in change dictated from above, which circumvents participation from below. Social processes that involve each person in the decisions which personally affect him or her have a dual theological basis: on the one hand, the impulse of love, which demands respect for every person, and on the other, the imperative to oppose the abuse that arises from the unchecked power of one person over another, which is one symptom of human depravity. Participatory democracy can be focused upon a centralized or a decentralized administration, depending upon the particular social and political situation. In recent cases of civil rights law, it has been centralized administration which has most often implemented justice and freedom. Centralization and decentralization do not involve basic principles of justice, however, but are variables to be used to promote social good, particularly for disadvantaged minorities.

Should one attempt to coerce adherence to Christian values? One writer sees little difference between forcing all citizens to be "their brothers' keepers" and the use of taxes to support preaching.[18] There are three things to be considered: the commands of Scripture, the criteria for Christian political decision-making, and the types of duties that are subject to legislation.

The Christian must be concerned about legislating the duties arising from responsibility for members of the community because Scripture teaches that the care of the needy is a matter of justice and therefore an obligation upon the whole.

The Christian must be guided by Christian values and duties in his or her participation in politics. What other set of values could guide a Christian? "Which morality" is what much of politics is about; behind the dispute in political issues lies disagreement about ethical values.[19] Christians with a sense of the sovereignty of God should not be reticent about the social necessity for their standard of justice. "Nobody in all the world is more qualified for political action than the child of God."[20]

But as we have indicated, work for justice is to be carried out through democratic processes. It is not a matter of the imposition of a minority's will (with the attendant necessity of endless restraints). If Christian ideals are to be embodied in the regulations of a secular society like the United States, the process will need support from non-Christians. Christian reform is advanced by the fact that, while we do not live in a Christian society, neither do we live in a pagan society without any Christian heritage. Ours is a semi-Christian society, which has been influenced by past and present leavening of Christian influence, and in which Judeo-Christian social values are often advanced with more vigor by non-believers than by many believers. But whether one is with the majority or not, one can work democratically only from one's own social outlook. A pluralistic society would become sterile if all traditions were reduced to the least common denominator. How then does one deal with a question such as racism or slavery? Could one countenance a refusal to work for laws which would reflect the Christian ideal in such a situation? Would one back off from sanctions on slave masters in the name of *freedom* from coercion?

Yet the question of freedom is relevant because not all matters of right are appropriate for legislation. Legislation deals with matters of justice; it deals with matters which substantially involve *rights*. Legislation is also appropriate in order to regulate actions which may cause *harm* to individuals or to institutions; it does not pertain to private matters that do not either interfere with the well-being of another or diminish the well-being of the community as a whole.

Legislation is also not appropriately used to give special advantage to a private group, such as a church. Merely cultic values must not be imposed. Such coercion was part of the defect of the Constantinianism of the medieval *Corpus Christianum,* in which the state and the church formed one whole, each using the other for its own ends.[21] Payment of preachers' salaries by the state would be an obvious act of Constantinianism; there is a long democratic tradition which would distinguish that practice from legislating community responsibilities for the needy.

CREATIVE OR COOPTABLE REFORM

The kind of reform rightly condemned by many who are searching for action to deal with the basic problems of a society is a cooptable type of reform; slight improvements are proposed to deal with what are in fact the fundamental problems of the society.[22] The changes which are sought and allowed are only those compatible with the preservation of the present social and economic system. The needs of the system determine which actions are rational, practical, and possible.[23] The assumption is that the system is fundamentally sound.[24] The situation of the people may be improved, but no real alternatives to the present power relationships are considered.

Constantinianism lends itself to such palliative reform through the mutual approval and support of church and state, in its old form, or in the current secular version, between the church and "the establishment." In this relationship the church cannot preach judgment on the selfish purposes at the heart of society without condemning its own role in that society. The ethics taught are those which are feasible within the limits of the acceptance of the established society.[25]

The short-term cooptable perspective has characterized some of the reform movements which have received the most attention in our century. Many struggles to correct disproportionate economic power have resulted in the appointment of independent regulating commissions, to cite a leading example. The hope of many was that a commission would serve as an effective watchdog to protect the public interest from the industry regulated. Yet the regulating commissions become the captive of the industry to be regulated. In the Progressive reforms of the period 1900–1916 the very form of the regulating legislation was usually proposed by the industry involved.[26] The typical regulating commission goes through a life cycle of increasing control by the industry. As public and congressional attention is withdrawn after the creation of the commission, the agency drops its police role and begins to play more the role of a manager of an industry. It is accepted and supported as an essential part of the industry, providing stability and predictability. The attitude toward the public interest becomes one of passivity and cold neutrality. The close relations with the industry and the narrow definition of its activities hamper the commission from even discerning the public interest.[27]

But the discouraging history of regulating commissions was to be expected from the nature of the reforms. Gabriel Kolko argues that the reforms of the Progressive period were prototypical of the regulating reforms which followed. They were founded on the assumption of the soundness of the basic patterns of property relationships in the American economy. No serious alternatives to the actual power in the hands of economic elites were proposed for organizing society.[28] What has been sought is not a reordering of economic relationships but the elimination of flagrant abuses.[29] When the commissions dealt with the abuses and then became spokespersons for the industry, they were only fulfilling their original purpose of aiding the continuation of the established system of business, minus the practices that exposed it to serious public criticism.[30] Such reformers, operating in the "genteel tradition of middle-class reform" and lacking a deep conviction of the reality of economic evil, hope to modify basic economic institutions by "tinkering with the machinery of government."[31]

Similar observations need to be made about the palliative programs of the 1960s, disappointment with which has led to a "neoconservative" movement of reaction to governmental reform. As Michael Harrington has argued, despite the claims by the government and the fears of the conservatives, the Great Society programs never included a pervasive governmental intrusion into the private sphere. Nor was there a massive trend toward equality in the 1960s. The programs were oversold and underfinanced.[32] Not their prodigality, but their lack of a radical innovative character has contributed to the developing urban struggle between the have-nots and the have-littles. It is not governmental generosity which has created the incentive for recipients of welfare programs to remain dependent, but the timidity of government and the failure of a full-employment policy.[33] One can say of the whole climate of protest in the 1960s that the focus was upon a more open society in policy formulation and social movement with only peripheral concern to economic institutions and economic power.[34]

But there is another type of reform. It is built on the premise that many social changes, even revolutionary changes, come only through a cumulative series of partial steps.[35] Here the reformer's goals are dissonant with the current social structures, but he or she recognizes that these goals cannot be achieved all at once. One accepts concrete solutions to specific problems but only on premises that question the assumptions of the present order and only as leading in the general direction of a new order. The Christian reformer first of all has a vision of the new order of the Reign of God but also realizes that the Reign will be only partially realiz-

able in history. The Christian also operates with a vision of a community in history which is not the Reign of God but which is
more proximate to the Reign than is the present society. Specific
reforms are advanced as they reflect the ultimate and the historical
vision.

Creative reforms are addressed particularly to those changes
which modify power relationships, set forth a new order of priorities, and provide new models of life and culture.[36] They are
changes which limit the power of those currently holding disproportionate power, which make the weak more aware of their human rights, and which grant the poor and members of the working
class (both in capitalism and in state socialism) more control over
their lives.

In creative reform the limits of what is possible are redefined
so as not to reflect the needs, criteria, and rationales of the present
way of doing things but rather what should be made possible in
terms of human needs.[37]

But what should be possible often only becomes reality piece-
meal. I have found John Yoder's strategy in an Anabaptist perspective helpful for models of Christian political reform which reflect more direct participation of Christians in the political process.
There is a disparity between the demands of God and what is po-
litically possible, between a Christian ethic dependent upon regen-
eration and its political expression, particularly in a secular state.
Thus what is sought through creative reform cannot be the elimination of all evil or even the immediate structuring of a new social
order. Rather the political strategy is to seek changes toward what
should be made possible by concentrating upon identifiable concrete problems of justice which are capable of being dealt with at
present. The greatest possible step toward the desired restructuring
of society is what is always required for creative reform.[38]

We have no grounds for great optimism about the possibility
of far-reaching political reform. It is difficult to see the possibility
of wholesale radical structural changes. Yet the "neoconservative"
counsel of diminished public intervention in our economic and social problems is not the answer, for such timidity is a cause, not

the solution, of the failures in the reformist posture. There are no easy answers but "there are *some* solutions to some of our problems."[39] Small victories are important, especially as they advance toward what should be possible. One must evaluate political change in the light of the difficulty of creating change at any level of human behavior. In considering political possibilities, we should remember that the security possessed by individuals and major segments of our society rides the crest of past political struggles to distribute power and the fruits of technology.

The short-sighted perspective on reform, which does not confront the gravity of the problems of the current system, leads to short-run efforts. Some of the failures of reform have been due to a lack of vigilance on the part of the reformers. This failure, for example, has been damaging in the history of the regulatory commissions, where once regulation is legislated the reformers take what they view as an earned rest and fail to provide sustained vigilance over the administration of the regulation.[40] In the time of Lincoln Steffens Philadelphia was regarded as the worst-governed city in the country, but it reflected a condition which followed reform: "Reform with us is usually revolt, not government, and is soon over."[41] Bishop Francis J. McConnell once said, "The trouble is not that we don't get mad but that we don't stay mad."[42] "Never settle for winning," warns Dieter Hessel.[43] More should be expected from those with the Christian perspective of human society and the Christian grounds for concern.

YOU CAN'T LEGISLATE MORALITY?

Our view of human nature and of history makes us aware that we cannot guarantee or assume sufficient personal morality to control injustice in society. What then are we to do? One answer is enforceable law. Can morality be achieved through the legal process? A frequently heard answer is the slogan, "You can't legislate morality." This phrase is applied by many to matters of private activity or consumption that do not harm the well-being of others: in such cases legislation is indeed futile. Others, however, aware that morality extends to matters of justice and rights, hold legislation to be futile in such matters as well. It is to this attitude that we would respond.

There are two aspects to morality. One aspect is subjective— our dispositions, intentions, even perceptions; it would appear difficult to legislate subjective morality. But the other aspect of morality is objective—our external behavior. Biblical ethics gives considerable space to regulating external actions, and social policy is more concerned with objective behavior. For social policy, tangible justice is more important than intangible love (although the highest standard is the presence and interconnection of both). Harvey Cox wrote several years ago:

> The recent civil rights revolution in America has proved at least one thing: Negroes are not so much interested in winning whites to a less prejudiced attitude as they are in preventing them from enforcing the prejudice they do have. The Negro revolt is not aimed at winning friends but at winning freedom, not interpersonal warmth but institutional justice. . . . The inmates of the urban concentration camp do not long for fraternization with the guards; what they want is the abolition of the prison; not improved relations with the captors but "release from captivity."[44]

External actions can be legally controlled and motivated[45] even though inner motivations cannot. The slogan "You can't legislate morality" is often used to offer a rationale for government to do nothing; but governments always regulate public behavior, and the great majority of our laws are attempts to control human behavior.[46]

Law, however, also has an impact upon the subjective aspects of morality. Law has an educative factor. It communicates a standard of right which can function through the superego. Law can legitimate morality. Law also has a conditioning factor. Virtues are habits, and habits are formed by doing similar acts over a period of time. The habits that are formed from youth do make a difference. One can promote public behavior by encouraging the desired values legally.

> This is confirmed by what happens in the city states. For the
> lawmakers make the citizens do good by forming good habits in
> them and certainly this is the will of every lawmaker; and those
> who do not will miss the mark. (Aristotle, *Nicomachean Ethics*
> 1103b.2–6)

This viewpoint taken without qualification runs the risk of over-
reliance upon law (cf. pp. 197–98), but it is generally correct.
One cannot in this way make new creatures, but one can affect
character in ways that are socially perceptible. One can make a
better society even if not a wholly *well* society.

Coerced actions have an impact even upon basic values, perceptions, and attitudes. A case in point is the effects of the creative
civil rights legislation and judicial decisions in recent United
States history. Surveys at the University of Alabama from the time
of its forced desegregation in 1963 until 1969 showed an increasing acceptance of blacks. There was a growing willingness to include blacks with whites in activities over which the general society was in conflict, such as worship and travel. On campus there
was less reluctance to include blacks in activities involving close
relationships with whites. Traits traditionally associated with
blacks were viewed more positively and stereotypes were falling.
There was growing support of blacks having political and economic
equality with whites. The student majority in 1963 accepted the
"separate but equal" doctrine. The student majority in 1969 approved desegregation. In 1969 the majority had not yet accepted
social desegregation (rooming with blacks, double-dating, mixed
dating), but there were strong trends in that direction.[47]

Robert Coles studied the attitudes of Southern white teachers
in desegregated schools. Many found that their sentiments about
desegregation were changed by the experience of having to teach
black children. One said,

> At first he was a Negro, then he became just another pupil. I'm
> not against *him*, though I still feel loyal to the way we've always
> lived down here. It's two different problems, you know.[48]

There are still tensions, but feelings are being conditioned even by compulsory experiences. The new attitudes are becoming part of the way of life to which people later will come to feel some loyalty.

The impact of civil rights legislation upon a locality has been carefully examined in a model political essay by Frederick Wirt. It is an interesting, well-written work based on impeccable research in Panola County, Mississippi. National law and national law enforcement were instruments of change in voter registration, schools, and economic rights. There is no evidence that there would have been significant change without such enforcement. In 1960 two-thirds of the black population earned less than $2,000. Only one black could vote. Except as private household workers, blacks earned less than whites in every occupation. Expenditure for black pupils was one-half to one-third of that for white pupils; almost two-thirds of the blacks received no more than six years of education. That law enforcement was effective was due in a large part to the role played by the Justice Department in the 1960s in litigation, overcoming the breakdown in the adversary system, in which the white lawyer out-weighed his black opponent in power and status and the judge was connected with the interests of the whites. In 1967, 3,500 blacks (50 percent of those eligible) were registered to vote. Their votes were being sought by white candidates. There were gravelled roads to black homes for the first time in memory. The local press had more and better coverage of the black community. Official violence had been curbed. There was little impact in the area of economic rights, e.g., employment needs. The legislation was palliative here; the federal programs met symptoms and did not deal with the roots of the problem. While perception of blacks had changed little, behavior patterns had, which made it possible that the change in perception would follow.[49]

Such legislation and enforcement represented creative reform. The increase in the liberty of blacks led to an alteration in their perception of themselves and the possibilities in their community. The reform created new possibilities of change. A vote and better

schools can open out the old self-defeating perspective to a new
vision of life's potential. There follows a new belief in one's worth
as an individual.[50]

The direct path to this achievement of partial justice was creative reform through politics. This path was not the only one,
however. In the distant background was the teaching of the Christian church on the meaning of the life of everyone for whom Christ
died. Behind the civil rights legislation was the powerful witness
of those who had laid down their bodies and even their lives in
noncooperation with evil. And behind those witnesses were communities which sustained them.

These paths came together to provide a road to justice. It is a
road which can most easily be followed by those who at the beginning meet One who gives them in place of oppression a yoke that
is easy and a burden that is light.

NOTES

1. BIBLICAL FAITH AND THE REALITY OF SOCIAL EVIL

1. For this interpretation of *1 Enoch* 6–11, cf. George W. E. Nickelsburg, "Apocalyptic and Myth in 1 Enoch 6–11," *Journal of Biblical Literature* 96 (1977), 383–405. The Shemihaza material is basic to the passage and tentatively goes back to the wars of the Diadochi at the end of the fourth century B.C. The Azazel material was added later.

2. See, among others, John Howard Yoder, *The Politics of Jesus* (Grand Rapids, Eerdmans, 1972), 140–62; Jim Wallis, *Agenda for Biblical People* (New York, Harper, 1976), 63–77; Richard J. Mouw, *Politics and the Biblical Drama* (Grand Rapids, Eerdmans, 1976), 85–116; and Walter Wink, "Unmasking the Powers: A Biblical View of Roman and American Economies," *Sojourners* (Oct. 1978), 9–15. The work most influential upon this recent discussion is Hendrikus Berkhof, *Christ and the Powers* (Scottdale, Pa., Herald, 1962). The purpose of this chapter is to clarify and validate the thrust of these writers.

3. Cf. Hermann Sasse, "*Kosmos,*" *TDNT* (1965), 3.868; Tebtunis Papyri 45.20; 47.12 (113 B.C.); George W. Redding, "KOSMOS from Homer to St. John," *Asbury Seminarian* 4 (1949), 63.

4. Sasse, "Kosmos," 891.

5. *Bios* in 1 John 2.16 and 3.17 signifies *means of subsistence, property, wealth* (cf. Bauer, *Lexicon*[5], 142; Rudolf Schnackenburg, *Die Johannesbriefe* (Freiburg, Herders theologischer Kommentar zum Neuen Testament 13,3, 1970[4]), 130.

6. For a discussion of *cosmos* and the powers as structuring the hostile divisions of humankind, cf. Paul S. Minear, *To Die and To Live* (New York, Seabury, 1977), 66–106; cf. Amos N. Wilder, *Kerygma, Eschatology, and Social Ethics* (Philadelphia, Fortress, Facet Books, Social Ethics 12, 1966), 28.

7. C. H. Dodd, *The Johannine Epistles* (New York, Harper, Moffatt New Testament Commentaries, 1946), 42–44.

8. Sasse, "*Kosmos,*" 894. Cf. Paul in 1 Cor. 1.18–21, Hans Conzelmann, *A*

Commentary on the First Epistle to the Corinthians (Philadelphia, Fortress, Hermeneia, 1975), 43.

9. Martin P. Nilsson, *Geschichte der griechischen Religion* (München, Beck, Handbuch der Altertumswissenchaft, 5,2, 1961²), 2.539; Walter Grundmann, *"Dynamai/dynamis,"* TDNT (1964), 2.288.

10. Versus Berkhof, *Christ and the Powers,* 59, n. 6.

11. In Psalm 148.2 this translation results in *angels* and *powers* being parallel.

12. Cf. Wilhelm Bousset, *Die Religion des Judentums in späthellenistischen Zeitalter,* ed. H. Gressmann (Tübingen, Mohr, 1966⁴), 326.

13. Martin Rist correctly sees an analogy in Revelation 2 and 3 where angels are closely related to ecclesiastical social bodies. The angel and the corresponding church share the praise or censure of Christ; "The Revelation of St. John the Divine," *Interpreter's Bible* (1957), 12.379. Deuteronomy 32.8 states that when God separated the people of the earth, God set their boundaries "according to the sons of God." This translation follows the text found at Qumran (Patrick W. Skehan, "A Fragment of the 'Song of Moses' [Deut. 32] from Qumran," *Bulletin of the American Schools of Oriental Research* 136 [Dec. 1954], 12), which seems to be the reading inferred by the LXX rendering, "according to the number of the angels of God." (The MT has "according to the sons of Israel," which appears to be an anti-polytheistic alteration.) To the concept, cf. Deut. 4.19. It is represented in NT times by *Jubilees* 15.31f. Cf. G. B. Caird, *Principalities and Powers: A Study in Pauline Theology* (Oxford, Oxford U. Press, 1956), 5–12. The Book of Daniel describes angelic "watchers" who sit in judgment over the kingdoms and assert the sovereignty of God (Dan. 4.13, 17). Because the nations have these guardians, in the final days when God fights with and defeats the human rulers, there is a corresponding battle in the heavens (Isa. 24.21; 34.2, 4). This vision is vividly presented in the War Scroll of Qumran (1 QM).

14. Gerhard Delling, *"Archē, archōn,"* TDNT (1964), 1.488; Bousset, *Religion des Judentum,* 324, 237.

15. Bo Reicke, "The Law and This World according to Paul. Some Thoughts concerning Gal. 4.1–11," *Journal of Biblical Literature* 70 (1951), 270–71. H. Berkhof (*Christ and the Powers,* 13) interprets Rom. 8.38–39 as enumerating realities which dominate our lives. The context, however, is persecution, not domination or freedom—a specific situation of the church, not a general condition of society.

16. Revelation 13 and 17 speak of a coming great empire of evil. This coming empire is symbolized by the empire present to John, the Roman Empire: The empire is represented by a harlot who sits on a beast with seven heads (17.3), which are identified with seven hills (v. 9). Rome has been known from sixth century B.C. as "the city of seven hills"; G. B. Caird, *The Revelation of St. John the Divine* (New York, Harper, 1966), 216. The identification of the woman is clarified in 17.18; she is "the great city which has dominion over all the kings of the earth." The beast is disclosed more fully in chapter 13 when Satan (12.9) calls forth two beasts representing supernatural evil power, to whom he gives his power and authority. The first beast, an anti-Christ figure associated with Nero (13.3) (G. R. Beasley-Murray,

"The Revelation," *New Bible Commentary,* ed. F. Davidson [Grand Rapids, Eerdmans, 1954²], 1184), gains control of the government, and receives worship directed by the second beast, a Satanic priestly figure.

17. Not all scholars are agreed that the *stoicheia* are personal beings in these chapters, cf. Gerhard Delling, *"Stoicheion," TDNT* (1971), 7.685, who takes them as "that whereon man's existence rested."

18. Xenocrates, the second successor to Plato at the Academy (339–314 B.C.), developed extensively Plato's ideas about the demonic world and taught of the *stoichoi,* divine forces dwelling in the elements (Nilsson, *Geschichte der griechischen Religion,* 2.256). Jewish apologists criticized the pagan practice of worshipping the gods associated with elements (Philo, *Dec.* 53–54; Wisdom of Solomon 13.2).

19. Revelation 14.18 speaks of the angel "who has authority over the fire"; G. H. C. MacGregor, "Principalities and Powers: The Cosmic Background of Paul's Thought," *New Testament Studies* 1 (1954), 22, who also cites Rev. 7.1; 16.5; and 19.17. (MacGregor argues for an astral interpretation for the *stoicheia,* for which there is some evidence, but the stars also are related to angels and gods.) The *Book of Jubilees* speaks of angels of fire, winds, clouds, snow, the seasons, and other forces (2.2).

20. Cf. Reicke, "The Law and This World," 259–62. Also cf. Gal. 3.24 (Law) with Gal. 4.2 (*stoicheia*).

21. Cf. Helmut Koester, "Häretiker im Urchristentum," *Religion in Geschichte und Gegenwart* (1959³), 3.18–19. Berkhof (*Christ and the Powers*) misses this possibility when he argues that the powers are depersonalized by Paul, on the basis that it is difficult to understand how angels or astral powers could be related to dietary laws (59n.6).

22. Patrick Kerans, *Sinful Social Structures* (New York, Paulist, 1974), 74–75. Pages 55–82 have an excellent discussion of the meaning of social structures in the context of individual responsibility.

23. Jacques Ellul, *The Political Illusion* (New York, Vintage Books, 1972 [1965]), 143, 146–48. Hugh Heclo describes more moderately the ineffective leadership of the short-term political appointees of the American federal executive over "the tight, ingrown village life of the bureaucratic community," in *A Government of Strangers: Executive Politics in Washington* (Washington, D.C., Brookings Institution, 1977) (quotation from p. 112).

24. Gordon Sherman, "The Business of Business Is To Make a Profit," *Unauthorized Version* (The Divinity School, Harvard University, March 13, 1972), 10.

25. Kerans, *Sinful Social Structures,* 59.

26. Roger Mehl, "The Basis of Christian Social Ethics," in *Christian Social Ethics in a Changing World,* ed. J. Bennett (New York, Association, 1966), 45.

27. Reinhold Niebuhr, *Moral Man and Immoral Society* (New York, Scribner's, 1932), 40.

28. Jürgen Moltmann, *The Crucified God: The Cross of Christ as the Foundation and Criticism of Christian Theology* (New York, Harper, 1974), 293, 329. Using the example of the federal bureaucracy, Hugh Heclo shows that we are unwilling to eliminate the components that create the dilemma. To protect democracy, we keep the tenure short at the top levels of government; to

avoid patronage, we remove the bureacracy from political control (*Government of Strangers,* 109).

29. Günther Baumbach, "Gemeinde und Welt im Johannes-Evangelium," *Kairos* 14 (1972), 125.

30. Heinrich Schlier, *Principalities and Powers in the New Testament* (New York, Harper, Quaestiones Disputatae, 1964), 37.

31. Ernst Troeltsch, *The Social Teachings of the Christian Churches* (New York, Harper, 1960), 344, draws such a distinction.

32. John Hinton, *Memoirs of William Knibb,* 45, as quoted by Philip Wright, *Knibb "The Notorious": Slaves' Missionary 1803–1845* (London, Sidgwick, 1973), 24.

33. S. C. Lord's report from the Select Committee on Slave Laws in the West Indies, as quoted by Wright, *Knibb,* 31–32.

34. Leroy Cleveland, "Let's Keep the Law!" *Sword of the Lord* 40, 52 (1974), 5.

35. John C. Bennett, *Christian Ethics and Social Policy* (New York, Scribner's, 1946), 67.

36. In John 8.23 Jesus asserts that he "is not of this world-order," which means that he does not share its values. Yet he came "to take away the sin of the world" (John 1.29). The order is judged in Christ; the "ruler of the world will be thrown out" (John 12.31). Thus according to John 17, although the Christians cannot be taken out of the social order, opting for ascetic retreat, they are not to belong to it; their existence and values cannot have that source (vv. 14, 15, 18). Christ has come to "destroy the works of the Devil," and his followers are not to participate in them (1 John 3.8).

37. Wilder, *Kerygma, Eschatology, and Social Ethics,* 24–25; Alan Richardson, *An Introduction to the Theology of the New Testament* (New York, Harper, 1958), 214. Against the background of the apocalyptic materials, in which the defeat of the fallen angels is a victory for justice and truth (cf. Nickelsburg, "Apocalyptic and Myth," 391–93), Christ's victory over the powers is seen as a divine act achieving justice and liberation from oppression.

38. Schlier, *Principalities and Powers,* 50–52.

39. For Weber's discussion of inner-worldly asceticism, cf. Max Weber, "Religious Rejections of the World and their Directions," in *From Max Weber,* eds. H. Gerth and C. W. Mills (New York, Oxford U. Press, 1946), 323–59; and *The Protestant Ethic and the Spirit of Capitalism* (New York, Scribner's, 1958), ch. 4.

40. James Luther Adams, " 'The Protestant Ethic' with Fewer Tears," in *The Name of Life,* E. Fromm Festschrift, eds. B. Landis and E. Tauber (New York, Holt, 1971), 178, 185.

41. Troeltsch, *Social Teachings,* 604.

42. R. Tamisier, "La Séparation du monde dans l'Ancien et le Nouveau Testament," in *La Séparation du monde* (Paris, Cerf, Problèmes de la religieuse d'aujourd'hui, 1961), 29.

2. GOD'S GRACE AND OUR ACTION

1. Karl Barth, *Church Dogmatics* 2,2 (Edinburgh, Clark, 1957), 565.

2. B. M. Styler, "The Basis of Obligation in Paul's Christology and Ethics," in

Christ and Spirit in the New Testament, C. F. D. Moule Festschrift, eds. B. Lindars and S. Smalley (Cambridge, Cambridge U. Press, 1973), 178–79.

3. Cf. Otto Merk, *Handeln aus Glauben: Die Motivierungen der paulinischen Ethik* (Marburg, Elwert, Marburger Theologische Studien 5, 1968), 34.

4. Victor Paul Furnish, *Theology and Ethics in Paul* (Nashville, Abingdon, 1968), 218.

5. Ernst Käsemann, "Kritische Analyse von Phil. 2, 5–11," *Zeitschrift für Theologie und Kirche* 47 (1950), 313–60.

6. Verne H. Fletcher, "The Shape of Old Testament Ethics," *Scottish Journal of Theology* 24 (1971), 52.

7. George E. Mendenhall, *Law and Covenant in Israel and the Ancient Near East* (Pittsburgh, Biblical Colloquium, 1955), 31–34.

8. Ed. Jacob, "Les bases théologiques de l'éthique de l'Ancien Testament," *Vetus Testamentum Supplements* 7 (1960), 43, 47.

9. Furnish, *Theology and Ethics,* 195–96, 213.

10. Paul L. Lehmann, "The Foundation and Pattern of Christian Behavior," in *Christian Faith and Social Action,* ed. J. Hutchison (New York, Scribner's, 1953), 100, 107; cf. James M. Gustafson, *Christ and the Moral Life* (New York, Harper, 1968), 26.

11. Fletcher, "Shape of Old Testament Ethics," 52.

12. Wolfgang Schweitzer, "Glaube und Ethos im Neuen und Alten Testament," *Zeitschrift für Evangelische Ethik* 5 (1961), 130–31.

13. Furnish, *Theology and Ethics,* 226.

14. Amos N. Wilder, "The Basis of Christian Ethics in the New Testament," *Journal of Religious Thought* 15 (1958), 142.

15. John Wesley, "Justification by Faith," in *John Wesley,* ed. A. Outler (New York, Oxford U. Press, 1964), 201 ("what God *does for* us"; "what he *works in* us"); and Reinhold Niebuhr, *The Nature and Destiny of Man,* vol. 2: *Human Destiny* (New York, Scribner's, 1964), 104–5 (grace as "God's power over man" and "God's power in man").

16. Karl Holl, *The Distinctive Elements in Christianity* (Edinburgh, Clark, 1937), 22.

17. C. G. Montefiore, *The Synoptic Gospels* (London, Macmillan, 1909), 2.901, 903.

18. This ethical argument does not hold with the textual reading reflected in the KJV, "We love *him*. . . ." But this textual variant is secondary for the following reasons: 1. it is easier to explain how it might have been added, since it balances the statement, is more pious, and may have been influenced by the references to loving God in v. 20; 2. the MSS which support it are less weighty.

19. Barth, *Church Dogmatics* 2,2.576.

20. Styler, "Basis of Obligation," 184, 186–87.

21. Holl, *Distinctive Elements in Christianity,* 17–23. Holl also is the source for the reference to Celsus.

22. Barth, *Church Dogmatics* 2,2.579.

23. Liem Khiem Yank, "Enacting the Acts of God: One Important Aspect of the Life and Proclamation of Jesus and Paul," *South East Asia Journal of Theology* 14,2 (1973), 26.

24. Cf. Norman N. Snaith, *The Distinctive Ideas of the Old Testament* (Philadelphia, Westminster, 1946), 136.
25. Cf. also Exod. 22.21; 23.9; Lev. 19.33; Deut. 10.18–19; 15.14–15.
26. Moltmann, *Crucified God,* 317.
27. Richard J. Mouw, *Political Evangelism* (Grand Rapids, Eerdmans, 1973), 91.
28. Merk, *Handeln aus Glauben,* 232. There are ten occurrences of *charis* in 2 Cor. 8–9.
29. Stephen Charles Mott, "The Greek Benefactor and Deliverance from Moral Distress" (unpub. Ph.D. diss., Harvard University, 1971), 102–9.
30. Merk, *Handeln aus Glauben,* 155; cf. Dieter Georgi, *Die Geschichte der Kollekte des Paulus für Jerusalem* (Hamburg, Reich, Theologische Forschung 38, 1965), 78.
31. James Moffatt, *Grace in the New Testament* (New York, Long & Smith, 1932), 230.
32. Georgi, *Die Geschichte der Kollekte,* 60.
33. Cf. Georgi, *Die Geschichte der Kollekte,* 60–61.
34. Jonathan Edwards, "Christian Charity," in *Works of President Edwards* (New York, Franklin, Research and Source Work 27, 1968 [1817], 5.403.
35. Cf. Schnackenburg, *Johannesbriefe,* 118. Schnackenburg notes that *brother* can mean fellow Christian as a special group within Judaism. The Pharisees and Essenes spoke similarly of themselves.
36. J. Ramsey Michaels argues that when the text is interpreted in this way, several elements are parallel to other texts of the ancient church, "Apostolic Hardships and Righteous Gentiles: A Study of Matthew 25:31–46," *Journal of Biblical Literature* 84 (1965), 27–37. Michaels notes that even within the bounds of this exegesis, the passage has social relevance with respect to style of life. Noting the condition in which Jesus expected his teachers to be found, Michaels states, "For those who carry on the work of the apostles by preaching and teaching the word it is essential to follow Jesus' example by taking upon themselves the poverty, sickness, and suffering which they found in the world and in the church" (p. 36).
    We should note that Prov. 19.17, "he who is kind to the poor lends to the Lord," approximates the traditional interpretation of the identity of Jesus with the oppressed. Further, would not the basis of obligation to the needy missionaries be the general principle of justice to the weak? The text then would still reflect the universal character of the Old Testament demand for justice.
37. Schnackenburg, *Johannesbriefe,* 120. Schnackenburg sees a universal love in the "visible brother and sister" in 1 John 4.20, applying love to those who bear human countenance, and also in the reference to Jesus' double command of love in v. 21 (p. 121).
38. Furnish, *Theology and Ethics,* 204.
39. David Nehring, "Biblical Resources for a Theology of Poverty," *Christian Community Action Newsletter* 8,6 (New Haven, Conn., August 1976), 9.
40. Walter Zimmerli, *"Charis:* B. Old Testament," *TDNT* (1974), 9.386.

3. LOVE AND SOCIETY

1. Stanley Hauerwas, "Love's Not All You Need," *Cross Currents* 22 (1972), 227–28.
2. Victor Paul Furnish, *The Love Command in the New Testament* (Nashville, Abingdon, 1972), 92.
3. Ibid., 157–58. Troeltsch noted that since "what they do is not done by men but by God or Christ" the exercise of active love does not involve a superiority in the giver (*Social Teachings,* 77).
4. John Wesley, "Law Established through Faith," in *Wesley's Standard Sermons,* ed. E. Sugden (London, Epworth, 1956), 2.81.
5. Albert Rasmussen, *Christian Social Ethics* (Englewood Cliffs, N. J., Prentice-Hall, 1956), 164.
6. Gene Outka, *Agape. An Ethical Analysis* (New Haven, Yale U. Press, Yale Publications in Religion 17, 1972), 126–27.
7. Leander E. Keck, "Justification of the Ungodly and Ethics," in *Rechtfertigung,* E. Käsemann Festschrift, ed. J. Friedrich *et al.* (Tübingen, Mohr, 1976), 202.
8. Rudolf Bultmann, *The Gospel of John: A Commentary* (Philadelphia, Westminster, 1971), 475–76, 525–26; Bultmann, *Theology of the New Testament* (New York, Scribner's, 1955), 2.81–82; Furnish, *Love Command,* 138; C. H. Dodd, *Gospel and Law. The Relation of Faith and Ethics in Early Christianity* (New York, Columbia U. Press, 1951), 71: "an obligation to reproduce in human action the quality and direction of the divine action by which it was initiated."
9. Outka, *Agape,* 44.
10. Christian love is "self-inverted": Paul Ramsey, *Basic Christian Ethics* (New York, Scribner's, 1950), 243.
11. Professor Outka in his outstanding study raises some important objections to self-sacrifice as the highest form of love (*Agape,* 274–79). Nevertheless, the highest model of love is Christ's self-sacrificial death. In addition, the placement in Luke of the sayings on turning the other cheek and giving up the tunic (Luke 6.29–30) in the midst of the discussion of love for one's enemies (6.27–36) shows that they are understood as dealing with love. Their self-sacrificial character is heightened with the perception of Robert C. Tannehill that the essential garments would figure in a lawsuit only of the extremely poor who had no other valuable property, "The 'Focal Instance' as a Form of New Testament Speech: A Study of Matthew 5:29b–42," *Journal of Religion* 50 (1970), 378–79. Yet the clarification that love is the principle in these sayings on non-resistance at the same time gives support to Outka's qualification that self-sacrifice must be for the welfare of others and not for self-sacrifice in itself. We then can say that the quintessence of love is self-sacrifice for the good of others.
12. Ramsey, *Basic Christian Ethics,* 340.
13. Furnish, *Love Command,* 51, who cites 2 John 10–11 as an example of the significance of the greeting.
14. Outka, *Agape,* 130–32. Outka draws upon Donald Evans's distinction of the

verdictive and the *commissive, The Logic of Self-Involvement* (London, SCM, 1963). Outka also speaks of this distinction as *viewpoint about* the neighbor (recipient-evaluation) and *declaration of policy by* the lover (agent-commitment) (p. 10). Evans argues that both features are included in looking upon each person as one for whom Christ died. By deciding *that* each person is also loved by Christ, I am also deciding *to* think and behave in a corresponding way (Evans, *Logic of Self-Involvement,* 129, 136–37, as cited by Outka, *Agape,* 131).

15. W. C. Van Unnik, "Die Motivierung der Feindesliebe in Lukas VI 32–35," *Novum Testamentum* 8 (1966), 297–98; cf. James Moffatt, *Love in the New Testament* (London, Hodder and Stoughton, 1929), 202.

16. Furnish, *Love Command,* 60, 202.

17. Thomas J. Mullen, *The Renewal of the Ministry* (New York, Abingdon, 1963), 72.

18. Furnish, *Love Command,* 38–42.

19. Outka, *Agape,* 13, 161.

20. Cf. Jacob, "Bases théologiques de l'éthique," 47–51, who also cites Prov. 14.31; 17.5; 22.2; 29.13.

21. Outka, *Agape,* 157.

22. This illustration was kindly suggested by my colleague, Professor Roger R. Nicole of Gordon-Conwell Theological Seminary. Troeltsch makes this observation of Calvinism: "Since in dealing with one's fellow-men, at least, it is impossible to distinguish outwardly the elect from the reprobate, everyone is to be considered and exhorted as belonging to the elect . . ." (Troeltsch, *Social Teachings,* 598).

23. John Wesley, "On Pleasing All Men," in *Works of John Wesley,* ed. T. Jackson (Grand Rapids, Mich., Zondervan, 1872), 7.145–46.

24. Furnish, *Love Command,* 33–34, cf. 205.

25. Cf. Karl Rahner, "The 'Commandment' of Love in Relation to the Other Commandments," in Rahner, *Theological Investigations* (Baltimore, Helicon, 1966), 5.440–43.

26. Peter A. Bertocci, "Does the Concept of Christian Love Add Anything to Moral Philosophy?" *Journal of Religion* 38 (1958), 6, 8.

27. Hauerwas, "Love's Not All You Need," 236.

28. Outka, *Agape,* 12.

29. Søren Kierkegaard, *Works of Love* (New York, Harper, 1963), 72, quoted in Outka, *Agape,* 159.

30. Furnish, *Love Command,* 178.

31. James H. Cone, *God of the Oppressed* (New York, Seabury, 1975), ch. 2, p. 33.

32. Austin Farrer, "Examination of Theological Belief," in *Faith and Logic,* ed. B. Mitchell (London, Allen and Unwin, 1958), 23, quoted in Outka, *Agape,* 161.

33. Norman W. Porteous, "The Care of the Poor in the Old Testament," in Porteous, *Living the Mystery* (Oxford, Blackwell, 1967), 146.

34. Cf. Bernard Williams, "The Idea of Equality," in *Philosophy, Politics, and Society,* 2nd ser., eds. P. Laslett and W. G. Runciman (Oxford, Blackwell, 1962), 112, 114; Stanley I. Benn, "Egalitarianism and the Equal Consider-

ation of Interests," in *Equality,* eds. J. R. Pennock and J. Chapman (New York, Atherton, 1967), 71.

35. Che Guevara, in *Che: Selected Works of Ernesto Guevara,* eds. R. Bonachea and N. Valdes (Cambridge, Mass., MIT, 1969), 426.

36. William Ernest Hocking, *Man and the State* (Hamden, Conn., Archon, 1968 [1954]), 13.

37. Juan Luis Segundo, *A Theology for Artisans of a New Humanity.* vol. 5: *Evolution and Guilt* (New York, Orbis, 1974), 39–40.

38. Ramsey, *Basic Christian Ethics,* 247.

39. Cf. Hayim Simha Nahmani, *Human Rights in the Old Testament* (Tel Aviv, Chachik, 1964), 30–31, 53, 65, 71, 78.

40. Ramsey, *Basic Christian Ethics,* 243, 347.

41. The helpful suggestions of Outka regarding how special considerations can be worked out within the context of love seem to me to be more the work of justice (*Agape,* 268–74).

42. Daniel Day Williams, *The Spirit and the Forms of Love* (New York, Harper, 1968), 250.

43. Eduard Heimann, *Reason and Faith in Modern Society* (Middletown, Conn., Wesleyan U. Press, 1961), 293.

44. Troeltsch, *Social Teachings,* 64.

45. Carl Oglesby, "Democracy Is Nothing If It Is Not Dangerous," quoted from undated reprint from *The Peacemaker,* in Arthur G. Gish, *The New Left and Christian Radicalism* (Grand Rapids, Mich., Eerdmans, 1970), 32.

46. Emil Brunner, *Justice and the Social Order* (London, Lutterworth, 1945), 117.

47. Rahner, " 'Commandment' of Love," 451.

48. Dodd, *Gospel and Law,* 76.

49. Saul D. Alinsky, *Reveille for Radicals* (New York, Vintage Books, 1969²), x.

50. Reinhold Niebuhr, *Moral Man and Immoral Society* (New York, Scribner's, 1932), 248.

51. Ramsey, *Basic Christian Ethics,* 241–42.

52. William Booth, *In Darkest England and the Way Out* (London, International Headquarters of the Salvation Army, n.d.), 36.

53. R. W. Funk, "Structure in the Narrative Parables of Jesus," *Semeia* 2 (1974), 51–73. Roger Ruston shows Jesus' rejection of a justice understood in terms of ability or merit in favor of justice as the preservation and creation of community, "A Christian View of Justice," *New Blackfriars* 59 (1978), 344–58.

54. Keck, "Justification of the Ungodly," 199–200, 207.

55. Furnish, *Love Command,* 44–45.

56. Stephen Charles Mott, "The Power of Giving and Receiving: Reciprocity in Hellenistic Benevolence," in *Current Issues in Biblical and Patristic Interpretation,* M. Tenney Festschrift, ed. G. Hawthorne (Grand Rapids, Mich., Eerdmans, 1975), 60–72.

57. Dietrich von Oppen, *The Age of the Person: Society in the Twentieth Century* (Philadelphia, Fortress, 1969), 13, 16.

58. John R. W. Stott, "The Biblical Basis of Evangelism," in *Let the World Hear His Voice,* ed. J. D. Douglas (Minneapolis, World Wide, 1975), 68.

59. Troeltsch, *Social Teachings,* 112.

60. Eric S. Fife and Arthur F. Glasser, *Missions in Crisis. Rethinking Missionary Strategy* (Chicago, Inter-Varsity, 1961), 36–37.

4. GOD'S JUSTICE AND OURS

1. Snaith, *Distinctive Ideas of the Old Testament,* 69.
2. E.g., Carl F. H. Henry, *Aspects of Christian Social Ethics* (Grand Rapids, Eerdmans, 1964), 146–71.
3. Reinhold Niebuhr, *Christian Realism and Political Problems* (New York, Scribner's, 1953), 167.
4. Cf. H. Cazelles, "A propos de quelques textes difficiles relatifs à la justice de Dieu dans l'Ancien Testament," *Revue Biblique* 58 (1951), 185–88.
5. Wallace I. Wolverton, "The King's 'Justice' in Pre-Exilic Israel," *Anglican Theological Review* 41 (1959), 286; cf. José Porfirio Miranda, *Marx and the Bible: A Critique of the Philosophy of Oppression* (Maryknoll, N.Y., Orbis, 1974), 109–60.
6 Cf. H. Cazelles, "A propos de quelques textes," 168–88. In this article Cazelles examines texts where $\m\~ed\=aq\=ah$ is alleged to be punitive and rejects that interpretation. *Mišpaṭ,* and related words, however, acquire a use describing the judicial process associated with God's wrath (e.g., Jer. 25.31; Ezek. 39.21).
7. The wicked are condemned ($r\=aš\=a$' [to be wicked] in the Hiphil) (Deut. 25.1, cf. Prov. 17.15; Isa. 5.23. cf. Rom. 3.20 "by the works of the law no flesh will be justified [dikaiōthēsesthai]").
8. Ernst Käsemann, "God's Righteousness in Paul," *Journal for Theology and the Church* 1 (1965), 100, 103; Peter Stuhlmacher, *Gerechtigkeit Gottes bei Paulus* (Göttingen, Vandenhoeck, Forschungen zur Religion und Literatur des Alten und Neuen Testamentes 87, 1966²), 78, 83; Karl Kertelege, *"Rechtfertigung" bei Paulus. Studien zur Struktur und zum Bedeutungsgehalt des paulinischen Rechtfertigungsbegriffs* (Münster, Aschendorff, Neutestamentliche Abhandlunger, n.s. 3, 1967), 107–8; Marcus Barth, "Jews and Gentiles: The Social Character of Justification in Paul," *Journal of Ecumenical Studies* 5 (1968), 259.
9. Stuhlmacher, *Gerechtigkeit Gottes,* 80. Cf. the contrast in Rom. 1.17–18. The element of judgment both in the doctrine of the atonement as satisfaction or propitiation and in the eschatological future, which Carl Henry associates with his view of justice (*Aspects of Christian Social Ethics,* 169), would be expressed by terms other than *dikaiosynē.* For an example of the distinct uses of this terminology, cf. Rom. 8.33 (*RSV*), "It is God who justifies [dikaioun], who is to condemn [katakrinein]?"
10. Walter Zimmerli, *"Charis:* B. Old Testament," *Theological Dictionary of the New Testament* (1974), 9:378, 380, 386. God's favor is given specifically to the poor (Prov. 3.34).
11. Cf. Zimmerli, *"Charis,"* 381–86.
12. Cf. C. van Leeuwen, *Le développement du sens social en Israël avant l'ère chrétienne* (Assen, Van Gorcum, Semitica Neerlandica 1, 1955), 184. Van Leeuwen demonstrates the closeness of $\m\~ed\=aq\=ah$ to love rather than to the Graeco-Ro-

man view of "to each his own." Later *eleēmosynē* (*act of mercy, alms*) begins to replace *dikaiosynē* as its equivalent (pp. 184–89).

13. The words of Charles E. Curran in describing Paul Ramsey's view of justice, *Politics, Medicine, and Christian Ethics* (Philadelphia, Fortress, 1973), 19.

14. Cf. the defense of meritorian justice by Roger Hancock, "Meritorian and Equalitarian Justice," *Ethics* 80 (1970), 166, who questions the assumption of equal merit.

   Even John Rawls, in his effort to demonstrate a basis for democratic equality without recourse to self-evident principles or a theory of human nature, develops justice out of a situation which functions in a way which approximates Christian love. In his hypothetical situation representative persons contract a scheme of justice, but they are ignorant of their share in the eventual society. As a result, each has to consider what he or she would want if in the place of each other person; one accepts restrictions on oneself because of empathy with the situation of others. (*A Theory of Justice* [Cambridge, Harvard U. Press, 1971]).

15. Ramsey, *Basic Christian Ethics,* 13–14.

16. Cf. David Miller's argument that a conception of justice is held against a particular model of society; justice as "distribution according to needs" is correlative to society as a "solidaristic community" ("The Ideological Backgrounds to Conceptions of Social Justice," *Political Studies* 22 [1974], 387–99).

17. G. Ch. Macholz, "Noch Einmal: Planungen für den Wiederaufbau der Katastrophe von 587," *Vetus Testamentum* 19 (1969), 325–27. Elie Munk states that "the point of departure of the system of social economy of Judaism is the equal division of the land among all its inhabitants," *La justice sociale en Israël* (Boudry, Neuchâtel [Switzerland], Baconnière, Israël et le monde 3, 1948), 75.

18. Albrecht Alt, "Micha 2,1–5 GĒS ANADASMOS in Juda," in *Kleine Schriften zur Geschichte des Volkes Israel,* vol. 3 (Munich, Beck, 1959), 374.

19. W. T. Blackstone, "On the Meaning and Justification of the Equality Principle," *Ethics* 77 (1967), 240, 243.

20. Gregory Vlastos, "Justice and Equality," in *Social Justice,* ed. R. Brandt (Englewood Cliffs, N. J., Prentice-Hall, 1962), 40–41.

21. Stanley I. Benn, "Egalitarianism and the Equal Consideration of Interests," in *Equality,* eds. J. R. Pennock and J. Chapman (New York, Atherton, 1967), 61–62, 74; cf. Snaith, *Distinctive Ideas of the Old Testament,* 70.

22. E.g., Heinz-Horst Schrey *et al., The Biblical Doctrine of Justice and Law* (London, SCM, 1955), 51–52, 57, 141; John R. Donahue, "Biblical Perspectives on Justice," in *The Faith That Does Justice,* ed. J. Haughey (New York, Paulist, 1977), 68–112.

23. Bruce Vawter, "A Tale of Two Cities: The Old Testament and the Issue of Personal Freedom," *Journal of Ecumenical Studies* 15 (1978), 261–73; and Wolff, *Anthropology of the Old Testament,* 194–205; also *Interpretation* 27 (1973), 259–72. Wolff recognizes the toleration of conditions contradicting this ideal but also shows the intensification of criticism of slavery which ultimately led to a fundamental rethinking of the problem.

24. Ludwig Koehler, *Hebrew Man* (London, SCM, 1956), 153, 155; cf. Robert Gordis, "Primitive Democracy in Ancient Israel," in Gordis, *Poets, Prophets and Sages* (Bloomington, Indiana U. Press, 1971), 45–60, which describes a representative assembly not on the village level, but on the national and possibly originally also the tribal level. This right existed, but is not commanded in our texts as are the other rights listed above.

25. Cf. Herbert Spiegelberg, "A Defense of Human Equality," *Philosophical Review* 53 (1944), 113–14; Rawls, *Theory of Justice*, 100.

26. Snaith, *Distinctive Ideas of the Old Testament*, 70. Normally, God's justice is implemented by means of human justice, but when human institutions fail in this purpose God acts directly (Isa. 59.12–16).

27. D. Daiches Raphael, "Justice and Liberty," *Proceedings of the Aristotelian Society* 51 (1950/51), 188–89.

28. For the Law, cf. Deut. 19.14, where the command not to remove one's neighbor's landmark is tied to the fact that they were set up in a land (*naḥᵃlâ*) which has been portioned out by Yahweh (cf. 27.17). The original divisions are to be revered. For the wisdom literature, cf. Prov. 23.10–11: Yahweh the *go'el*, the redeemer and guardian, enters the field of the fatherless in the case of the right of redemption (cf. Prov. 15.25). As in Deut. 19, justice is tied to possession of the land and the ancient provision of it. Walter Zimmerli, *The Old Testament and the World* (Atlanta, Knox, 1976), 95.

29. Cf. Walter Rauschenbusch, *Righteousness of the Kingdom* (New York, Abingdon, 1968), 228.

30. Walter Zimmerli, "Planungen für den Wiederaufbau nach der Katastrophe von 587," *Vetus Testamentum* 18 (1968), 246.

31. Macholz, "Noch Einmal," 330, 336, 338, 341.

32. Alt, "Micha 2,1–5," 377–78, 379–81.

33. Raphael, "Justice and Liberty," 170, 193.

34. Cf. Blackstone, "On the Meaning and Justification of the Equality Principle," 242.

35. Vlastos, "Justice and Equality," 35.

36. Outka suggests that of all the conceptions of justice, the one which overlaps the most with agape is "to each according to his needs" (*Agape*, 91). We have seen the rectifying bias of love toward the handicapped and defenseless.

37. Snaith, *Distinctive Ideas of the Old Testament*, 68.

38. Cf. Rawls, *Theory of Justice*, 91.

39. Miller, "Ideological Backgrounds," 389.

40. Cf. Rawls, *Theory of Justice*, 15.

41. H. McKeating, "Justice and Truth in Israel's Legal Practice. An Inquiry," *Church Quarterly* 3 (1970), 55.

42. Robert Davidson, "Some Aspects of the Old Testament Contribution to the Pattern of Christian Ethics," *Scottish Journal of Theology* 12 (1959), 379.

43. Zeev W. Falk, "Two Symbols of Justice," *Vetus Testamentum* 10 (1960), 72–73. As the king became more distant from the village, his responsibilities increasingly were delegated to princes and elders (Wolverton, "The King's 'Justice,' " 281–82).

44. Koehler, *Hebrew Man*, 153, 155. Cf. his Appendix, "Justice in the Gate," pp. 149–75.
45. Cf. similar teachings in Matt. 12.7; 19.16–22 par.
46. Otto Bird, *The Idea of Justice* (New York, Praeger, 1967), 168, 171.
47. Snaith, *Distinctive Ideas of the Old Testament*, 73.
48. Cf. Rawls, *Theory of Justice*, 4, 62, 259.
49. Ibid., 3; cf. 7, 54–55, 58.
50. Ibid., 259.
51. Koehler, *Hebrew Man*, 157.

5. THE LONG MARCH OF GOD

1. Bousset, *Religion des Judentums*, 314.
2. Herman Ridderbos, *The Coming of the Kingdom* (Philadelphia, Presbyterian and Reformed, 1962), 3–4.
3. Ibid., 13.
4. Rudolf Schnackenburg, *God's Rule and Kingdom* (Freiburg, Herder, 1963), 12–13.
5. Ibid., 18.
6. Amos Niven Wilder, *Eschatology and Ethics in the Teaching of Jesus* (New York, Harper, 1939), 27.
7. Ridderbos, *Coming of the Kingdom*, 5.
8. Wolverton gives the following examples: Isa. 5.16; 28.17; 30.18; 32.16; 33.22 ("The King's Justice," 285).
9. Schnackenburg, *God's Rule and Kingdom*, 41.
10. Klaus Koch, *The Rediscovery of Apocalyptic* (London, SCM, Studies in Biblical Theology 22, 2d ser., 1972), 131.
11. C. René Padilla, "The Kingdom of God and the Church," *Theological Fraternity Bulletin*, nos. 1 and 2 (1976), 1.
12. Günther Bornkamm, *Jesus of Nazareth* (New York, Harper, 1960³), 92.
13. Wilder, *Eschatology and Ethics*, 19, 153f.
14. Cf. ibid., 47, 197.
15. Cf. Ridderbos, *Coming of the Kingdom*, 521.
16. Ibid., 55.
17. Other interpretations are offered for this passage. The interpretation, "the Reign is inside you," as a purely spiritual reality, is hindered by the fact that Jesus' audience are the Pharisees and by the use of *entos* rather than *en*, the normal word for *in*. *Entos* often means *among* when the object is plural. The other leading interpretation, that Jesus is referring to a statement which will be made in the future, is more persuasive. But if this is taken to mean that it will be sudden, rather than something which can be calculated, then one must note that there is nothing in the passage to suggest suddenness. Cf. Werner Georg Kümmel, *Promise and Fulfillment: The Eschatological Message of Jesus* (Naperville, Allenson, Studies in Biblical Theology 23, 1957³), 32–36. If it means that the Reign would then already be present as a religious, ethical, and social reality, then that assumes a coming of the Reign into

history. The most plausible time for such a nonobservable coming would be
with the work of Jesus.

18. Cf. Wilder, *Eschatology and Ethics,* 192.
19. Ibid., 196.
20. H. Richard Niebuhr, *The Kingdom of God in America* (New York, Harper
    Torchbooks, 1959), 26.
21. Ibid., 131, cf. 26–28.
22. Schnackenburg, *God's Rule and Kingdom,* 266.
23. Karl Mannheim, *Ideology and Utopia* (New York, Harcourt, Harvest Book,
    1936), 104.
24. Walter Rauschenbusch, *Christianity and the Social Crisis* (Boston, Pilgrim,
    1907), 346.
25. Miracles motivated by compassion: Mark 1.41 (the text is questionable, how-
    ever); Matt. 14.14/Mark 6.34; Matt. 15.32/Mark 8.2; Matt. 9.36 (cf. 9.35
    and 10.1); 20.34; Mark 5.19; Luke 7.13. Miracles in response to a plea for
    compassion: Matt. 9.27; 15.22; 17.5/Mark 9.22; Matt. 20.30–31/Mark
    10.47–48/Luke 18.38–39; Luke 17.13.
26. Augustine, *Of the Morals of the Catholic Church,* ch. 27, in *Christian Social
    Teachings,* ed. G. Forell (New York, Doubleday, Anchor Books, 1966), 78.
27. Booth, *In Darkest England,* 221 (italics mine).
28. Cf. Bornkamm, *Jesus of Nazareth,* 67–68; Schnackenburg, *God's Rule and
    Kingdom,* 124–26.
29. Moltmann, *Crucified God,* 24.
30. Cf. René Padilla, "Evangelism and the World," in *Let the Earth Hear His
    Voice,* ed. J. D. Douglas (Minneapolis, World Wide, 1975), 122.
31. Cf. Schnackenburg, *God's Rule and Kingdom,* 297.
32. Paul Tillich, "The Kingdom of God and History," in *Church, Community and
    State,* vol. 3: *The Kingdom of God and History,* by H. G. Wood *et al.* (London,
    Allen & Unwin, 1938), 115, 124–31.
33. Cf. Tillich, "Kingdom of God and History," 119, 132–35.
34. Cf. Schnackenburg, *God's Rule and Kingdom,* 333.
35. Scholars differ about the meaning of the preposition *into* (*eis*) in this verse
    (literally, "co-workers *into* the Reign of God"). I have followed Bauer's inter-
    pretation that it indicates the field in which the cooperation takes place (*Lex-
    icon*[5], 787). Schnackenburg represents the view that it indicates the goal:
    toward the Reign of God (*God's Rule and Kingdom,* 288; cf. *RSV: for*). The
    parallels in 2 Cor. 8.23 and 1 Thes. 3.2 seem to favor Bauer.
36. Arthur Rich, "Die Radikalität des Reiches Gottes," *Zeitwende* 43 (1972),
    254.
37. Sasse, *"Kosmos,"* 885.
38. Bauer, *Lexicon*[5], 546.
39. Sasse, *"Kosmos,"* 885.
40. N. H. Cassem, "A Grammatical and Contextual Inventory of the Use of
    kosmos in the Johannine Corpus with Some Implications for a Johannine
    Cosmic Theology," *New Testament Studies* 19 (1972), 84–85.
41. Edward Schillebeeckz, "Foi chrétienne et attente terrestre," in *L'Eglise dans*

le monde de ce temps, 151–58, as cited by Gustavo Gutiérrez, *A Theology of Liberation* (Maryknoll, N.Y., Orbis, 1973), 284.

42. Niebuhr, *The Kingdom of God in America,* 10, 23, 28.
43. John Calvin, *Institutes of the Christian Religion* (Grand Rapids, Mich., Eerdmans, 1957), 4.20.2 (vol. 2, p. 652).
44. Niebuhr, *The Kingdom of God in America,* 40.
45. John Saltmarsh, *Smoke in the Temple* (1646), in *Puritanism and Liberty,* ed. A. S. P. Woodhouse (Chicago, U. of Chicago Press, 1951), 184–85.
46. Hedda Hartl, "Die Aktualität des Gottesreiches nach Lk. 17, 20f," in *Biblische Randbemerkungen,* R. Schnackenburg Festschrift, eds. H. Merklein and J. Lange ([Würzburg], Echter, 1974²), 30.
47. Cf. John G. Gibbs, *Creation and Redemption: A Study in Pauline Theology* (Leiden, Brill, *Novum Testamentum Supplements* 26, 1971), 76.
48. Gibbs, *Creation and Redemption,* 37, 40.
49. Rich, "Radikalität des Reiches Gottes," 254.
50. Padilla, "Evangelism and the World," 145.
51. Hans Heinrich Schmid, "Rechtfertigung als Schöpfungsgeschehen. Notizen zur alttestamentlichen Vorgeschichte eines neutestamentlichen Themas," in *Rechtefertigung,* E. Käsemann Festschrift, ed. J. Friedrich *et al.* (Tübingen, Mohr, 1976), 405.
52. Frank Moore Cross, *Canaanite Myth and Hebrew Epic. Essays in the History of the Religion of Israel* (Cambridge, Harvard U. Press, 1973), 135–37.
53. Cf. also Isa. 41.20; 43.7; 48.7; Gutiérrez, *Theology of Liberation,* 155. The merging of creation and redemption, however, is not as common as suggested by some. Many of the texts cited seem to praise God's power in creation as evidence of God's sufficiency for salvation rather than actually to merge the two functions.
54. Ibid., 159–60, 169.
55. T. W. Manson, *The Servant Messiah. A Study of the Public Ministry of Jesus* (Cambridge, Cambridge U. Press, 1953), 98.
56. Wolfgang Schweitzer, "Das Reich des Gekreuzigten in exegetischer und sozialethischer Sicht," *Zeitschrift für Evangelische Ethik* 20 (1976), 188.
57. Schnackenburg, *God's Rule and Kingdom,* 315.
58. Rauschenbusch, *Righteousness of the Kingdom,* 87, cf. 86, 88, 110.
59. Bernard Zylstra, "The Bible, Justice and the State," *International Reformed Bulletin* 16,55 (fall 1973), 3.
60. Washington Gladden, *Social Salvation,* in *Christian Social Teachings,* ed. Forell, 362.
61. James M. Gustafson, "Christian Conviction and Christian Action," in Gustafson, *The Church as Moral Decision-Maker* (Philadelphia, Pilgrim, 1970), 102.
62. The reader may object that in some of these NT passages, *dikaiosynē* represents the total obligation in interhuman relations and is not as specific as when it means *justice.* Even where this objection might be valid, however, justice still must be included as a central part of the whole.
63. The finder's joy in Matt. 13.44 relates to acquiring a treasure for which he

has not toiled; J. Duncan Derrett, *Law in the New Testament* (London, Darton, 1970), 14–15; cf. Philo, *Quod Deus* 91–92.

64. Schnackenburg, *God's Rule and Kingdom,* 194, cf. 251–54.
65. Eduard Schweizer, "Versöhnung des Alls. Kol. 1,20," in *Jesus Christus in Historie und Theologie,* H. Conzelmann Festschrift, ed. G. Strecker (Tübingen, Mohr, 1975), 500.
66. Ridderbos, *Coming of the Kingdom,* 356.
67. Padilla, "Kingdom of God and the Church," 1, 10.
68. Mehl, "Basis of Christian Social Ethics," 53.

6. EVANGELISM

1. Julius Schniewind, "The Biblical Doctrine of Conversion," *Scottish Journal of Theology* 5 (1952), 271.
2. Stow Persons similarly characterizes the American Puritan understanding of conversion as reorientation of the personality and moral engagement, *American Minds: A History of Ideas* (New York, Holt, 1958), 12–13.
3. Cf. William Temple, *Nature, Man and God* (London, Macmillan, 1934), 394, 397.
4. Timothy L. Smith, *Revivalism and Social Reform in Mid-Nineteenth Century America* (New York, Abingdon, 1957).
5. Henry V. Jaffa, *Crisis of the House Divided* (Garden City, N.Y., Doubleday, 1959), 74.
6. Erich Fromm, *The Sane Society* (New York, Rinehart, 1955), 264.
7. Gutiérrez (*Theology of Liberation,* 176–77) makes this distinction between the coming and growth of the Kingdom.
8. Elton Trueblood, *The New Man for Our Time* (New York, Harper, 1970), 61.
9. Cf. Maurice B. Reckitt, *Faith and Society: A Study of the Structure, Outlook and Opportunity of the Christian Social Movement in Great Britain and the United States* (London, Longmans, 1932), 30.
10. Jessie Rice Sandberg, *Sword of the Lord,* Dec. 27, 1974, 5.
11. Martin Luther, "Secular Authority: To What Extent It Should Be Obeyed," in *Martin Luther. Selections from His Writings,* ed. John Dillenberger (Garden City, N.Y., Doubleday, Anchor Books, 1961), 370–74.
12. Emilio Castro, "Conversion and Social Transformation," in *Christian Social Ethics in a Changing World,* ed. John C. Bennett (New York, Association, 1966), 363.
13. Henry, *Aspects of Christian Social Ethics,* 59. This author speaks elsewhere from a broader perspective than appears in this quotation.
14. John Bennett, *Social Salvation. A Religious Approach to the Problems of Social Change* (New York, Scribner's, 1935), 46.
15. Rudolf Bultmann, "Paul," in Bultmann, *Existence and Faith* (New York, Meridian, Living Age Books, 1960), 130; Hans Walter Wolff, *Anthropology of the Old Testament* (Philadelphia, Fortress, 1975), 7–8.
16. Ibid., 8.
17. Augustine, *The City of God* (New York, Modern Library, 1950), 14.2–3, pp. 443, 446.

18. Bo Reike, "Body and Soul in the New Testament," *Studia Theologica* 19 (1965), 202. In *The Vitality of the Individual in the Thought of Ancient Israel* (Cardiff, U. of Wales Press, 1964), Aubrey R. Johnson shows that various organs and parts of the body—bones, heart, bowels, kidneys, face, head, flesh *et al.*—have psychical properties in Old Testament usage. They have emotions, make ethical responses, have rational activity.

19. Wolff, *Anthropology of the Old Testament,* 29.

20. Reike, "Body and Soul," 203.

21. Ibid., 202.

22. This is the interpretation of Professor Helmut Koester.

23. Cf. Augustine, *City of God,* 446: "Man living according to man."

24. Bultmann, *Theology of the New Testament,* 1.195. Paul never calls a corpse *body (sōma).*

25. Nicolas Berdyaev, *Solitude and Society* (New York, Scribner's, 1938), 104.

26. Gibbs, *Creation and Redemption,* 142.

27. Leonard Audet, "Avec quel corps les justes ressuscitent-ils? analyse de 1 Corinthiens 15:44," *Studies in Religion/Sciences Religieuses* 1 (1971), 172–75.

28. Audet, "Avec quel corps?" 166.

29. Jürgen Moltmann, *Theology of Hope: On the Ground and the Implications of a Christian Eschatology* (New York, Harper, 1967), 214.

30. Audet, "Avec quel corps?" 175.

31. G. Ernest Wright, *The Biblical Doctrine of Man in Society* (London, SCM, Ecumenical Bible Studies 2, 1954), 47.

32. Wolff, *Anthropology of the Old Testament,* 217–19.

33. Michael Harrington, *The Other America: Poverty in the United States* (Baltimore, Penguin, 1971[2]), 81.

34. Erich Fromm, "The Dogma of Christ," in Fromm, *The Dogma of Christ and Other Essays on Religion, Psychology and Culture* (New York, Holt, 1963), 3.

35. Karl R. Popper, *Objective Knowledge* (Oxford, Oxford U. Press, 1972), 106, 159; Bryan Magee, *Popper* (Glasgow, Fontana, Modern Masters, 1975), 59; Peter L. Berger and Thomas Luckmann, *The Social Construction of Reality. A Treatise in the Sociology of Knowledge* (Garden City, N.Y., Doubleday, 1966), 21–23.

36. George H. Mead, *Mind, Self, and Society* (Chicago, U. of Chicago Press, 1934) 152–64; Alfred Schutz, "The Dimensions of the Social World," in Schutz, *Collected Papers,* vol. 2: *Studies in Social Theory* (The Hague, Nijhoff, Phaenomenologica 15, 1964), 3, 32; Berdyaev, *Solitude and Society,* 90; H. Richard Niebuhr, *The Responsible Self* (New York, Harper, 1963), 76–79.

37. Berger and Luckmann, *Social Construction of Reality,* 150; Mannheim, *Ideology and Utopia,* 3, 269; Mead, *Mind, Self, and Society,* 161–62.

38. Ibid., 215; Berdyaev, *Solitude and Society,* 89–91; Niebuhr, *Responsible Self,* 85.

39. Mannheim, *Ideology and Utopia,* 206–207; Mead, 168, 215; Popper, *Objective Knowledge,* 147, 149.

40. Rollo May, *The Art of Counseling* (New York, Abingdon, 1939), 33.

41. Booth, *In Darkest England,* 48.

42. Stott, "Biblical Basis of Evangelism," 67; and Stott, *Christian Mission in the Modern World* (Downers Grove, Ill., Inter-Varsity, 1975), 29.

43. Cf. Jimmy R. Allen, "Urban Evangelism," in *Toward Creative Urban Strategy*, ed. G. Torney (Waco, Tex., Word, 1970), 119.

44. Michael Green, "Evangelism in the Early Church," in *Let the Earth Hear His Voice*, ed. J. D. Douglass (Minneapolis, World Wide, 1975), 176.

45. Cf. Reinhold Niebuhr, *An Interpretation of Christian Ethics* (New York, Harper, 1935), 128; Bernard Iddings Bell, *Crowd Culture* (Chicago, Gateway, 1952), 79; Gilbert Haven, "The State a Christian Brotherhood" (address, 1863), in Haven, *National Sermons* (Boston, Lee & Shephard, 1869), 342.

46. Thomas Luckmann, *The Invisible Religion. The Problem of Religion in Modern Society* (New York, Macmillan, 1967), 85.

47. Plutarch, *Praecepta gerendae reipublicae*, 30 (822b).

48. George W. Webber, *God's Colony in Man's World* (Nashville, Abingdon, 1960), 38.

49. Philippe Maury, *Politics and Evangelism* (Garden City, N.Y., Doubleday, 1959), 104 (speaking out of his personal experience in French underground activities against the Nazis).

50. Mr. Douglas Ganyo.

51. David O. Moberg, *The Great Reversal: Evangelism versus Social Concern* (Philadelphia, Lippincott, Evangelical Perspectives, 1972), 159.

52. Allen, "Urban Evangelism," 118.

53. Cf. Samuel Escobar, "Evangelism and Man's Search for Freedom, Justice and Fulfillment," in *Let the Earth Hear His Voice* (cf. n.44, above), 310.

54. Roberto Barbosa, "The Gospel with Bread: An Interview with Brazilian Pentecostalist Manoel de Mello," in *Missions Trends No. 2: Evangelization*, eds. G. Anderson and T. Stransky (New York, Paulist, 1975), 150–51.

55. Thomas Guthrie, *The City: Its Sins and Its Sorrows* (Glasgow, 1862), as quoted in Smith, *Revivalism and Social Reform*, 167–68.

56. Reckitt, *Faith and Society*, 58–59.

57. Booth, *In Darkest England*, 233, 256.

58. Also Bauer, *Lexicon*[5], 567.

59. Furnish, *Love Command*, 26–27, 30–31.

60. Ronald J. Sider, review of *The Evangelical Renaissance* by Donald G. Bloesch, *Christianity Today* 18 (1974), 1161.

61. Padilla, "Evangelism and the World," 144–45.

62. *Partnership* (newsletter by Partnership in Mission, Abingdon, Pa.), no. 5 (Sept. 21, 1976), 3.

63. James Daane, "The Primary Task of the Church," *Reformed Journal* 24,7 (Sept. 1974), 7. It should be noted that priorities in this chapter are treated on the level of the basic goals of an organization and not on the administrative level of rationally combining the skills and opportunities at hand in planning toward those goals. So in the church we must not make a basic command for God's people to be a secondary goal, but we will still make strategies that will at a given time assign priority to a particular task in working towards the goals.

7. THE CHURCH AS COUNTER-COMMUNITY

1. John Howard Yoder, *The Politics of Jesus* (Grand Rapids, Mich., Eerdmans, 1972), 157.
2. Ernst Käsemann, *Das wandernde Gottesvolk* (Göttingen, Vandenhoeck, Forschungen zur Religion und Literatur des Alten und Neuen Testaments 37, n.s., 1961⁴), 8.
3. Rudolf Schnackenburg, *The Church in the New Testament* (New York, Herder, 1965), 167.
4. Hendrikus Berkhof, *The Doctrine of the Holy Spirit* (Richmond, Va., Knox, 1964), 57–59.
5. Robert A. Evans, "The Quest for Community," *Union Seminary Quarterly Review* 30 (1975), 197.
6. Berkhof, *Doctrine of the Holy Spirit,* 65.
7. Cf. F. W. Dillistone, *The Structure of the Divine Society* (Philadelphia, Westminster, 1951), 37.
8. "An Interview with Reba Place Fellowship," *Post American* 2,4 (Sept./Oct., 1973), 10, quoting David Jackson.
9. Jay Ogilvy and Heather Ogilvy, "Communes and the Reconstruction of Reality," *Soundings* 55 (1972), 91; Troeltsch, *Social Teaching of the Christian Churches,* 339.
10. Cf. Elizabeth O'Connor, *Journey Inward, Journey Outward* (New York, Harper, 1968) and other works by this member and interpreter of the Church of the Saviour. She states, "There is no Christian community not rooted in service, no Christian service not rooted in relationship" (40).
11. Cf. John Howard Yoder, *The Christian Witness to the State* (Newton, Kan., Faith and Life, Institute of Mennonite Studies 3, 1964), 17.
12. Schnackenburg, *Church in the New Testament,* 174–75.
13. Calvin Redekop, "Church History and the Contrasystem: A Case Study," *Church History* 40 (1971), 58. Redekop's term is *contrasystem*.
14. Yoder, *Politics of Jesus,* 47.
15. Cf. Rosemary R. Ruether, *Radical Social Movement and the Radical Church Tradition* (Oak Brook, Ill., Bethany Theological Seminary, Colloquium 1, 1971), 25.
16. Paul Mininger, "The Limitations of Nonconformity," *Mennonite Quarterly Review* 24 (1950), 169.
17. Cf. ibid., 164.
18. Mead, *Mind, Self, and Society,* 167–68; Berger and Luckmann, *Social Construction of Reality,* 144–45.
19. Theodore Newcomb, *et al., Persistence and Change: Bennington College and Its Students after Twenty-Five Years* (New York, Wiley, 1967), 53.
20. Gish, *New Left and Christian Radicalism,* 129–30.
21. Quoted by Evans in "Quest for Community," 197.
22. Dale W. Brown, *The Christian Revolutionary* (Grand Rapids, Eerdmans, 1971), 127–28.
23. Käsemann, *Wandernde Gottesvolk,* 24.

24. Jim Wallis, *Agenda for Biblical People* (New York, Harper, 1976), 53, 68, 135.
25. John Howard Yoder, "Living the Disarmed Life," *Sojourners* 6,5 (May, 1977), 19.
26. Gish, *New Left and Christian Radicalism*, 130.
27. Koinonia Partners newsletter (Americus, Ga., Spring, 1977), 1–2. It should be noted that this example does not belong to the pure type. This demonstration is not what the community is doing for each other but what it is doing for and with its neighbors. And even in its voluntary action, it has made an intervention in the society's housing system.
28. Yoder, *Christian Witness to the State*, 20–21; and "Christ the Hope of the World," in Yoder, *The Original Revolution* (Scottdale, Pa., Herald, Christian Peace Shelf, 1972), 164.
29. Cf. Yoder, *Christian Witness to the State*, 21.
30. Stanley Hauerwas, "The Nonresistent Church: The Theological Ethics of John Howard Yoder," in Hauerwas, *Vision and Virtue* (Notre Dame, Ind., Fides, 1974), 221 (italics mine).
31. Larry Christenson, *A Charismatic Approach to Social Action* (Minneapolis, Bethany Fellowship, 1974), 75, 93.
32. "Glorifying God" in 1 Peter 2.12 and Matthew 5.16 means acclaiming his presence in the action carried out by the believers: C. Spicq, *Les Epîtres Pastorales* (Paris, Gabalda, Etudes Bibliques, 1969⁴), 681.
33. The triumphant image in Matt. 5.14 is even stronger if one accepts, as have many, Gerhard Von Rad's suggestion, in "Die Stadt auf dem Berge," *Evangelische Theologie* 8 (1948/49), 447, that the city on the mountain is the eschatological city of God on the world mountain of Isa. 2.1–4 (cf. Mic. 4.1–4); Isa. 60; Hag. 2.6–9. In these passages the nations are in willing political and spiritual submission to Zion. The syntax of Matt. 5.14, however, does not indicate that Matthew was aware of this allusion (absence of article with *city* [*polis*] and the separation of *city* and *mountain* [*oros*]). To deal with a separate concern, *city* as a symbol separable from the metaphor drawn in the text should not be interpreted as indicating the nature of the church any more than *salt* or *candle*.
34. Rudolf Schnackenburg, " 'Ihr seid das Salz der Erde, das Licht der Welt': Zu Mt. 5,13–16," in Schnackenburg, *Schriften zum Neuen Testament* (Munich, Kösel, 1971), 190–94.
35. J. Lawrence Burkholder, "The Anabaptist Vision of Discipleship," in *Recovery of the Anabaptist Vision*, H. Bender Festschrift, ed. G. Hershberger (Scottdale, Pa., Herald, 1957), 137, 142; Franz Heimann, "The Hutterite Doctrine of the Church and Common Life, A Study of Peter Riedemann's Confession of Faith," *Mennonite Quarterly Review* 26 (1952), 22–23, 32.
36. Harold S. Bender, "The Anabaptist Vision" (1944), in *The Recovery of the Anabaptist Vision*, 53–54.
37. Berkhof, *Doctrine of the Holy Spirit*, 41.
38. Ibid., 31.
39. Cf. Richard Shaull, "The Church and the Making of a Counter Culture," *Chicago Theological Seminary Register* 61,4 (May 1971), 26.

40. Gish, *New Left and Christian Radicalism,* 131.
41. R. Newton Flew, *Jesus and His Church. A Study of the Idea of the Ecclesia in the New Testament* (London, Epworth, 1938), 115–16.

8. STRATEGIC NONCOOPERATION

1. The translation of Edward Gordon Selwyn in *The First Epistle of St. Peter* (London, Macmillan, 1946), 172.
2. Etienne de La Boétie, "Discourse de la servitude voluntaire," quoted by Gene Sharp in *The Politics of Nonviolent Action* (Boston, Porter Sargent, Extending Horizons Books, 1973), 11.
3. Sharp, *Politics of Nonviolent Action,* 63–64.
4. John M. Swomley, Jr., *Liberation Ethics* (New York, Macmillan, 1972), 186–87. Cf. ch. 10, "Strategies of Liberation," 183–207.
5. Sharp, *Politics of Nonviolent Action,* 151. All systems operate within a "zone of compliance." Much of life's activity occurs not by reason of great thought or special motivation, but by habit, convention, or mere compliance. P. J. D. Wiles states, "Mere routine . . . is the mightiest force of all" (*Economic Institutions Compared,* 19). The Birmingham children's action forced people to think about that which had not needed thought. Sharp's book describes almost 200 methods of nonviolent direct action (119–433); the table of contents is an education in itself.
6. Sharp, *Politics of Nonviolent Action,* 111; Elliot M. Zashin, *Civil Disobedience and Democracy* (New York, Free Press, 1972), 260.
7. Zashin, *Civil Disobedience,* 124–25.
8. Sharp, *Politics of Nonviolent Action,* 68.
9. Ibid., 47.
10. Cf. Swomley, *Liberation Ethics,* 193.
11. James Luther Adams, "Civil Disobedience: Its Occasions and Limits," in *Political and Legal Obligation,* eds. J. R. Pennock and J. Chapman (New York, Atherton, Nomos 12, 1970), 329.
12. Cf. the survey of literature on the black struggle in the South in Zashin, *Civil Disobedience,* 250–58.
13. Ibid., 251, cf. 244.
14. Marcus Borg, "A New Context for Romans xiii," *New Testament Studies* 19 (1973), 205–18.
15. Johannes Friedrich, Wolfgang Pöhlmann, and Peter Stuhlmacher, "Zur historischen Situation und Intention von Röm. 13, 1–7," *Zeitschrift für Theologie und Kirche* 73 (1976), 131–66.
16. Cf. Michael Grant, *Nero* (London, Weidenfeld, 1970), 60.
17. Ibid., 56–64; A. Momigliano, "Nero," in *Cambridge Ancient History* (1934), 10.704.
18. George La Piana, "Foreign Groups in Rome during the First Centuries of the Empire," *Harvard Theological Review* 20 (1927), 374–75; Henry J. Leon, *The Jews of Ancient Rome* (Philadelphia, Jewish Publication Society, Morris Loeb Series, 1960), 27–28, 37.

19. Robert J. Karris, "Rom. 14:1–15:13 and the Occasion of Romans," *Catholic Biblical Quarterly* 35 (1973), 155, with bibliography.

20. Ibid., 174–77. Karris's article is reprinted on pp. 75–99 of *The Romans Debate,* ed. K. Donfried (Minneapolis, Augsburg, 1977), where Karris also responds (pp. 149–51) to Donfried's criticism (pp. 120–48) of his argument.

21. It is important to note that the responsibilities Paul sets forth for slaves are not set over against a quest for justice but rather a quest for release from social obligations. Paul, in common with all other writers of his time, does not deal with slavery as an institution which is unjust in itself; cf. S. Scott Bartchy, *First Century Slavery and the Interpretation of 1 Corinthians 7:21* (Missoula, Mont., Council on the Study of Religion, Society of Biblical Literature Dissertation Series 11, 1973), 299–300. Paul does not consider slavery in terms of justice; therefore his failure to accost it more directly does not stem from an opposition on his part to struggles for justice. It is invalid, therefore, to cite Paul's treatment of slavery as a norm opposing Christian efforts for social justice.

22. Selwyn, *First Epistle of St. Peter,* 174.

23. Recent advocates of this position are Ernst Käsemann, "Principles of the Interpretation of Romans 13," in Käsemann, *New Testament Questions for Today* (Philadelphia, Fortress, 1969), 209–12; and Gerhard Delling, *Römer 13, 1–7 innerhalb der Briefe des Neuen Testaments* (Berlin, Evangelische, 1962), 66.

24. W. C. van Unnik, "Lob und Strafe durch die Obrigkeit: Hellenistisches zu Röm. 13.3–4," in *Jesus und Paulus,* W. Kümmel Festschrift, eds. E. Ellis and E. Grässer (Göttingen, Vandenhoeck, 1975), 334–43; cf. Selwyn, *First Epistle of St. Peter,* 87, 173.

25. I owe the comparison of the two phrases to Selwyn, ibid., 172.

26. Richard A. Wasserstrom, "The Obligation to Obey the Law," in *Contemporary Political Theory,* ed. A. de Crespigny and A. Wertheimer (New York, Atherton, 1970), 270, describes this viewpoint while rejecting it.

27. Yoder, *Politics of Jesus,* 208.

28. Rawls, *Theory of Justice,* 383.

29. Käsemann, "Principles of Interpretation of Romans 13," 213–14 (both quotations).

30. Bornkamm, *Jesus of Nazareth,* 122.

31. Cf. Ellis Rivkin, "Beth Din, Boulé, Sanhedrin: A Tragedy of Errors," *Hebrew Union College Annual* 46 (1975), 183–89; T. A. Burkill, "Sanhedrin," *Interpreter's Dictionary of the Bible* (1962), 4.215–16.

32. Charles C. Ryrie, "The Christian and Civil Disobedience," *Bibliotheca Sacra* 127 (1970), 160. Professor Ryrie, however, sees this conflict only where the government forbids one to worship God (162).

33. Harold J. Berman, *The Interaction of Law and Religion* (Nashville, Abingdon, 1974), 52–53.

34. William G. McLoughlin, "Civil Disobedience and Evangelism among the Missionaries to the Cherokees, 1829–1839," *Journal of Presbyterian History* 51 (1973), 118–25, 139.

35. Stephen J. Akangbe, "The Effect of Christian Social Action Change in Oro

Community (Oro Ago, Ilorin, Kwara State, Nigeria, Africa)," (unpub. course paper prepared for me, 1975), 13.

36. W. D. Ross, *The Right and the Good* (Oxford, Oxford U. Press, 1930), 20–21, 38.

37. William K. Frankena, *Ethics* (Englewood Cliffs, N.J., Prentice-Hall, Foundations of Philosophy, 1963), 2.

38. Herbert McCabe, *What Ethics Is All About* (Corpus, 1969), 33, quoted in Hauerwas, "Love's Not All You Need," 230.

39. Ross, *Right and the Good*, 41.

40. Ross, *Right and the Good*, 29.

41. Norman L. Geisler, *Ethics: Alternatives and Issues* (Grand Rapids, Zondervan, 1971), 107.

42. Matt. 19.5–9; 1 Cor. 7.12–16; Helmut Thielicke, *Theological Ethics*, vol. 1: *Foundations* (Philadelphia, Fortress, 1966), 610–11.

43. Examples by Charles Hodge, *Systematic Theology*, 441–45, cited by Geisler, *Ethics*, 91.

44. Frankena, *Ethics*, 24.

45. Ross, *Right and the Good*, 28, 41.

46. Harvey Seifert, *Ethical Resources for Political and Economic Decision* (Philadelphia, Westminster, 1972), 22.

47. Cf. Ross, *Right and the Good*, 28.

48. Geisler, *Ethics*, 116.

49. Rawls, *Theory of Justice*, 6.

50. Rawls, *Theory of Justice*, 339.

51. Ross, *Right and the Good*, 34–35.

52. Frankena, *Ethics*, 53.

53. John Rawls, "The Justification of Civil Disobedience," in *Civil Disobedience*, ed. H. A. Bedau (New York, Pegasus, 1969), 247.

54. Zashin, *Civil Disobedience*, 127.

55. James F. Childress, *Civil Disobedience and Political Obligation: A Study in Christian Social Ethics* (New Haven, Yale U. Press, Yale Publications in Religion 16, 1971), 8.

56. Sanford Jay Rosen, "Civil Disobedience and Other Such Techniques: Law Making through Law Breaking," *George Washington Law Review* 37 (1968/69), 454.

57. James Luther Adams was the first to note the similarity between the criteria for civil disobedience and for just war ("Civil Disobedience," 302). In both cases concern for basic prima facie duties imposes strict qualifications upon the actions taken.

58. Cf. Kent Greenawalt, "A Contextual Approach to Disobedience," in *Political and Legal Obligation*, (cf. n. 11 above), 347.

59. Thomas Aquinas, *Summa Theologica*, 1.2, qu. 96, art. 4.

60. Michael Bayles, "The Justifiability of Civil Disobedience," *Review of Metaphysics* 24 (1970), 13; cf. Thielicke, *Theological Ethics*, 1.533.

61. Rauschenbusch, *Christianity and the Social Crisis*, 325.

62. Booth, *In Darkest England*, 174.

63. Bayles, "Justifiability of Civil Disobedience," 17–18.

64. Ibid., 11.
65. Cf. Adams, "Civil Disobedience," 304–305.
66. Rosen, "Civil Disobedience," 455.
67. Bayles, "Justifiability of Civil Disobedience," 13–14.
68. Adams, "Civil Disobedience," 306–10.
69. Bayles, "Justification of Civil Disobedience," 20.
70. Greenawalt, "Contextual Approach to Disobedience," 347.
71. Wasserstrom, "Obligation to Obey the Law," 287.
72. Adams, "Civil Disobedience," 328.
73. Ibid., 330.
74. Childress, Civil Disobedience, 239.
75. Zashin, Civil Disobedience, 315. On this point, cf. 313–16.

9. AFTER ALL ELSE—THEN ARMS?

1. Norman Gottwald's tribute "to the memory and the honor of the first Israelites," The Tribes of Yahweh (Maryknoll, N.Y., Orbis, 1979), dedication
   page; taken from "an anonymous tribute to the people of Vietnam."
2. J. G. Davies, Christians, Politics and Violent Revolution (London, SCM, 1976),
   165.
3. Käsemann, "Principles of the Interpretation of Romans 13," 216.
4. Cf. Brown, Driver, Briggs, Lexicon, 953–54, 246–47.
5. Jean Lasserre, War and the Gospel (Scottdale, Pa., Herald, Christian Peace
   Shelf 7, 1962), 169–70.
6. Cf. Solomon Zeitlin, "Prolegomenon," to The Jewish Sources of the Sermon on
   the Mount, by Gerald Friedlander (New York, Ktav, Library of Biblical Studies, 1969), xxii–xxiii.
7. Matt. 5.38–48 was "the key passage" for G. H. C. MacGregor, The New
   Testament Basis of Pacifism (Nyack, N.Y., Fellowship, 1954[2]), 31–37; cf.
   John Ferguson, The Politics of Love. The New Testament and Non-Violent Revolution (Greenwood, S.C., Attic, n.d.), 3–6; Lasserre, War and the Gospel, 30.
8. Robert C. Tannehill, "The 'Focal Instance' as a Form of New Testament
   Speech: A Study of Matthew 5:39b–42," Journal of Religion 50 (1970), 372–
   85.
9. Baba Kamma 8.6; cf. Herman L. Strack and Paul Billerbeck, Kommentar zum
   Neuen Testament (Munich, Beck, 1926), 1.342; James Moffatt, Love in the
   New Testament (London, Hodder & Stoughton, 1929), 118; Job. 16.10.
10. Stuart D. Currie, "Matthew 5:39A—Resistance or Protest?" Harvard Theo-
    logical Review 57 (1964), 140–45, argues that even the expression often ren-
    dered "resist not the evil person" refers concretely to not protesting wrong in
    court. In Deuteronomy 19.15–21, the law of talio is applied to one who has
    given false testimony against a person in court. As in several other places in
    the Septuagint, the word for resist (anthistanai, Matt. 5.39) appears in 19.18
    as "to testify against someone." (The word for evil person [poneros, Matt. 5.39]
    appears in 19.19, where it does not refer to the enemy as an outsider or a
    foreign enemy.) With this background in the law of talio, it can be argued

persuasively that Matthew 5.39a forbids speaking against someone in court in one's own defense.

11. William A. Beardslee, "New Testament Perspectives on Revolution as a Theological Problem," *Journal of Religion* 51 (1971), 28.

12. This terminology is that of R. M. Hare, *Freedom and Reason* (New York, Oxford U. Press, Galaxy Books, 1965), 117. For the following discussion, cf. Lewis Smedes' argument that "love does not seek its own" (rights) (1 Cor. 13.5) except when assertion of one's own rights is only a means to protect or foster a neighbor's rights and not an end in itself; *Love Within Limits: A Realist's View of 1 Corinthians 13* (Grand Rapids, Mich., Eerdmans, 1978), 36–41.

13. MacGregor, *New Testament Basis of Pacifism*, 46; Lasserre, *War and the Gospel*, 63; cf. Ferguson, *Politics of Love*, 20.

14. Oscar Cullmann, *Jesus and the Revolutionaries* (New York, Harper, 1970), 39; J. Andrew Kirk, "The Messianic Role of Jesus and the Temptation Narrative: A Contemporary Perspective," *Evangelical Quarterly* 44 (1972), 97–98.

15. Cf. Birger Gerhardsson, *The Testing of God's Son* (Lund, Gleerup, Coniectanea Biblica, New Testament Series 2, 1966).

16. Yoder, *Politics of Jesus*, 30. The rejection of violence at Jesus' Temptation is a keystone in the argument of this book; in several instances references to it carry the argument about other passages (cf. 42, 57, 98, 100, 242–43). Professor Yoder bases his case for kingship in the temptation narrative upon the fact that Jesus is there twice addressed as Son of God and that in the baptismal narrative (which precedes immediately in Matthew but not in Luke) the title has its background in the messianic royal Psalm 2. Even with that understanding of the baptismal narrative (not all scholars agree that there messiahship is stressed), it does not follow methodologically that Son of God in the distinct temptation pericope would have the same nuance. Son of God in the Gospels has a variety of nuances, reflecting various types of backgrounds; see the survey by I. H. Marshall, "The Divine Sonship of Jesus," *Interpretation* 21 (1967), 87–103. (Interestingly, the temptation which would seem most kingly, or messianic, is the one lacking the title [Matt. 4.9 par.].) The conclusion of Marshall's study is that the roots of the NT designation of Jesus as Son of God lie in his consciousness of having a unique filial relationship with the Father; the filial relationship is the basis of his mission and task as Messiah (Marshall, 93, 103). (Matthew 11.27 par. would be the key text; but also important are the prayers of Jesus and the birth narrative, cf. Luke 1.34, which shows sonship to be a characteristic of his nature and not simply an expression of function; Marshall, *The Origins of New Testament Christology* [Downers Grove, Ill., Inter-Varsity, 1976], 122.) Thus the stress on filial loyalty in the temptations is consistent with the term Son of God (particularly with the reference to Israel as *son* in Deut. 8.5). The identification of the particular nuance of Son of God is controlled by exegesis of the passage.

17. The OT provides examples of battles won or kingships changed by direct acts of God rather than human effort (2 Kgs. 7.6; 19.35; Dan. 5). One can

think of the examples of victories won in holy war without any fighting on
the part of the Israelite army; cf. Millar C. Lind, "Paradigm of Holy War in
the Old Testament," *Biblical Research* 16 (1972), 16–31. The prophets described by Josephus apparently revived the hope that God would directly
intervene—by knocking down the walls of Jerusalem, parting the Jordan, or
unspecified "signs of freedom" (Josephus, *Jewish War* 2.259). Satan could
be expected to act in an analogous manner.

The worship of the Devil can be understood as direct worship of God's
rival in the struggle for the world as in Rev. 13.4, or it can refer to the
great struggle with polytheism. Jewish apologetics confuted idolatry either
by denying the reality of the gods or, as in the tradition upon which Paul
draws in 1 Cor. 10.20, by identifying the gods as in fact demons. This latter
alternative would be consistent with the worship of the gods of the land in
the context of Jesus' citation from Deut. (6.14). To understand the passage
in light of the mind of that day, it is not necessary to reduce worship of the
Devil to a disobedient moral course not specified in the text.

18. Cf. Morton Smith, "Zealots and Sicarii, Their Origins and Relation," *Har-
    vard Theological Review* 64 (1971), 1–19; and the modification and critique of
    Smith's position in Valentin Nikiprowetzky, "Sicaires et Zélotes—Une re-
    considération," *Semitica* 23 (1973), 51–64. Smith's argument for greater dis-
    cernment of chronology and diversity is a sharp critique particularly of Mar-
    tin Hengel, whose *Die Zeloten* (Leiden, Brill, 1961) had been the basic
    authority on the subject and which remains valuable for its ideological treat-
    ment. A similar criticism can be made of S. G. F. Brandon's stimulating yet
    less widely accepted treatise, *Jesus and the Zealots* (New York, Scribner's,
    1967).
19. Josephus certainly has an axe to grind in his historical works. But it is
    difficult to see why his agenda would lead him to cover up earlier outbreaks
    of the insurgent movement. In the *Antiquities* (the real theme of the *Jewish
    War* is the war which started in A.D. 66) in light of his concern to dispel
    dislike and mistrust of the Jewish people and to explain the disaster in
    A.D. 70 in terms of the pernicious activity of those whom he calls Sicarii,
    Zealots, or "brigands" (cf. Brandon, *Jesus and the Zealots,* 30–31), Josephus
    could be expected to put the blame on the latter, if possible, for public
    disorders earlier in the century. Such an explanation would also support his
    description of a "Fourth Philosophy" beginning with Judas of Galilee.
20. Cf. P. W. Barnett, " 'Under Tiberius All Was Quiet,' " *New Testament Stud-
    ies* 21 (1974/75), 564–71; Jean Giblet, "Un mouvement de résistance armée
    au temps de Jésus?" *Revue Théologique de Louvain* 5 (1974), 422–26; David
    M. Rhoads, *Israel in Revolution* (Philadelphia, Fortress, 1976), 64–68, 174–
    75.
21. Smith, "Zealots and Sicarii," 5, 13; cf. Giblet, "Mouvement de résistance,"
    422.
22. Rhoads, *Israel in Revolution,* 64.
23. Cf. M. Stern, "Aspects of Jewish Society: The Priesthood and Other Classes,"
    Compendia Rerum Iudaicarum ad Novum Testamentum, Section 1: *The Jewish Peo-
    ple in the First Century,* eds. S. Safrai and M. Stern (Philadelphia, Fortress,

1975), 2.563–64, 577; and S. Applebaum, "Economic Life in Palestine," in ibid., 2.663–64, 692.

24. Josef Blinzler, "Die Niedermetzelung von Galiläern durch Pilatus," *Novum Testamentum* 2 (1957), esp. 30, 37–40, 47.

25. Richard A. Horsley, "Ancient Jewish Banditry and the Revolt against Rome, A.D. 66–70," *Catholic Biblical Quarterly* 43 (1981), 409–32, and "Josephus and the Bandits," *Journal for the Study of Judaism* 10 (1979), 37–63. In "The Sicarii: Ancient Jewish 'Terrorists,' " *Journal of Religion* 59 (1979), 435–58, Horsley adds support to the argument in these pages that the Fourth Philosophy may have lain dormant, perhaps even gone out of existence, until the Sicarii sprung up in the 50s.

26. Cf. Giblet, "Mouvement de résistance," 413–14.

27. John Pairman Brown, "Techniques of Imperial Control: The Background of the Gospel Event," in *The Bible and Liberation*, eds. N. Gottwald and A. Wire (Berkeley, Calif., Community for Religious Research and Education, 1976), 74–75, 83, n.17.

28. Cf. MacGregor, *New Testament Basis of Pacifism*, 37, 73–74; Yoder, *Politics of Jesus*, 127, 183; and on 1 Pet. 3.16–18, Ferguson, *Politics of Love*, 15–16.

29. Cf. n.10 above.

30. Ronald Sider, "To See the Cross, To Find the Tomb, To Change the World," *The Other Side* 13, 1 (February 1977), 18.

31. For Rudolf Bultmann, *The History of the Synoptic Tradition* (New York, Harper, 1968[2] [1931]), 282, the saying about the angels involved legendary elements with an apologetic motive.

32. Cf. Ferguson, *Politics of Love*, 43–44.

33. Ernst Haenchen, "History and Interpretation in the Johannine Passion Narrative," *Interpretation* 24 (1970), 199–201.

34. Georg Richter, "Die Deutung des Kreuzestodes Jesu in der Leidensgeschichte des Johannesevangeliums (Jo. 13–19)," *Bibel und Leben* 9 (1968), 25. The theocentric interpretation in John of Christ's death and the paraenetic interpretation are so distinct that Richter attributes the former to the Evangelist and the latter to the Redactor. He argues that the paraenetic texts without exception are found in verses or passages which the literary criticism of the Gospel has on other grounds considered secondary (p. 30).

Theofried Baumeister observes that the concrete situation in relation to which laying down one's life would be understood in the Johannine church is not evident, "Der Tod Jesus und die Leidensnachfolge des Jüngers nach dem Johannesevangelium und dem Ersten Johannesbrief," *Wissenschaft und Weisheit* 40 (1977), 88.

35. Yoder, *Politics of Jesus*, 56.

36. John Howard Yoder, *The Christian Witness to the State* (Newton, Kan.: Faith and Life, Institute of Mennonite Studies 3, 1964), 49.

37. Lasserre, *War and the Gospel*, 55.

38. Cf. the choice that Professor Sider presents: either to accept the way of nonviolence or to abandon the principle of Scriptural authority (Sider, "To See the Cross," 18).

39. This contrast is noted by Yoder (*Christian Witness to the State*, 31). The text

does not, however, support his contention that *Christians* are therefore not to participate in this function of the state (*Politics of Jesus*, 199). The grounds for Yoder's interpretation lie in his helpful perception that "Christian ethics is for Christians" and that there is a lower demand for nonbelievers who cannot understand or fulfill God's ultimate standard (*Christian Witness*, 28–32). The stress in Romans 13, however, is that the authorities are to be obeyed because they are channels of God's purpose for human community. The argument would be undercut by an accompanying contention that, because they are pagan, there is a lower expectation of their performance; in fact, there is no evidence in the passage of this contention.

40. Paul Ramsey, *War and the Christian Conscience. How Shall Modern War Be Conducted Justly?* (Durham, N.C., Duke U. Press, 1961), 38–40.

41. Cf. ibid., *xvi, xviii,* 40, 305; Ramsey, *The Just War. Force and Political Responsibility* (New York, Scribner's 1968), 143, 159; Claude J. Peifer, "Jesus and Violence," *Bible Today* 46 (1970), 3209–10.

42. John H. Yoder, "If Christ Is Lord," in Yoder, *The Original Revolution* (Scottdale, Pa., Herald, Christian Peace Shelf 3, 1970), 87.

43. Yoder, "If Christ Is Lord," 85, 90; cf. Yoder, "The Political Axioms of the Sermon on the Mount," in *Original Revolution*, 48.

44. Davies, *Christians, Politics*, 91, 132. Cf. *Update Latin America* Sept./Oct. 1979), 7.

45. Cf. the similar interpretation of violence in Scripture by José Míguez Bonino, "Violence: A Theological Reflection," *Ecumenical Review* 25 (1973), who says that whether violence is approved or renounced is secondary to its direction in the conflict of oppression and liberation as to whether or not it opens up the existence of human beings (pp. 471, 474). It was Professor Harry A. Hoffner, Jr. of the Oriental Institute who pointed out to me the character of the Old Testament terminology for violence.

46. H. J. Stoebe, *"Ḥāmās,"* in *Theologisches Handwörterbuch zum Alten Testament* (1971), 1.586, notes the broad range of injustice, including the abandonment of duty to the neighbor and the restriction of right and space for life, with which the term is connected. Somewhat similarly, *biazein* in Josephus is associated with the deprivation of rights; Ernest Moore, "BIAZŌ, ARPAZŌ and Cognates in Josephus," *New Testament Studies* 21 (1975), 522, 524, 536, 538.

47. Paul Ramsey, "The Just Revolution," *Worldview* 16, 10 (Oct., 1973), 37.

48. Ralph B. Potter, *War and Moral Discourse* (Richmond, Knox, 1969), 45–54.

49. Ramsey, *War*, 127.

50. Karl Marx, "The Civil War in France," in Karl Marx and Friedrich Engels, *Basic Writings in Politics and Philosophy*, ed. L. Feuer (New York, Doubleday, Anchor Books, 1959), 386.

51. Cf. Sharp, *Politics of Nonviolent Action*, 423–33.

52. Ramsey, *War and the Christian Conscience*, xix–xx, 72, 127; *Just War*, 154, 159.

53. Cf. Herbert Marcuse, "Ethics and Revolution," in *When All Else Fails*, ed. IDO-C (Philadelphia, Pilgrim, 1970), 220.

54. Rosemary Radford Ruether, *Liberation Theology* (New York, Paulist, 1972), 13.
55. Paul Lehmann, *The Transfiguration of Politics* (New York, Harper, 1975), 271.
56. Beardslee, "New Testament Perspectives on Revolution," 32.
57. Ruether, *Liberation Theology*, 12–13.
58. Rolland F. Smith, "A Theology of Rebellion," *Theology Today* 25 (1968), 10–22.

10. CREATIVE REFORM THROUGH POLITICS

1. Berkhof, *Christ and the Powers*, 55; Yoder, *Politics of Jesus*, 144–46; Wallis, *Agenda for Biblical People*, 65, 71.
2. Yoder, "If Christ Is Truly Lord," 63; Yoder, *Christian Witness to the State*, 12; Wallis, *Agenda*, 74–75.
3. Gish, *New Left and Christian Radicalism*, 138.
4. Yoder, *Christian Witness to the State*, 14.
5. Calvin, *Institutes*, 4.20.6 (vol. 2, p. 655).
6. Francis John McConnell, *Christianity and Coercion* (Nashville, Cokesbury, 1933), 34.
7. Berkhof, *Christ and the Powers*, 23, cf. 49.
8. I owe this perspective on the Puritans to Professor Talcott Parsons of Harvard University. He saw the Puritans as the first group in history with an ideology of modernization because of the combination of their stress on personal decisions with a social organization in which there is a goal-setting process through a democratic conception of the needs of the group.
9. Thomas Case, *Two Sermons to the Commons* (1641), 21–22, as quoted by A. S. P. Woodhouse in "Introduction," to *Puritanism and Liberty*, ed. Woodhouse (Chicago, U. of Chicago Press, 1951), 43. For the Puritan view of history, cf. pp. 39–51, 95–97 of Woodhouse's introduction.
10. Kenneth Willis Clark, "The Meaning of [Kata]kyrieyein," in *Studies in New Testament Language and Text*, G. Kilpatrick Festschrift, ed. J. K. Elliott (Leiden, Brill, *Novum Testamentum Supplements* 44, 1976), 100–105.
11. Mott, "The Greek Benefactor," 95, 104–5, 146–76. Despite its usage in the benefactor cult, of which "emperor worship" was an expression, the mere title of *euergetēs*, as in Luke 22.25, does not connote a claim of deity.
12. Cf. Bauer, *Lexicon*[5], 498, 726. The Markan account also restates *the rulers* as *the great ones (hoi megaloi*, "those with high rank and dignity," Mark 10.42 par.).
13. Marver H. Bernstein, *Regulating Business by Independent Commission* (Princeton, N.J., Princeton U. Press, 1955), 289.
14. John S. Jackson III, "Shall We Legislate Morality?" *Review and Expositor* 73 (1976), 175.
15. Yoder, "Christ the Hope of the World," 177–78.
16. Cf. Yoder, *Christian Witness to the State*, 40; Yoder, "If Christ Is Truly Lord," 77; Berman, *Interaction of Law and Religion*, 25–29, 144.

17. Richard J. Mouw, *Politics and the Biblical Drama* (Grand Rapids, Mich., Eerdmans, 1976), 109; Wallis, *Agenda for Biblical People*, 139; Yoder, *Christian Witness to the State*, 27.

18. Christenson, *Charismatic Approach to Social Action*, 87.

19. Jackson, "Shall We Legislate Morality?" 176.

20. William M. Pinson, Jr., "Why All Christians Are Called into Politics," in *Politics*, ed. J. Dunn (Dallas, Christian Life Commission of the Baptist General Convention of Texas, 1970), 18.

21. Fritz Blanke, "Anabaptism and the Reformation," in *The Recovery of the Anabaptist Vision*, H. Bender Festschrift, ed. G. Hershberger (Scottdale, Pa., Herald, 1947), 68.

22. Denis Goulet, *Is Gradualism Dead?* (New York, Council on Religion and International Affairs, Ethics and Foreign Policy Series, 1970), 12. The term "cooptable reform" is that of Peter Dreier, "Power Structures and Power Struggles," *Insurgent Sociologist* 5 (1975), 238–40.

23. André Gorz, *Strategy for Labor* (Boston, Beacon, 1967), 6.

24. Cf. Rosemary Ruether, "The Reformer Versus the Radical: The Problematic of Social Change," *Lutheran Theological Seminary Bulletin* 51, 1 (Feb., 1971), 23.

25. Yoder, "Christ the Hope of the World," 151–52; Yoder, "Let the Church Be the Church," in Yoder, *Original Revolution*, 119; Yoder, "If Christ Is Truly Lord," 82.

26. Gabriel Kolko, *The Triumph of Conservatism: A Reinterpretation of American History, 1900–1916* (New York, Free Press, 1963), 5, 283.

27. Bernstein, *Regulating Business by Independent Commission*, 82–83, 87–88, 90, 156–57, 276, 296.

28. Cf. J. Philip Wogaman, *The Great Economic Debate: An Ethical Analysis*, (Philadelphia, Westminster, 1977), for consideration of the premises involved in this economic critique.

29. Kolko, *Triumph of Conservatism*, 279, 281–83, 305; Bernstein, *Regulating Business*, 76.

30. Theodore Caplow, *Toward Social Hope* (New York, Basic, 1975), 127–28.

31. Bernstein, *Regulating Business*, 129–30.

32. The total programs were underfunded but scattered and short-term local grants were often overfinanced, particularly in relation to the services provided. Local grants had the character of too much money for the level of planning (cf. Caplow, *Toward Social Hope*, 165). The Great Society programs can also be criticized for their failure to make use of available knowledge about social improvement (cf. ibid., 164–68).

33. Michael Harrington, *The Twilight of Capitalism* (New York, Simon & Schuster, 1976), 268–69, 271–72, 281.

34. Caplow, *Toward Social Hope*, 151–52.

35. Goulet, *Is Gradualism Dead?* 12, 31.

36. Gorz, *Strategy for Labor*, 8, 12.

37. Goulet, *Is Gradualism Dead?* 15; Gorz, *Strategy for Labor*, 6.

38. Cf. Yoder, *Christian Witness to the State*, 32, 38, 42.

39. Harrington, *Twilight of Capitalism*, 266.

40. Bernstein, *Regulating Business,* 82–83.
41. Lincoln Steffens, *The Shame of the Cities* (New York, Hill and Wang, American Century Series, 1957 [1904]), 137, cf. 134.
42. Francis J. McConnell, as quoted in James Luther Adams, "Introduction," to *Political Expectation,* by Paul Tillich (New York, Harper, 1971), xx.
43. Dieter T. Hessel, *A Social Action Primer* (Philadelphia, Westminster, 1972), 108.
44. Harvey Cox, *The Secular City* (New York, Macmillan, 1965), 140–41, 143. C. Willie similarly writes that the quality of race relations in cities is a function less of attitudes than of institutional arrangements that limit or facilitate opportunity; in a review of *Race in the City* by J. Aberbach and J. Walker, *Contemporary Sociology* 5 (1976), 495.
45. The coercive impact of law is not only to control those who are opposed to the values expressed in the law but also to control those who agree with these values but who otherwise might not be willing to pay the cost of compliance; Malcolm Feeley, "Coercion and Compliance: A New Look at an Old Problem," *Law and Society Review* 4 (1970), 505–19.
46. Jackson, "Shall We Legislate Morality?" 173–74.
47. Donal E. Muir, "Six-Year Trends in Integration Attitudes of Deep-South University Students," *Integrated Education* 9 (Jan./Feb. 1971), 21–27.
48. Robert Coles, "How Do the Teachers Feel?" *Saturday Review,* May 16, 1964, 90.
49. Frederick M. Wirt, *The Politics of Southern Equality: Law and Social Change in a Mississippi County* (Chicago, Aldine, 1970).
50. Wirt, 312.

INDICES

SCRIPTURAL PASSAGES AND OTHER ANCIENT
SOURCES (Selective)

OLD TESTAMENT

Genesis:

1.28, p. 46; 2.24, p. 116; 3.13-15, p.
97; 3.17-18, p. 97; 3.17, p. 101; 4.9,
p. 43; 9.6, p. 46; 22.1-14, p. 155;
37.27, p. 116.

Exodus:

1.15-21, p. 153; 3.7-8, p. 153; 14.8, p.
153; 15.11, 18, p. 83; 18.21, p. 72;
20.2, p. 25; 20.6, p. 171; 22.21, p.
214n.25; 23.1-3, 6-8, p. 67; 23.7, p.
63; 23.8, p. 72; 23.9, pp. 50, 214n.25.

Leviticus:

19.15, p. 71; 19.18, pp. 42, 43; 19.33,
p. 214n.25; 25, p. 68; 25.25-28, p. 68;
25.35-36, p. 67; 25.35, p. 67; 25.39,
42, p. 67; 25.49, p. 116.

Numbers:

23.21, p. 83; 26, p. 66.

Deuteronomy:

1.17, p. 60; 4.19, p. 210n.13; 6-8, p.
173; 6.10-13, p. 174; 6.14, p.
234n.17; 6.16, p. 174; 8.2-3, p. 174;
8.2, 5, p. 174; 8.5, p. 233n.16;
10.18-19, pp. 43, 60, 64, 214n.25;
10.18, p. 67; 15.4, p. 69; 15.10, p. 70;
15.14-15, p. 214n.25; 16.18-19, p. 72;
16.20, p. 71; 17.12, p. 120; 19.14, p.

220n.28; 19.15-21, p. 232n.10;
23.15-16, p. 67; 24.17-18, p. 30; 25.1,
p. 218n.7; 27.17, p. 220n.28; 32.8, p.
210n.13.

Judges:

6.1-6, p. 187; 7.19-25, p. 187.

1 Samuel:

2.4-10, p. 68; 2.8, p. 67; 8.11-17, p.
67.

1 Kings:

21, p. 67.

2 Kings:

7.6, p. 233n.17; 9.6-7, p. 170; 19.35,
p. 233n.17.

2 Chronicles:

19.7, p. 72.

Job:

16.10, p. 232n.9; 19.7, p. 187; 29.14,
16, p. 72; 29.14, 17, p. 73; 31.13-15,
p. 46; 31.21, p.72.

Psalms:

2, p. 233n.16; 10.18, p. 61; 22.28-29,
p. 84; 25.6, p. 120; 35.10, p. 61;
55.9-11, p. 187; 72.1-4, pp. 71, 193;
72.12-14, p. 187; 76.9, p. 61;
77.16-19, p. 102; 84.2, p. 116;
89.10-11, p. 102; 93.1-4, p. 102;

PERSONS

SUBJECTS